Martin Nakata's book, *Disciplining the Savages: Savaging the Disciplines* represents the most focussed and sustained Indigenous critique of anthropological knowledge yet published. It is impressive, rigorous, and sometimes poignant: a must-read for anyone concerned with the troubled interplay of Indigenous issues and academic institutions in Australia today.
Professor Nicholas Thomas, University of Cambridge

Speaking as a Torres Strait Islander Nakata renders a deeply unsettling account of the Haddon anthropological expedition into Torres Strait, from which he constructs an 'Indigenous standpoint' that becomes the theoretical core of the book, and from which he explores the anger and dis-ease indigenous students regularly experience in university classrooms. Nakata here reveals himself as an Indigenous philosopher of the first rank.
Associate Professor Regina Ganter, Griffith University

Disciplining the Savages
Savaging the Disciplines

Martin Nakata

ABORIGINAL
STUDIES
PRESS

First published in 2007
by Aboriginal Studies Press

Reprinted 2008, 2026

© Martin Nakata

All rights reserved. No part of this book may
be reproduced or transmitted in any form or by
any means, electronic or mechanical, including
photocopying, recording or by any information storage
and retrieval system, without prior permission in
writing from the publisher. The *Australian Copyright
Act 1968* (the Act) allows a maximum of one chapter
or 10 per cent of this book, whichever is the greater,
to be photocopied by any educational institution for
its education purposes provided that the educational
institution (or body that administers it) has given a
remuneration notice to Copyright Agency Limited
(CAL) under the Act.

Aboriginal Studies Press
is the publishing arm of the
Australian Institute of Aboriginal
and Torres Strait Islander Studies.
GPO Box 553, Canberra, ACT 2601
Phone: (61 2) 6246 1183
Fax: (61 2) 6261 4288
Email: asp@aiatsis.gov.au
Web: www.aiatsis.gov.au/aboriginal_studies_press

National Library of Australia
Cataloguing-In-Publication data:

> Nakata, Martin N.
> Savaging the disciplines: disciplining the savages.
>
> Bibliography.
> Includes index.
> ISBN 9780855755485.
> ISBN 9780855756925 (ebook PDF).
>
> 1. Anthropology — Research — Queensland —
> Torres Strait Islands — Evaluation. 2. Ethnology
> — Methodology — Evaluation. 3. Torres Strait
> Islanders — Study and teaching. 4. Critical
> pedagogy — Queensland — Torres Strait Islands.
> 5. Torres Strait Islands (Qld.) — Colonies —
> Research — Evaluation. I. Title.
>
> 306.0720994

Front cover image: © Crocodile Dance Headdress
by James Eseli, photograph courtesy of the
Queensland Museum.
Part-title illustration by James Boyd
Index by Michael Harrington

Contents

Acknowledgments	vi
Map: Islands of the Torres Strait	vii
Introduction	1

Part One

1. Missionary inscriptions of the 'lost soul'	15
2. Domesticating the savage	26
3. Linguistic inscriptions of the language	32
4. Psychological inscriptions of the mind	42
5. Physiological inscriptions of the senses	76
6. Anthropological inscriptions of the community	101
7. Disciplining and regulating the body	129

Part Two

8. Disciplining the Islander in formal education	155
9. Disciplining Indigenous Knowledge	182

Part Three

10. The Cultural Interface	195
11. An Indigenous Standpoint theory	213
Concluding remarks	218
References	226
Index	237

Acknowledgments

I thank my family Vicky, Sana and Lucy for their support throughout this journey. I also thank Professor Mary Kalantzis for giving me the courage to explore a topic in an academic institution on Islander terms, for stating up front her confidence in my ability to finish the task, and for dragging me over the line at times when I doubted myself. I wish to thank Lorraine Murphy, Kate Leeson and Patrick Sullivan for their editorial advice and assistance, and all those, too numerous to mention, who have read drafts or have provided suggestions. Thanks also to Sue Sifa for the F. Scott Fitzgerald quote.

Chapters One to Seven of this book draw from research work I undertook during my PhD studies, and here I would like to acknowledge the Federal Government's ABSTUDY program for providing financial support during my studies. Chapter Seven also draws in part from an article I published in H. McGlade (ed.), *Treaty: Let's Get it Right*.

Chapter Eight, 'Disciplining the Islander in formal education', draws from articles I published in the *International Journal of Qualitative Studies in Education*, *The Aboriginal Child at School* and in N. Loos & T. Osanai (eds.), *Indigenous minorities and education: Australian and Japanese perspectives of their Indigenous peoples, the Ainu, Aborigines and Torres Strait Islanders*.

Chapter Nine, 'Disciplining Indigenous Knowledge', was the basis for a publication in the *International Federation of Library Associations & Institutions (IFLA) Journal* and in A. Hickling-Hudson, J. Matthews & A. Woods (eds.) *Disrupting Preconceptions: Postcolonialism and Education*.

Chapters Ten and Eleven of this book, 'The Cultural Interface' and 'An Indigenous Standpoint theory', was the basis for a keynote address delivered at the (Re)contesting Indigenous Knowledge and Indigenous Studies Conference, 28–30 June 2006, Gold Coast, Queensland, Australia, and will be published as part of its proceedings in a special issue of the *Australian Journal of Indigenous Education*.

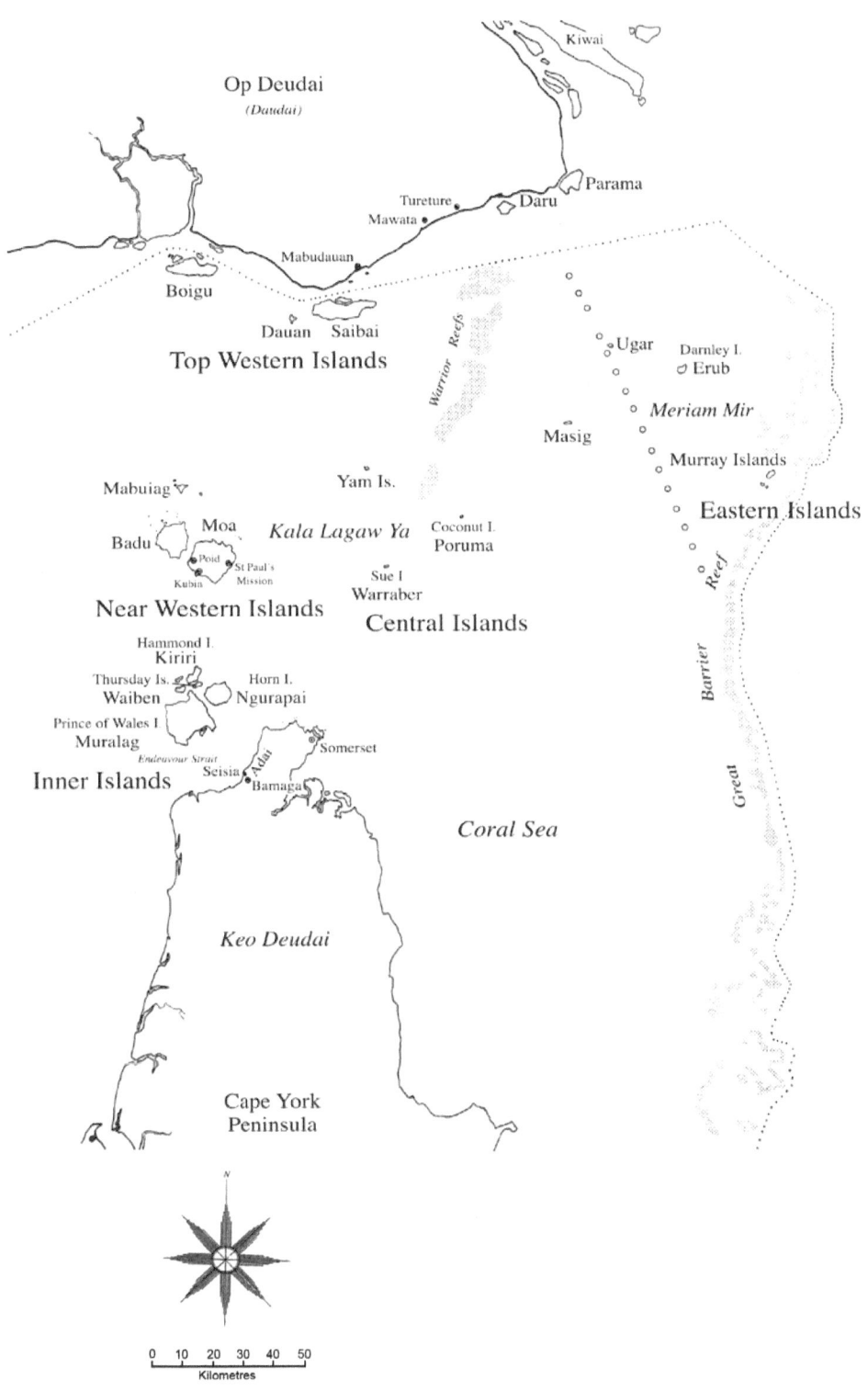

Islands of the Torres Strait and their neighborhood.
Drawn by John Waddingham. Reproduced with permission from
© Sharp, N, No Ordinary Judgement, 1996, Aboriginal Studies Press.

Anton (1979–1997)

This book is dedicated to my nephew, Anthony Philemon Nakata, who contracted sub-acute sclerosing pan-encephalitis (SSPE) at the age of sixteen, and fought on for two years before dying on Friday 20 June 1997.

In one of his quiet moments of frustration, 'Anton threatened to go to university just to write a book', his mother reflects, 'because he felt people at school really didn't understand who he was or what it was like growing up today'. This book is for you, Anton.

Introduction

> Their condition might be called the tragedy of the inarticulate. They could not make the intruder understand the injustice which had been inflicted upon them. They were left confused and hopeless.
>
> (Bleakley, 1961, p. 140)

When I commenced my studies in education, I was motivated not by a desire to teach, but by a need to understand the knowledge that teachers possessed. As an Education Officer on Thursday Island in the Torres Strait I interacted with both teachers and principals and continually felt my ignorance of educational matters in a very personal way — one that seemed to diminish both me and my contribution as an Islander to the educational needs of Torres Strait Islander students. It seemed clear to me at that time that local knowledge was not enough to make the meaningful contribution I wanted to make. By local knowledge I mean not only having an understanding of the background of Islander students but also having an understanding of what I knew, through personal experience, about the difficulties they were experiencing in schooling.

While my local knowledge had meant that I, as an 'unqualified' Islander, had gained the position of Education Officer in preference to a person with educational qualifications, it also meant that my views were often patronised or discounted by those in the school system. In short, I felt that my position was merely a token offering and that my local knowledge was not really respected at all. As a result I was determined to change that tokenism by learning more about the knowledge systems from which teachers viewed and understood the difficulties that Islander students experienced. These things together, I thought, would enable me to make a more effective contribution to improving the schooling experiences of Torres Strait Islanders.

Introduction

Enrolling at university, it did not take long for me to feel a sense of disquiet. My initial success brought with it only subdued elation because of the sense of alienation I felt, in particular from much of the cross-cultural and Australian Indigenous components of my course. To me, they seemed to be less about 'me', 'us' or 'our situation' and more about what people with academic knowledge — the 'experts' — thought about these things. It was as if Indigenous people were an object of study viewed from the confines of a fixed vantage point. Our perspective — the Islanders' point of view — was mostly obscured from view and, it would seem, irrelevant as it could always be explained away by theoretical knowledge. Yet, I felt, this large body of theoretical knowledge was only able to chart the surface level of our historical experience; it could never penetrate within and illuminate the shadowy corners. This was what I had unconsciously felt working as an Education Officer in the Torres Strait when any insights my local knowledge could have given were refused any priority in the scheme of things. I had also felt it on numerous occasions when interacting with experts from outside of the islands who seemed, at the time, to 'know' more about my history and my 'situation' than I did and who thought nothing of correcting my own understandings with their own explanations. If, in my cross-cultural interactions, I had always been reminded of my ignorance, why, when I was seeking to address that ignorance, did I feel such disquiet about the knowledge that I was being taught?

Around this time, my mother, in course of conversation, told me her understanding of her own history and, in particular, about her family's pursuit of knowledge through education. My mother had not read any accounts of Torres Strait history. In those terms she knew nothing about it at all, for she did not even know what had been written about it. But she had lived it. Her brief account showed her understanding about the place education held in her family's life. She did not offer an analysis of why or how this was constrained by the oppressive administrative apparatus of the time. Quite simply, she did not know all the details. However, despite this historical 'ignorance', in a personal sense she had absorbed the analyses of her father and grandfather which ensured that education and higher knowledge continued to be valued in her own household.

At the time of my undergraduate studies, I hadn't read many accounts of Torres Strait history either. In retrospect, I am glad that I hadn't because I gained instead a different perspective that helped me to uphold Islander responses to the interventions which disrupted our lives; responses that were all too easily submerged in other accounts which came from 'accredited sources' only and were 'solidly grounded' in scholarship. Consequently, when, as a student, I first came to read the historical literature and the educational literature on the Torres Strait Islanders, I did not read them from a position of 'ignorance' or 'neutrality' or as an 'onlooker'. Rather I read them from a position of awareness that this literature was an attempt to re-present my experience and my forebears' experience, as well as an attempt to re-present an analysis of my or my fellow Islanders' situation. This brought to light a significant omission. The readings and analyses brought down through family and collective consciousness, from which my own position was derived, were invariably absent or bypassed, or, more often, re-explained in such a way as to negate the validity of my own understanding as an Islander.

When trying to redress these practices, Islanders are accused by implication of 'getting it wrong' because, it is said, we do not fully understand all that has influenced the context that shaped our experiences. The implication is that, in the passing down of our understandings of events via the oral tradition, 'popular memory' distorts, exaggerates, misunderstands, fabricates or simply 'forgets' the actual 'facts' of what was experienced. This growing awareness of the uneasy relationship between my lived experience and that ascribed to me by the texts produced about Islanders led to the focus of my studies over the years. I wanted to investigate the way these two 'realities' have met historically at the interface of Islander experience and Western knowledge systems. I wanted to come to an understanding of how this had come about. And I wanted, through this knowledge, to change this situation.

My mother is a Torres Strait Islander who grew up on Naghir Island in the central Torres Strait region. Her grandfather, Mr James Mills (Jimmy Samoa), was a relatively prosperous and enterprising Samoan who owned a successful pearling fleet. He was educated in boyhood by the London Missionary Society (LMS) at Upolo in Samoa, was widely travelled as a ship's bosun and had spent time in both England and South Africa before coming to the Torres Strait. Because he had a wider knowledge of the world when he married into the Torres Strait side of the family, he secured a lease over the family's islands. At the time he may have thought that this secured and legitimated his position; certainly, it prevented these islands being gazetted by the Queensland government as 'Reserves' in 1912. Recent investigations (Peterson, 1996) into the lease arrangements, however, show that he was charged far in excess of what European entrepreneurs who held leases in other parts of the Strait were required to pay.

Introduction

As an intruder himself, an analysis of the situation would, perhaps quite fairly, position my great-grandfather as another exploiter of the local population. In fact, he was a non-European, inserted into a racial hierarchy just above the local natives and viewed by the family as a man who used this position to gain as much advantage as he could for the community. He was remembered as speaking 'good English' and he valued education enough to employ teachers for his children. Who these teachers were, and to what standard they taught, is not remembered in detail but a visitor who stayed with the family in 1946 on Naghir Island commented on the extensive English vocabulary of his son — my grandfather, Mr Frank Mills (Raven-Hart, 1949). This same visitor also noted that, in general, there was a high standard of English in the younger generation on this island.

When my great-grandfather died, his assets (which, according to the family, included the lease and £10,000) were left to his family. The family saw none of this money. Investigations into the official records (Peterson, 1996) revealed that although he had made good money over his lifetime he did not, in fact, possess very much at the time of his death. The family, having an historical understanding that there were assets (a pearling fleet) and a view that the Queensland government had never been completely trustworthy when dealing with Islander finances fail to be convinced by this investigation. At the time, the family, of course, felt that they had been robbed, but were not quite sure how it was done.

For my mother's father, who became the next leader on Naghir Island, education — that is, knowledge and understanding about the world outside of the islands — continued to be a matter of great importance. It appeared obvious that education, and English literacy in particular, were needed not just for the development of our own community, but also for us to understand and master the system so that the bastards could not rob us again. We needed to know how it was that Western regimes did things that always seemed to advantage them but not us.

My grandfather was so keen for his children, including his daughters, to receive the best education that they could, that my mother and her twin sister were sent away, at the age of seven, to board at the Catholic Convent School on Thursday Island. My mother learnt to read and write and do basic maths and received an education to Year 4 standard. This was in the mid-thirties, well before Islanders were considered citizens, and the family funded their education themselves. My mother also learnt to boil up the nuns' habits and linen in the copper; to scrub, starch, iron and mend clothes; to prepare food; to wait on priests at tables; to garden and milk goats, and so on. As a teenager she became, without any training, the teacher at the small school on Naghir Island and remained there until her marriage in the early 1950s.

This school had been conceived, built and paid for by her grandfather in 1904 (Lawrie, 1984). His only negotiation with the Queensland government, who held the primary responsibility to provide schools for the education of Islanders, was for the appointment of a fully qualified European teacher. Unfortunately the first one left within a year, enrolments having fallen to a level that did not officially warrant a government teacher. Unable to maintain enrolments by taking children from nearby islands, my great-grandfather confined himself to the education of his own community and employed his own teachers. Over the years, various teachers, mostly Islanders, were employed, including older family members such as my mother. At other times the children were sent away to other schools. Thus this family (and the story is repeated with variations in other parts of the Strait, for example at Masig Island) was actively pursuing education for its children, and responding to changing circumstances, in an independent manner.

Continuing the pursuit for the children to have a better education and better life chances, my grandfather made the momentous decision to abandon his island in 1964. Anyone who understands the attachment Islanders have for land, sea and the island way of life can perhaps come close to understanding the incredible pain and pressure he had to confront in doing this. But the Second World War and the decline in the pearling industry brought a lot of changes for Torres Strait Islanders and economic and educational opportunities were certainly much better on Thursday Island, the administrative centre for the Strait (Beckett, 1987; Prideaux, 1988; Ganter, 1994). It was the future of the younger generation — that is my generation — with which he was concerned.

When I struggle with academic work, I often think of my grandfather. I think of his generous nature and his intelligence. I think about his bitterness and suppressed anger and confusion over the intrusions of colonial regimes in his community. I also think of his efforts to build on his own father's perceptions of the situation and the aspirations he held for his children and subsequent generations. I think of the high hopes he had for all his grandchildren — that we could do 'better'. And I think of his sadness towards the end of his life in 1988 when he realised that, despite some successes, we were not really in a much better position than we had been all those years ago. Yes, things had changed and we were able to go away to schools on the Australian mainland. We had more education and some of us eventually made it to tertiary level. Yet, relatively speaking, we were still educationally disadvantaged in comparison to other Australians and this educational disadvantage reduced our ability to gain control over our own destinies.

His biggest sadness, though, was the self-doubts he had about giving up his island and his community for this other life. To this day, Naghir Island remains abandoned. To this day, there is no longer a community of our people. As a community our legal status remains questionable precisely because of the lease arrangements and because of relocation; the very decisions made by us to improve our position all those years ago have dislocated us from our heritage. Today, in our separate isolations, the image of this community of people exists only in our thoughts and memories. But we still remain optimistic about building a better future for ourselves. We took risks and as a result we have lived with the positive and negative outcomes that accrued from those decisions.

My own early education occurred mainly on Thursday Island, first at the convent school that my mother had attended and then at the state primary and secondary schools. This period between the early 1960s and the early 1970s was a period of change for Torres Strait Islanders. As the pearling industry was in decline, the Queensland government began to allow Islanders more freedom of movement to find work in other regions. Islanders from other islands in the Strait were now allowed to reside on Thursday Island. The right to vote in Federal elections was granted in 1962 and in Queensland State elections in 1965. There was desegregation of schools and repeated requests for secondary education were finally answered with the extension of schooling to Year 10 on Thursday Island in 1966. In the early 1970s, access to schools on the Australian mainland for Years 11 and 12 was also provided.

My education occurred within this changing context. We were taught the Queensland curriculum — by teachers who probably did not know we existed until they found out they had a transfer to the region. There was no recognition at that time that English was a second — or even third — language to us. In those days Torres Strait Creole, our local language, was not even considered to be a language. It was just 'bad' English — broken English (Shnukal, 1988). Like my mother, my Japanese father was very keen for us to have the best education that was possible. To this end, he always spoke English to us as best he could and encouraged us at every moment to speak and read it, even buying us the *Encyclopaedia Britannica* at considerable expense to help us with our schoolwork. All that I know of the Japanese language was learnt from other Japanese people, not from my father.

Both my parents worked hard to provide their eight children with the material means to participate and do well and we were continually exhorted to do better. My memories of school are always of trying, trying, trying but never quite getting it right. Of never knowing what it was that I did not quite get right. Of never being able to make myself understood. Of always knowing that even when I was understood it was not in the ways that I meant it to be.

Despite this, I was able to do relatively well on Thursday Island and it was not until I attended school in Maroochydore and Yeppoon on the Australian mainland that I had a credible measure of my real educational position. I found then that I understood nothing in the classroom. I understood nothing of what the teacher was teaching. I understood nothing of what we were required to read, nor why. I began to understand nothing of myself, feeling nothing but confusion. This was the time when I first drifted into using drugs and, later, turned to sports as a survival strategy. Yet academically it made no difference. At the end of Year 11, I disappointed my parents and gave school away for good. I was to work for fifteen years before entering university.

I think that my family's history and my own experiences provide a sharp edge to my perceptions of the outside world and our position in it. As I look back on it, this edge was part of what drove me to see our position as political when I first approached academic work. This historical trajectory shows a community which was, since at least the 1880s, actively engaging with the changing world around it; a community intent on working in its own interests but, nevertheless, positioning these by necessity in relation to those larger forces which pulled and tugged from both inside and outside the community. Despite being unable to satisfactorily bring those forces to account, particularly in relation to financial and legal matters, my family did not remain blind or indifferent to their differential treatment but absorbed their perceptions into a view that oriented them to the future rather than the past. While some may mourn the loss of pure lineage and tradition from former times, perhaps my forebears considered that the flexibility necessary for autonomy and independence was preferable to being rigidified, patronised and subtly shaped in the mould of dependence. Perhaps also, tradition was seen to be both transportable and transplantable, while yielding independence was an intolerable and humiliating burden. Perhaps, indeed, independence was our tradition.

It can be seen from this small part of our history that the Islander lifeworld has long been positioned in relation to colonial institutions and knowledge. Our lives were always grounded in our relationship to these influences. This is not to say, however, that daily life was not grounded in other relationships as well but it is to make the point that Islander orientation to the outside world and a Western economy was, in fact, a very real organising structure in our lives. The degree to which success in relation to these factors was valued was firstly grounded in material necessity. Like parents everywhere, mine worked to provide the means to give their children a chance to live a reasonable life. Education was seen to be necessary for economic security. The bottom had fallen out of the marine industry and there were now fewer prospects for uneducated labour. Apart from this, success was a measure of stature and indicated an understanding of the knowledge of that world beyond the Strait — an understanding that would enable us to improve our position in relation to that outside world, which in turn would reduce the constant struggle in our day-to-day lives.

My experiences as an Islander and the analyses and understandings I derived from these, my family's, and the collective Torres Strait Islander experience have enabled me to hold one tenet central to the investigations that led to this book. This is the idea that Islander experience and the analysis derived from that experience — however ignorant of historical fact; or however ignorant of the context of events; or however much it derived from just mere popular memory — are grounded in something that is significant to the ways that we have historically viewed our predicament and have enacted our lives. This experience continues to shape our ongoing responses and it cannot simply be re-explained or re-interpreted by informed, educated or expert people outside of our communities. To do so is a negation or denial of our experience and our understanding of our own position as we confront alien — and alienating — practices and knowledge.

It was from this lifeworld that I emerged to confront the knowledge inscribed in academic institutions. Despite having failed my last engagement at the secondary school level, having engaged with a new and clearly more sensitive and appropriate educational bureaucracy through my job, I arrived at the university in 1988 with a political, although largely unarticulated, view of my situation. I struggled to articulate, using the tools I was in the process of learning, what I thought people did not understand about the position of Islanders in relation to colonial processes and institutions — indeed, in our relation to the wider Australian community, its many disciplines, and its knowledge and practices that have become commonplace. Yet, even with a First Class Honours degree in Education, I still felt completely alienated and isolated within the walls of this inclusive and enlightened institution, simply because I still could not articulate my position in a way that others were able to understand.

To find fault with a university that was outwardly supportive, encouraging and generally understanding was clearly self-defeating, especially when it was the very institution that I had to engage with successfully if I was going to contribute to improving the position of Islanders. My position in the university seemed to mirror the position of all Torres Strait Islanders as they, too, in ways that would better serve their interests and the interests of their community, attempted to articulate themselves with the external forces which shaped their lifeworld. Indeed, it was our relationship with the wider Australian community and its institutions that drove Islanders in the pursuit of improved educational outcomes in the first place (Torres Strait Islander Regional Education Committee, 1985).

Islanders have long understood their need to be educated in the ways of the world developing outside of our islands. Facility with the English language, and understanding of knowledge and practices associated with the developing world, have long been recognised as the path to effectively negotiating our position in a changing order which is otherwise outside of our control. But in this engagement there has always been a need to defend our own position as well, while incorporating and making effective use of the new. However, educating ourselves has also meant running the risk of blindly taking on the knowledge and practices that have served to keep us in a subjugated position. We lose some of ourselves in the process, for educating ourselves via these institutions to overcome our subordinate position brings the risk of submerging or erasing those elements of our own lifeworlds that define us as a distinct group — the Torres Strait Islanders.

Within the university system, I found there was a lot of sympathy, combined with expressions of understanding, for people in our position. Much has been written across academic disciplines about the dilemma of marginalised people who need to articulate their position by deploying knowledge of the centre (e.g. Trinh, 1989), and there have been many attempts to find ways around this perplexing problem by people at the so-called 'margins' (e.g. Bishop, 1995) as well as the centre (e.g. Weedon, 1999; Henriques, Holloway, Urwin, Venn & Walkerdine, 1984). The assumption is that, as an Islander, I will be able to use existing academic conventions to articulate what I think others do not fully understand. But it turned out to be not so straightforward for me.

Two incidents in my undergraduate years provide insights into why I became more focused in interrogating the theoretical underpinnings of the disciplinary approaches to Torres Strait education and Indigenous Studies generally. What I call the cultural paradigm and which is now more generally referred to as culturalism (following McConaghy, 2000) has framed both policy and practice in Torres Strait education since the 1980s. This posits Islanders primarily as culturally different subjects and from this flows an array of theorising about the most appropriate ways to educate us. In practice, somewhat arbitrary tests of cultural appropriateness are applied where they are seen to fit or be relevant to curriculum and other decisions.

I felt an unease at the unquestioned acceptance, on the part of both academics and Islanders, of this paradigm as the answer to our educational problems. Was it not still rooted in others' understanding of us, in others' ways of knowing us? This unease crystallised into an oppositional stance in an undergraduate tutorial when, in dispute with other students over the merits of bilingual education for Islanders, it was suggested I might not really be able to call myself an Islander because I had been on the mainland for too long. I remember as well an education meeting on the same topic in the Torres Strait where an Islander questioned my commitment to Torres Strait culture and language after prompting from the linguist seated beside her. Such experiences led me to wonder just where I had to begin in order to articulate my own unease cogently and to have my questions and concerns considered more seriously. I felt my questions were legitimate ones that needed to be raised and such easy dismissals frustrated me to say the least. Indeed, I felt I was being 'disciplined' and brought into line on each occasion.

It seemed that as I gained knowledge, a deeper problem persisted. I was being called in to agree with accepted positions and if I couldn't agree then the problem must lie with my own thinking and lack of appropriate knowledge. If this was the case, then what was my education for? What I brought to my learning, that standpoint derived from within my own lived experience of my world, was not considered admissible unless I could explain and defend it according to the content, logic and systems of thought of others. Once again, my understandings were discounted and for the experts there were many Islanders more 'authentic' than me who could provide support to the educational orthodoxy.

Ironically, my time at the university was giving me confirmation of what I had been struggling to come to terms with — that I would never be able to argue my position cogently and coherently until I understood it in its totality, and that I would never be able to do this from within the confines of that knowledge system. I would have to find a better way to toggle between representations of Islander experience in the disciplines and my understandings of who we were that were derived from lived experience. I would not understand my position until I accepted that it was only and always being seen in relation to the order of things validated in the Western knowledge system. My task was not simply to know my position but to know first how I was positioned in and by Western disciplines and knowledge practices. My task then was to know how such a knowledge system created a position for Islanders through which we have all come to view Islanders and their problems. Only then could I, a Torres Strait Islander, understand why my viewpoint was never understood and how I could go about changing this situation.

This book is in three parts.

Part One looks at various inscriptions of the Islander into Western disciplines. In Chapter One I explore the presence of Western systems of thought through the London Missionary Society's seminal text, *Among the Cannibals of New Guinea*, published in 1888, of their mission in the Torres Strait to uncover how it is that Islander people come to be inscribed in a historical schema that is not their own, how it is that Islander people come to be seen as only having some distant and timeless past, and how this smooths over the voice of the people as active agents within developing traditions. This and the following five chapters offer an in-depth explication of the different practices of Western disciplines to apply some authority to the constitution of racial characteristics of the Islander people so that they could be understood in the West not as animals but as a people in a lower stage of development, 'as savages'. The reports of the *Cambridge Anthropological Expedition to the Torres Strait* in 1898 form the basis of this explication into Western disciplines.

In Chapter Seven I explicate what such inscriptions meant for the regulation and disciplining of Islander bodies. The administrative regimes of colonial bureaucracies extended the inscriptions of Islanders as 'lost souls' and 'savages' and deployed a new 'commonsense' that constituted Islanders as 'overgrown children', as 'dependents' of the state who needed protection from 'outside influences'. The bodily circumscription of Islanders into webs of government legislation and policy, and the imperatives of commercial and economic interests linked to global markets is the literal embodiment of a commonsense produced via knowledge inscriptions.

Part Two deals with knowledge production in more recent times to consider how accepted disciplinary practices come to both inform and delimit how we can understand Islanders today. In Chapter Eight I dig into the educational corpus to provide some insight into how the textual and inter-textual layers of educational discourse produce discursive positioning and re-positioning of Islanders in more contemporary times. Chapter Nine considers a broader Indigenous position in recent preoccupations with Indigenous Knowledge to exemplify similar disciplinary practices in current times.

Part Three considers a new way forward. Chapter Ten is about a priority to see the everyday world of the Islander as a productive theoretical space, the Cultural Interface, which is a re-theorisation of the lived position as the space where generations of Islander people make and remake themselves as they encounter competing and changing traditions. This conceptualisation of the lived space challenges the simple binary constructions of Islander people as cultural 'others' and ruptures theorising of 'problems' as arising out of 'clashes' between traditional and Western values.

In Chapter Eleven I draw on some of my current work around an Indigenous standpoint theory as a potential theoretical schema for undertaking future explication of disciplinary and knowledge practices between ongoing colonial regimes and Indigenous Australians.

In my Concluding Remarks I draw the key issues together and outline how that would translate in relation to Indigenous education issues in the higher education sector that could improve opportunities and outcomes for Australian Indigenous people.

The lived space of Indigenous people in colonial regimes is the most complex of spaces and one of the goals of this book is to persuade the reader that understandings of the Indigenous position must be 'complicated' rather than simplified through any theoretical framing. The possibilities for this are more open than at any time over the last century. In this historical moment, when political autonomy is a possibility, it is critical that Indigenous people and those who are committed in their support for us develop deeper understandings of how we are positioned at the interface of different knowledge systems, histories, traditions and practices.

PART ONE

1

Missionary inscriptions of the 'lost soul'

> We can understand you captains, you come and trade with us, and then return to your own country to sell what you get: but who are these missionaries? Have they done something in their country, that they dare not return?
>
> (A Lifuan of the Loyalty Islands cited in MacFarlane, 1888, p. 41)

Despite the many thousands of years Islanders have spent developing complex and diverse cultures in the islands of Torres Strait, and in their interactions with mainland Australia and Papua New Guinea, in 1871 it appeared obvious to missionaries from England that the souls of the Islander people needed to be rescued. In this chapter, I chart one particular missionary's rationalisation of his actions — his founding principles — to gain a broader understanding of the motivations that appeared to justify this major intervention into other people's lives. Of course, this is not to find out who was responsible for the missions in the 1870s and apportion blame accordingly; nor is it to evaluate the obviously massive impact the missionaries have had on Islander communities retrospectively. My aim here is purely to explore and chart the way in which the Islander was transformed into both the subject and object of this early missionary endeavour, and provided from without with an inner soul that needed to be rescued and reshaped.

In his book *Among the Cannibals of New Guinea* — the first major publication dealing with the London Missionary Society's (LMS) work in the Torres Strait — Rev Samuel MacFarlane (1888) has provided an interesting account of his mission to evangelise 'New Guinea'. At the time the New Guinea Mission was established in 1871, the islands of the Torres Strait had not yet been annexed by the Queensland government so MacFarlane, quite arbitrarily, included them as part of New Guinea.

Despite twelve years of evangelising in the South Sea Islands, missionaries from the LMS did not know much about the region at all, so MacFarlane, in his own words, found it necessary to set out 'at once to collect information and mature plans...*to spy out the land*' (1888, pp. 12–13). Although knowing little, MacFarlane took with him a considerable body of assumptions which were to prove hard to shift. He believed that in Torres Strait he would find a fantastic, primitive, timeless world inhabited by people who were, seemingly all at once, cannibals, noble savages and lost souls.

> It would be difficult to describe our feelings as we sailed towards that great land of cannibals, a land which, viewed from a scientific, political, commercial, or religious point of view, possesses an interest peculiarly its own. Whilst empires have risen, flourished, and decayed; whilst Christianity, science, and philosophy have been transforming nations, and travellers have been crossing polar seas and African deserts, and astonishing the world by their discoveries, New Guinea has remained the same...where the natives may be seen in the cocoanut groves [*sic*] mending their bows and poisoning their arrows, making their bamboo knives and spears, and revelling in war and cannibalism as they have been doing for ages. (MacFarlane, 1888, pp. 14–15)

MacFarlane's reasoning posited a particular concept of the unknown in relation to what was already known about the outside world. By using developments in the civilised world as a benchmark, the 'uncivilised' world he was approaching was easily conceptualised as static, implying a society that knew no change or progress, a society from the past rather than with a past. What appeared to be commonsense provided the only possible conceptualisation for what had already been observed elsewhere in the region and what he felt sure he would be observing on arrival. Perhaps what was not so evident to MacFarlane was that his own views of progress and his own partial interests in the inhabitants of this 'unknown' part of the world would colour his observations to such a degree that his subsequent accounts of Islanders, who they were and why they were, would be a fiction. In the process, the view of Islanders with their own histories could be submerged, indeed rendered invisible, without challenge.

On 1 July 1871, MacFarlane and his crew arrived at Darnley Island in the Torres Strait. MacFarlane had chosen this island not randomly but quite deliberately. For him it possessed, in fact, a rich evangelical symbolism.

1. Missionary inscriptions of the 'lost soul'

> A consideration of the known, as well as the unknown and probable difficulties, led me to select Darnley Island as the most safe, central, and in every way the most suitable place at which to commence our mission. For such a work as we were beginning, we required a central station, which we might make our sanatorium, city of refuge, and educational centre. As a Scotchman, I remembered Iona and its history in connection with the evangelization of Scotland, and hoped that Darnley would prove the Iona of New Guinea. (MacFarlane, 1888, p. 28)

Like a latter day Saint Columba building an Iona-in-the-South-Seas, MacFarlane set out to do battle with the devil for the souls of these apparently primitive people. Like Saint Columba before him, MacFarlane was clear that he would need to establish a safe haven in what he foresaw as an inevitably hostile world. He needed a strong strategic base from which to mount his evangelical offensive.

Twenty years earlier John MacGillivray, who had been the naturalist on the HMS *Rattlesnake*'s expedition to survey the waters of the Torres Strait, had also considered the idea of establishing strategic settlements both on Cape York and to the east on Darnley (Erub to the Islanders) and Murray Islands (Mer to the Islanders). He, too, was thinking in terms of a strategic base, although in his usage this had at once a military and a religious sense.

> In a military point of view the importance of such a post has been urged upon the ground, that in the event of war, a single enemy's ship stationed in the neighbourhood, if previously unoccupied, could completely command the whole of our commerce passing through the Strait...
>
> 5th. From what more central point could operations be conducted with the view of extending our knowledge of the interior of New Guinea by ascending some of the large rivers of that country, disemboguing on the shores of the Great Bight?
>
> 6th and lastly. But on this point I would advance my opinion with much diffidence — I believe that were a settlement to be established at Cape York, missionary enterprize, *judiciously conducted*, might find a useful field for its labours in Torres Strait, beginning with the Murray and Darnley Islanders, people of a much higher intellectual standard...and consequently more likely to appreciate any humanizing influence which might be exercised for their benefit. (MacGillivray, 1852, p. 320)

It would be helpful here to understand that the narrow waterway known as Torres Strait, which lies between Australia and Papua New Guinea, is less than 200 kilometres wide, a narrow bottleneck between two great oceans: the Arafura Sea to the west and the Coral Sea to the east. It is considered such a bottleneck because of the many islands dotted throughout its waterway, the maze of coral reefs that span the length and breadth of the Strait, the shallow waters, and the dangerous tidal surges and currents that run between them. The scores of ships that lie wrecked on reefs in the Strait are testimony to the difficulties sailors faced in manoeuvring through the narrow passages. Introducing a settlement to this region would have the effect of taming and civilising the unknown; it would eliminate the isolation and make the region part of the known world.

Adding to the perception of danger at this time were the stories of sailors who survived shipwrecks only to be attacked and eaten by natives. One of these tales had, in fact, become something of a preoccupation with travellers and voyagers in the nineteenth century. Thomas Wemyss (1837), for example, retells, in sickening detail, the story of a group of intrepid sailors and travellers who were 'massacred…by natives addicted to thieving' (p. 36) and 'addicted to cannibalism' (p. 24). Unfortunately, the mud was to stick for a very long time. Over a century later McInnes (1983), a historian who specialises in north Australian maritime history, continues to typecast the Islanders as cannibals, using — still in gory detail — the undisputed evidence from the wreck of the *Charles Eaton*:

> [t]hey [the shipwrecked survivors] plodded around the island in search of food and water but were so exhausted by fatigue and hunger they could scarcely crawl and fell to the ground in despair. At this time the peaceful attitude of the natives changed alarmingly. The natives stood grinning and laughing in the most hideous manner and it soon became evident that they were exulting in anticipation of their murder…At a short distance off, making the most hideous yells, the other savages were dancing round a large fire before which were placed in a row the heads of their victims; whilst their decapitated bodies were washing in the surf on the beach, from which they soon disappeared. (McInnes, 1983, pp. 36–37)

In this way, the stain is still there in the records, intact and relatively undisputed.

In his narrative of the gruesome fate of the surviving members of the shipwreck *Charles Eaton* in the Torres Strait Islands, Wemyss suggests there could be four possible responses to the massacre:

> To send a suitable force from India and New South Wales to seize these islands, to exterminate their inhabitants, and to take possession of them in the British name, so as to form settlements or colonies, in which the shipwrecked mariner may in future find a secure refuge.
>
> To invade the islands as before, and without exterminating, to expatriate the natives, by landing them on the coast of New Holland [Australia], leaving them to find their own way in that vast continent.
>
> To subdue the islands, and to preserve the inhabitants, making them tributary, and using such efforts to civilise and improve them, as would render them less formidable to all who might visit them.
>
> But, as all efforts to civilise, by merely introducing the arts of life, have proved either very tedious or absolutely ineffectual, there remains only another plan, and that is, to introduce the Gospel among them by means of missionaries, and by translating the Scriptures into their language. (Wemyss, 1837, p. 34)

The first two responses were clearly rather drastic and, indeed, would have been counterproductive in terms of the established framework of Christian beliefs about preaching the gospel in 'heathen' lands. In contrast, the last two pointed the way towards the more acceptable response of introducing civilisation and improvement as well as the notion that communities 'destitute of the light of the Gospel' (p. 39) could be reformed and that such intervention was 'the proper province of missionary exertion' (p. 39). Whatever else motivated these early concerns with the souls of Islanders, it was essentially the strategic need to find a safe passage through the Strait from countries to the west to the eastern seaboard of Australia that had brought them into contact and created the problem in the first place.

Although MacFarlane (1888) could say, seemingly without intentional irony, that '[i]t was this terra incognita that we were approaching, with its primeval forests and mineral wealth and savage inhabitants' (p. 15), he appears to have had very definite ideas about what he would find there:

> It comes with a sense of relief to visit a country really new, about which little is known, a country of *bonâ fide* cannibals and genuine savages, where the pioneer missionary and explorer truly carries his life in his hand. A land of promise, capable of sustaining millions of people, in which however the natives live on yams, bananas, and cocoa-nuts [*sic*]. A land of mighty cedars and giant trees, where notwithstanding the native huts are made of sticks, and roofed with

palm leaves. A land consisting of millions of acres of glorious grass, capable of fattening multitudes of cattle, where however neither flocks nor herds are known. A land of splendid mountains, magnificent forests, and mighty rivers, but to us a land of heathen darkness, cruelty, cannibalism, and death. We were going to plant the gospel standard on this, the largest island in the world, and win it for Christ. (MacFarlane, 1888, pp. 15–16)

The missionary's task operated on two basic premises. The first was the need to inculcate Islanders into a moral world through what MacFarlane termed 'a pure simple religion' and the second was the need to insulate them from any encroachment from the civilised worlds which could prove pernicious. MacFarlane (1888) was convinced that he had a God-given mission to rescue 'the multitude of souls who have lost the image of God' (p. 24). Indeed, for these 'lost souls', he believed that the gospel was not 'only the best civilizer, the best reformer, and the best handmaid to science, but that it…[was] the only way to eternal life' (p. 24). It was the only means of preventing the natives from being overcome by human progress and civilisation.

So much was anticipated by this imaginative visionary and yet so little was actually known, as MacFarlane's colleagues later found to their detriment. Before departing Lifu for the southern coast of Papua New Guinea in 1871, MacFarlane had recruited a fellow missionary, Mr Murray, as well as four native pastors and their wives. Illness and ailments claimed approximately half of their South Sea Islander recruits, especially in western areas of New Guinea where it was low and swampy. Far from being a land of promise, capable of sustaining millions of people, MacFarlane found what he was to later describe as a 'sickly country' (p. 160). It took a while, however, for him to accept the defeat of his initial blueprint, and it was only with reluctance that he resolved to train Islanders in the Torres Strait as missionaries. These Islanders, it was reasoned, would be more resistant to ailments in New Guinea and were also more akin to the people of its coastline communities than the Lifuan recruits from the Loyalty Islands. He thus moved to establish the Papuan Institute on Murray Island in 1880 as the central training ground, rather than on Darnley Island where he had first landed nine years prior. As far as MacFarlane was concerned, Murray Island was just that bit further off the main route yet still central to the New Guinea communities. Most importantly to the mission, it was reasoned, Torres Strait Islanders could be recruited from other islands and brought to Murray Island so that they were far enough away from both 'their evil surroundings' (p. 81), and the damaging influence of explorers, travellers and traders. That way there was little chance to stall his efforts to 'win it for Christ'.

Nowhere in his later writings does MacFarlane cite any direct observation to support the practice of cannibalism in the islands and his worst fears, it would seem, were never realised. Indeed, the reality portrayed in his later writings and in the earlier writings of people who had spent some time in the region, was quite different. Joseph Beete Jukes (1847) and John MacGillivray (1852) had, in fact, found the Islanders to be mostly hospitable and helpful. They had, they said, welcomed them, willingly sharing their water and food supplies and demonstrating experience as traders. Far from being cannibals, MacFarlane was to find, these Islanders possessed all the attributes of 'the noble savage'.

Although the idea of the noble savage has not weathered as well, it has, we will see, brought with it even further-reaching consequences for Islander people. Certainly, the original concept of the noble savage was at the time a very powerful one in Western thought, with its image of mankind living in a primitive state of innocence in nature; their own nature as yet unspoiled by the depredations and contaminations of civilisation. In MacFarlane's writing the image is tied up with what he defined as the ideal 'social state' (p. 129) and rests on his inability to recognise, as evolved forms and structures, the complex societies that existed in New Guinea and the Torres Strait Islands. As a missionary, he contended that '[t]here must be some goal, some state of perfection which we may never reach, but to which all true progress must bring us nearer' (pp. 129–30). There is a crucial distinction in his mind between progress towards a distorted goal ingrained in civilised and developing nations and true progress to the ideal social state.

Observing Islander society he initially saw it thus:

> It is a state of individual freedom and self-government, rendered possible by the equal development and just balance of the intellectual, moral, and physical parts of our nature — a state in which we shall each be so perfectly fitted for social existence by knowing what is right, and at the same time feeling an irresistible impulse to do what we know to be right, that all laws and all punishments shall be unnecessary. In such a state every man would have a sufficiently well-balanced intellectual organisation to understand the moral law in all its details, and would require no other motive but the free impulses of his own nature to obey that law. (MacFarlane, 1888, p. 130)

Such a state of affairs closely resembled what had earlier been known as utopia; a state of perfection that is not of place but of imagination

— a state of being; a state of grace. MacFarlane's view of Islanders is, in this way, related to the accepted view of the ideal state of humanity. He described

> the 'noble savage'...in New Guinea [and the Torres Strait], where the natives are found in their primitive simplicity, the undisputed lords of the soil, displaying a proud independence, their lives void of care, and with little to excite either ambition or jealousy, as they see every one around them sharing the same lot, enduring the same hardships, feeding on the same food, and arrayed in the same rude garments. They have no laws or law courts (so far as we know), but the public opinion of the village freely expressed. Each man respects the rights of his fellows, and any infraction of those rights very rarely takes place. In these communities all are nearly equal. There are none of those wide distinctions of education and ignorance, wealth and poverty, master and servant, which are the product of our civilisation. There is none of that widespread division of labour, which, while it increases wealth, produces also conflicting interests. There is not that severe competition and struggle for existence, or for wealth, which the dense population of civilised countries inevitably creates. All excitements to great crimes are thus wanting, and petty ones are suppressed, partly by the influence of public opinion, but chiefly by that natural sense of justice and of his neighbours' rights which seems to be in some degree inherent in every race of man. (MacFarlane, 1888, pp. 131–32)

This was an extremely idealised description and, although a far cry from his anticipated worries about cannibalism, just as unrealistic. Islander people were now seen as living in an isolated, idyllic, utopian society, uncontaminated by the evil of civilised worlds; a pristine wilderness in which the people existed free of either want or the need to own possessions. In their childlike simplicity, with their lives void of care, MacFarlane considered them to be affluent, for instead of competition and division, he contended, there was sharing, equity and a natural sense of justice. He could see no social foundations for any distinctions to be made on the basis of wealth, status, education or work. There was no conflict, he argued, because there were no competing interests; no reasons for opposition and antagonism; indeed no 'excitement to great crimes'. The state of such a utopian society, he suggested, had no need for regulatory devices such as laws or law courts. Through MacFarlane's eyes, the society he viewed had no recognisable form or structure and he took this, therefore, to mean that it actually had no form or structure at all.

1. Missionary inscriptions of the 'lost soul'

Based on these theories, MacFarlane set about establishing his own personal Iona. The missionaries established sixty mission stations and six churches along six hundred miles of coastline communities. Training institutions for native evangelists were also established at Murray Island and Port Moresby to assist the mission to rescue the lost souls. And, after a few short years of their occupation in these parts, the missionaries documented six languages or dialects — MacFarlane was not able to distinguish in his text which was a language and which was a dialect — whereupon they produced translations of the New Testament, hymn books, catechism and curriculum materials for teaching 'the natives'.

> In our mission work in New Guinea we have had to contend with difficulties quite peculiar to the place. We have had to sail in unknown and dangerous waters in order to reach the natives. We have had to contend with savages and cannibals, who regard strangers generally as enemies to be killed, cooked, and eaten. We have had to pass through sickly swamps and be exposed to deadly fevers in planting and superintending our mission stations. We have had to reduce the languages to writing, and translate portions of the Scriptures, school books, and hymn books into them. We have had to battle with the evil influences of abandoned sailors, although we have been helped rather than otherwise by many of the visitors and travellers who have come to New Guinea. We have had to guide the natives in making and administering laws, in developing the resources of their country, in building houses, making roads, and, in fact, in everything connected with their material as well as their spiritual progress. (MacFarlane, 1888, pp. 184–85)

The goal of the mission was to bring the gospel to the people, rescue the lost souls, and guide them back towards the ideal state. Given that MacFarlane could not recognise any of the social structures then in place, it seemed to him that there was an obvious need to introduce recognisable ones — new laws, new belief systems, new ways of living and working. Not realising what they were subjugating, the missionaries regarded this as a justifiable act. With no understanding of 'native' structures, they imposed remedies and reforms that they saw as universal. Indeed, because the missionaries intended the reforms to be well ordered, they were proud of their achievements:

> Let the present appearance and condition of some of the towns and villages where we have mission stations be compared with what they were fifteen years ago, and the difference is truly wonderful. Instead

of the war song, the cannibal feast, and the night dance, churches and schools and family worship are established. Instead of the wild-looking appearance of the people, dressed in feathers and shells and paint, they are now respectably clothed, and ashamed of their former appearance and habits. Instead of dirt huts, lazy and cruel husbands, and neglected children, there are now well built houses, industrious and kind husbands, and bright and intelligent children. Instead of every man doing as he liked, which led to village quarrels, plunder, and war, there are now laws established, magistrates and policemen appointed, and law and order prevail...Instead of heathenism and cannibalism, there is springing up a growing education and a thriving trade. Side by side with the preaching of the gospel goes the social improvement of the natives. (MacFarlane, 1888, pp. 188–89)

In each of these instances the missionaries overlaid what was unrecognisable to them with structures that they could recognise; they replaced the unknown with the known. The Islanders' culture was replaced with the fundamental accoutrements of Western culture; Christianity replaced their religion; English apparel and taboos replaced Islander ideas about clothing the body; English-style buildings replaced the Islanders' homes; English concepts of law, education and work replaced the complex evolutions of the Islanders' social, political and economic structures; the customs and structures of the English lifeworld began to influence that of the Islanders. That this was done intentionally but in ignorance makes no difference to the final result.

Despite the theoretical underpinnings there was no way, of course, that these people could be returned to an 'ideal state'. In practical terms the mission strove instead to shape them as recognisably civilised by 'furnish[ing] [them] with the useful appliances of civilized life' (MacFarlane, 1888, p. 189) while shielding them from the evil influences created by the degeneration of those same civilised societies. The mission's approach was based on education and protection; it was aimed both at re-educating Islanders from their own ways and insulating them from the evils of civilisation:

> our primary project in going there was not that we might render it safe to land upon its shores...it was not that we might render life and property secure whilst the miner digs for coal, iron, and gold, which are known to exist there...although we are fully persuaded that the introduction of Christianity will do this more effectually than anything else: it was not the treasures of the country, but the inhabitants that we sought. (MacFarlane, 1888, p. 24)

1. Missionary inscriptions of the 'lost soul'

Understandably, the missionaries saw the role of Christianity in a positive not a negative way. Yet at the same time the process of cultural destruction and the exploitation of a people necessarily went hand in hand with the appropriation of their land, their natural resources and their labour in the secular domain.

MacFarlane's mission, to save the souls of the Islanders through Christian guidance, came quite clearly from his own worldview. They came from his own critique of the civilisation of which he was a part; his own conceptual view of the noble savages and their historical evolution; his resolute belief in the transformative power of the gospel; and his belief that missionary 'good works' could stem the pernicious influence of creeping civilisation.

What his missionary view did not include, of course, was crucial: this was the lived reality of Islanders in all its complexity, with its own history and its own goals. The Islanders represented in the missionary's text are not the Islanders as they would have described themselves and their world at that time. Instead, here was an Islander whose own understanding of history was not recognised and who was, therefore, re-configured in relation to the religious and historical knowledge of an alien culture.

MacFarlane's writing documents the beginning of a systematic way of thinking about the Islanders — who and what they are and what should be done 'for' them to enrich their lives in recognisable and validated ways. In MacFarlane's case this was a particular and narrow view of Islanders as 'lost souls' needing to be rescued and remade. In his descriptions of Islanders outlined above as cannibals, noble savages and lost souls, he builds a logical argument that missionary intervention was a good and worthy project.

As this nineteenth-century St Columba and his missionaries came ashore on Darnley Island to found this new Iona, they not only altered the course of Islander history but they also brought with them a 'new' biblical history which took no account of what the Islanders knew about their own history; a new history, ready-made from pre-digested ideas about the inhabitants of lost utopias. With their hands they changed the landscape irrevocably, building settlements that they could recognise and value as outposts of a crusading civilisation. With their minds they sowed the seeds which would change the mental landscape as well, for they brought with them, again ready-made, a set of philosophical principles — a new explanation of the universe; a new way of seeing the world; a new point of view.

2

Domesticating the savage

> ...it was a principal object of our work to discover, if possible, racial characteristics.
>
> (McDougall, 1903, p. 189)

The detailed findings published by the scientists who were members of the Cambridge Anthropological Expedition to the Torres Strait in 1898 represent a very different site of investigation from those of the missionaries. For these are the works of university-based scholars — academic reports based on the scientific analysis of data they collected from observations and testing of and interviews with Torres Strait Islanders themselves. In fact, it is precisely because the collection and analysis of the data adhered to the underlying principles of scientific method, that the various Cambridge reports carry a degree of weight. Here at least, we might well suppose, the representations of Torres Strait Islanders should provide us with 'accurate' and 'objective' representations of who and what Islanders were at the time of the expedition.

A superficial reading of the reports that they wrote on their return to Cambridge may well confirm for the scientific and scholarly community the validity of much of the contents. In such a reading, any peculiarities would now be understood in terms of the historical context of the expedition with the data re-interpreted from a late twentieth century perspective. Indeed, the centenary of this expedition has already been marked by a renewed academic interest in both its history and its findings (Hart, 1998; Whittle, 1997). Anthropologists and experimental psychologists in particular are even now rediscovering and reconsidering the importance of this expedition in the formation of their disciplines and 'revisiting a formative event of one hundred years ago... to throw light on our own contemporary search for a new paradigm'

(Hart, 1998, p. 3). For this was an ambitious, groundbreaking expedition not only in terms of proportion and logistics but also in terms of its theoretical and methodological innovations. It was an expedition at the cutting edge of the social sciences — those new scientific disciplines and knowledge emerging at the turn of last century.

The Cambridge expedition had been stimulated by an earlier collection of ethnographical data gathered by Alfred Cort Haddon. A marine zoologist, Haddon had relinquished his position as Professor of Zoology to pursue his new-found intellectual and research interests in cultural anthropology after visiting the Torres Strait in 1888. He was convinced that anthropology should be grounded in rigorously collected and collated scientific data and, as such, was one of the new breed of ethnographically centred anthropologists who became the model for the twentieth-century discipline (Hart, 1998, p. 6). Arguing that 'no investigation of a people was complete that did not embrace a study of their psychology, and being aware of the paucity of our knowledge of the comparative physiology and psychology of primitive people' (Rivers, 1901, preface), Haddon determined that a team of psychologists should also be part of the expedition. These men were the 'founding fathers' of these disciplines, revolutionaries who were drawing the boundaries of academic theory in the early years of the twentieth century. The expedition, and their ideas, were to have a major significance long after their reputations had vanished from academic consciousness and been replaced by later 'founding fathers' such as Malinowski and Radcliffe-Brown (Hart, 1998; Whittle, 1997).

Haddon's approach challenged the boundaries of what was already known and understood about primitive people, and his expedition to the Torres Strait stands as one of the most comprehensive early attempts to document the lives and characteristics of a primitive society before the onslaught of colonial expansion changed Torres Strait society forever and before the previous skills and knowledge of the Islanders were lost to the world.

However, in terms of this book, these scientific texts represent a different site in another sense as well. For, unlike the missionaries, the scientists did leave — and what they deduced and wrote went with them. Their findings were not relayed to the Islanders daily; they were not drummed into their heads as were the ideas of the missionaries. Although the six volumes of their reports took decades to publish — 1901, 1904, 1907, 1908, 1912, 1935 — the scientists themselves were present in the Torres Strait for only a few months. Drs William HR Rivers, Charles S Myers and William McDougall spent from May to September

1898 carrying out tests and observations on Murray Island, while from May to July Sidney H Ray, Anthony Wilkin, Charles S Seligmann and Haddon were in Papua New Guinea. In October the expedition officially broke up although Myers, McDougall, Seligmann, Ray and Haddon did not go on to Sarawak until the end of April 1899. Until recent years, few Islanders — including myself — knew little about these findings, let alone how to access them.

While many authors on Torres Strait issues (e.g. Beckett, 1987; Singe, 1989; Sharp, 1993) make reference to the content of these reports, there is no direct evidence that any material effect on the lives of Islanders directly resulted from this huge body of writing. For these were academic treatises designed to expand the intellectual landscape of the then infant social sciences. Their purpose was to objectively observe and document, not to change or distort what they were observing and documenting. Yet, in effect, the work of these scientists was later to do precisely this. For they were to shape and inform disciplines, leaving behind a legacy embedded in knowledge that has not yet been properly recognised or acknowledged (e.g. Roldan, 1993). As such, this invisibility makes the legacy of their work all the more insidious.

Now, more than ever, these reports are being consulted by authors writing on the Torres Strait (e.g. Beckett, 1987; Singe, 1989; Sharp, 1993; Mullins, 1995) — as historical sources and as authoritative accounts of what Islanders once were and the way they once lived. They are considered to contain data that provide accurate snapshots of a vanished culture. Now, more than ever, these reports are accessible to Islanders who can use them in the search for their own antecedents. Islanders interested in their history can now find details once lost to them from the genealogies, collected in particular by Rivers, which help them to authoritatively trace their connections to each other and to past generations. They are able to do this from the descriptions, painstakingly collected by Haddon, of past practices and customs that provide an understanding of tradition and heritage; and from the linguistic studies, compiled in detail by Ray, that provide insights into languages that were spoken a century ago 'before they were corrupted by outside influences'. In this light in particular it is important for researchers to have an accurate measure of the significance of these reports both to their own and to others' understanding of Islanders' past and present. Most importantly, the analysis of these authoritative texts can be used to determine how the forms and processes of the scientists' rationale and methods have provided both the conditions and the limits to the way Islanders could be understood historically and can be understood now and in the future.

2. Domesticating the savage

The seven-member research team landed on Thursday Island on 22 April 1898. On their arrival, the scientists found to their dismay that things had already considerably changed for the Islanders in the Torres Strait. The Islanders' lives had been adversely affected by a burgeoning marine industry that harvested the bêche-de-mer (sea cucumber) and the mother-of-pearl shell. This had attracted a lot of people with financial interests who were exploiting the Islanders as a cheap labour force. As we have seen, in the eastern region of the Torres Strait, where the islands were more isolated, missionaries from the London Missionary Society (LMS) in England had control of the communities and were busily introducing a new moral order designed to retrieve the Islanders' souls from the devil. By this time the Queensland government had also stepped in to regulate disorder in the commercial sector and to protect the welfare of all Islanders in the Torres Strait, including those under missionary control. The Islanders, in this way, found themselves invaded and besieged from a number of quarters, overwhelmed by the different regimes and new forms of regulation as commerce, Christianity and an emerging colonial bureaucracy combined to usher them into the alien world of twentieth-century capitalism.

Undaunted, the project for the Haddon-led expedition was simply given an added and, if anything, more urgent purpose. The Cambridge team was now 'to recover the past life of the islanders, not merely in order to give a picture of their former conditions of existence and their social and religious activities, but also to serve as a basis for an appreciation of the changes that have since taken place' (Haddon, 1935, p. xiv). The accurate charting of native languages, the natives' primitive psychology, as well as their traditional culture, were now priorities for the team who knew that there would be no second chance. The new sense of purpose required concentrated efforts to extricate and describe what constituted the Islander before the arrival of the marine industries, government agencies and missionaries, as the project had never been about assessing the impact made by intruders from the West on Islanders or documenting the damage done to whole communities by the inroads of commercial enterprises, Christianity and an early colonial bureaucracy. In this way, the expedition gained its first overtly political overtones.

It is important in the context of this book to stress that by no means were these Cambridge scientists testing and observing in a theoretical vacuum. They came from a university already hundreds of years old, a university that had seen the knowledge it was producing increasing exponentially during the nineteenth century. They left their book-lined libraries to travel halfway around the world to test their theories.

And they returned to their libraries to assess their data, consult with the relevant literature on the subject and write their reports. They also lectured, debated and produced seminal works in developing disciplines. Their aim was to produce a comparative study — a sort of 'before and after' chapter of the human race.

To chart the characteristics of 'the savage mind', the team proposed to directly compare Islanders and Europeans on a broad range of validated scientific tests. They then cross-referenced their data with the scientific knowledge gleaned from other studies of different groups before drawing their conclusions. By this process the scientists did much more than describe and report on the characteristics of Islanders and their society. They inscribed the Torres Strait Islander in a particular and already prescribed relation with European people, with 'other savage people', and with European knowledge. In doing so, they embedded the Islanders in an evolutionary history that they felt explained the continuing inequality between the different racial groups of the world. It is this action, and the subsequent relation that it engendered at the level of knowledge which is with us still, that limits understandings about Islanders and defines the parameters of the position that was constructed for them.

To missionaries and scientists alike, Islanders were a people from the past. The position of Islanders has been framed, pre-conditioned and subsequently described, explained and understood — disciplined — by a scientific community of scholars. It is to illustrate how these pre-conditions infiltrated and shaped the scientists' interpretation of data as well as how this circumscribed, informed and limited the conclusions they were able to draw on Torres Strait Islander characteristics. Scientific research is embedded in mental abstractions, hypothetical constructs and illusions concerning the natural world. It is both imbued with personal bias and riddled with unacknowledged and unrecognised subjectivities. What scientists 'know' or 'investigate', and what they consequently 'understand' about the objects of their study, is built up using the ideas, images and shapes they have recorded within their emerging disciplines. What they have learned and validated provides a limit to their personal perceptions and the questions they pose for themselves, which in turn restricts their ability to develop abstractions and construct hypotheses about their objects of study which remain alien to their comprehension. They cannot 'know' something if they do not possess either the vocabulary or experience to recognise and position that knowledge in either an accurate or even a truly meaningful way. Through these references scientists consciously and unconsciously construct their illusions — their view of the reality of the world in which they live, or, in this instance, the world in which the people they are observing live. I will attempt to illustrate this over the next four chapters; first in relation to linguistics, then in turn psychology, physiology and anthropology. The objective is to highlight how disciplinary practices as well as the thinking of the day on civilised and uncivilised people come together to domesticate the Islanders as savages.

3

Linguistic inscriptions of the language

> The former grammars (based on translations of the Gospels) had left many expressions to be elucidated and explained…The difficulties had been simplified, or as my informant Pasi [*sic*] described the process, 'they cut it short'. (Ray, 1907, p. 5)

Ray's linguistic work on the Cambridge expedition represents a concerted attempt to hear and describe in depth the formal aspects of the traditional languages as they were spoken in the Torres Strait at the turn of the century. Spanning 528 pages, the report describes the languages of the eastern and western Islanders, the languages of the people of Cape York, and the languages of the southern people of Papua New Guinea.

At first glance, the extensive descriptions of the grammar of the Islander languages that Ray produced are impressive. On scrutiny they are, however, less remarkable and tell us more about Ray and the emerging discipline of linguistics than they do about the languages he was studying. Historically, linguists have a location in the production of knowledge. In the period in which Ray was writing, major expeditions around the globe were attempting to scientifically taxonomise all aspects of difference — an idea that had great intellectual currency at the time — and researchers were comparing such differences on an evolutionary scale.

If linguistic positioning was an important social indicator, linguistic progress was also of vital importance. For this reason, it is clear that while Ray's study was mostly centred on capturing the formal elements of the grammar of the two traditional languages of the Strait, his location in history led him to propose that the knowledge gained in his study was primarily a tool with which to ascertain the maturation stages in the grammar by comparing it with other languages. In this way the linguistic nuts and bolts could position the people in a universal sequence which would define them in an evolutionary history. For this reason, although he couldn't find the evidence he was looking for, he was sure of its existence and his report was constructed around his conviction rather than around his data. His conclusions, therefore, owe more to his original question and his intellectual point of departure than they do to the material he so painstakingly collected.

Ray published his work in 1907 but it was not until Ferdinand de Saussure's ground-breaking lectures delivered between 1906 and 1911 that a scientific basis was evolved that could possibly locate psychology in linguistics. Comparing the psychology of languages was, at the time of the expedition, only at a speculative stage.

Ray was studying the two traditional languages of the Torres Strait at a time when there were multiple theoretical shifts being made in the study of languages. Scientific theories were being proposed which sought to overthrow established wisdoms. Linguists such as Ray were attempting to redefine their discipline. The questions that they asked were based on drawing the boundaries of the paradigms they were in the process of constructing — boundaries that were already, in theoretical terms, basically decided upon.

Up until then there had been two clear positions on linguistics: grammar and philology. Grammar, at the initiation of the Greeks and later taken up by the French, was oriented to the formal elements of a language and was heavily reliant on the logic of grammatical rules to elaborate the use and misuse of a language. As such, it had become a very prescriptive discipline. Philology, on the other hand, was oriented to written texts rather than the language used in daily discourses. The main preoccupation was literary histories and especially forms and styles of writers over different periods, with criticism at the centre of its discipline.

By the time Ray was gathering data, however, there was a growing position in linguistic studies, which held that languages not only could be compared but that they should be compared. To Saussure, '[w]hat was new was the elucidation of one language by reference to a related language, explaining the forms of one by appeal to forms of the other' (1972, p. 2). Those who proposed that one language could be compared with another looked towards the 'living language' and subsequently moved to develop those standpoints that became known as comparative philology and comparative grammar.

Comparative philology continued its earlier stand on styles and the focus was on the ideological creativity of language as used in speech acts. Underlying all forms of verbal expressions were elements that provided for correspondence between speakers. How else would there be coherence between speakers, it was asked. Coherence in communicative events, it was contended, comes about because they are aligned by elements of phonetics (familiar sounds), grammar (recognised ways of making meaning), and lexical forms (a shared vocabulary). Language, seen in these ways, corresponded with a normative system borne out of communal usage — an agreed system of ways to structure and make common meanings.

To grammarians, the living language was seen to be embedded in 'a stable, immutable system of normatively identical linguistic forms which the individual consciousness finds ready-made and which is incontestable for that consciousness' (Volosinov, 1973, p. 57). It was not, it was argued, a contortion of some ideological creativity. In short, grammatical features of a confined linguistic system not only determined but also delimited forms of communication between speakers.

Ray had definite opinions about his own theoretical positions that he wanted to prove. Confronted with a theoretical standpoint based on a normative system of phonetic, grammatical and lexical forms as the basis for describing languages on the one hand, and on the other with the philologists pointing to instances and thus 'facts' in communicative events, he was determined to build his career by overturning established wisdoms. He rejected such positivism, which uses facts as a basis for its standpoint.

For Ray, the stage of development in the grammar of a language had to be identified and fully understood. Once a language was known in these ways, he claimed, comparisons with another could then be contemplated. He thus moved to provide the following examples to demonstrate the 'true principles upon which linguistic comparisons can be made' (p. 507):

> The process by which a thought is expressed in a language and the changes of form or position by which the words in a sentence are fitted to one another, are the only safe guides in establishing the connection of languages. There can be no relationship in the speech of the Murray Islander who says, *Nako ma-ra nei?* (What thee-of name), of the Banks Island Melanesian who says, *I-sei na-sasa-ma?* (Person-who the-name-thy), or the Hindu who says, *Terá kyá nám hai?* (Yours what name is). But the language of the Micronesian who says, *Ia ito-m?* or *Ia ato-m?* (Who (is) name-thy) uses exactly the same formula of words as the Loyalty Islander who says, *Iâ iâ-m?* and we may regard them as related to one another just as the Solomon Islander who asks,

3. Linguistic inscriptions of the language

A-hei na aha-mu? is speaking a language akin to that of the Fijian who asks, *O d'ei na yad'a-mu?* (Person-who the name-thy), identical in construction with the expression of the Banks Islander just given. (Ray, 1907, p. 507)

Ray qualified this however by noting that 'a similarity of structure is not evidence of linguistic connection unless there is also an identity of formative particles' (p. 507). He subsequently moved to provide the following example:

The Turkish words *el-in, el-e, el-den* are translated exactly by the Miriam [Murray Islander language] *tag-ra, tag-em, tag-lam,* or the Mabuiag *geta-u, geta-ka, geta-ngu* (of hand, to hand, from hand), but there is no connection between the languages. But when, as in the words given above for 'name-thy', the Banks Islander says *sasa-ma*, the Micronesian *ito-m* or *ato-m*, the Loyalty Islander *iâ-m*, the Solomon Islander and Fijian *aha-mu* and *yad'a-mu*, and it can be shown by comparison with languages spoken between them that not only are *sasa, ito, ato, iâ, aha, yad'a*, related words for 'name', but that the same suffix *-ma, -m, -mu* is used in these, and in the languages between, we may safely assume that we are dealing with related languages. (Ray, 1907, p. 507)

Finding connections between languages for Ray required the consideration of root words, the formative particles used with them, as well as the effects they had on meaning when words and particles were compounded (what he termed as 'word-building'). This approach, to Ray, required no less than a close examination of all the grammatical features that provided the basic structure of the traditional languages in the Torres Strait.

Ray maintained that the process by which speech acts are formally structured and expressed in a language, and particularly their stage of development in grammatical terms, are the only primary organising principles by which language connections can legitimately be made. Isolated cases of a similar word or words appearing in different languages, as far as he was concerned, did not prove language connections. The priority was for a more extensive consideration of grammatical features and syntactical rules. What was crucial to his approach was the view that a language had to be treated at the outset as a static entity in a temporal space, contextualised only by its grammatical rules. In other words, connecting languages in these ways affords no view to ideological creativities and thus no view to a history of language. Just as

Ray queried the early enterprise of basing connections exclusively on the style and sound of words, and particularly of not factoring in at least some position on the formal aspects of a language, so in turn we need to question his method of giving exclusive attention to the charting of developments in grammatical rules and structures without including the people in the making and remaking of their language.

From his review of extant practices in the literature, however, Ray resolved that a more focused effort was needed in the gathering of data because what was needed, he felt, was more evidence of the grammar of the traditional languages. Likewise, from his consideration of the theoretical trends, he resolved to focus on analysing the Islander languages by their grammar. His approach was to collect as many language encounters from the Islanders as he could. It was only through a very labour-intensive process that he was able to put together, with what he felt was some certainty, the grammar of the traditional languages as they were spoken in the western islands (for example pp. 6–48) and the eastern islands (pp. 49–87).

Ray gathered statements used in day-to-day conversations and studied them individually for their grammar. From these, he was able to document a variety of ways of saying things, all the time checking and double-checking his data. To ensure scientific accuracy, he had his notes and descriptions checked not only by informants but also by the older members of the community, whose assistance he found particularly important to verify whether those things said by informants were stated correctly. This also helped him to authenticate the data he gathered as 'traditional language' and not some contemporary form adjusted to suit the changing times.

Ray also contended with dialectical variations. He considered in depth the phonology of the words (sounds of vowels, consonants, syllables, etc.), word-formations (roots and particles of words), and classes of words (demonstrative words and particles, adjectives, nouns, pronouns, verbs, adverbs, connective words, exclamations and numerals). From his efforts he was able to conclude, for instance, that word formation in the western Islander language was 'in the agglutinate stage, the significant roots and modifying particles being clearly distinguishable. The particles have no meaning when separated from the root word' (1907, p. 9). By contrast, he was able to resolve that the eastern Islander language was also 'in the agglutinate stage, but the significant roots and modifying particles…[were] not so clearly distinguishable as in the language of the western Islanders. The particles have no meaning when separated from the root word' (p. 53). That is, from Ray's findings it appeared that the traditional grammar of the western Islander language was not as complex as that of the eastern Islanders. For this reason, the eastern Islander language was, he noted, 'more difficult to analyse' (p. 49) than the western Islander one with its 'simple construction' (p. 7).

Clearly Ray's work was very carefully carried out and its scholarly exactitude has enabled it to provide useful information — particularly as a counter to the derogatory claims that Islander people did not have a systematic, grammatical language. Certainly, the contemporary need to establish the fact that Islanders were fully human has long since passed and Ray's desire to position Islanders on an evolutionary scale is just as obsolete. But his work is, of course, significant to Islanders of today because it now provides a record of the linguistic features of the Torres Strait languages spoken a century ago. However, what needs to be clearly noted about linguistic studies of this kind is that the information produced by such linguists has been built around their own terms of reference. Despite its scholarly nature, Ray's findings did not give any thought to the contemporary position of the speakers and, therefore, there was little understanding of the traditional languages beyond their perceived grammatical order.

In fact, throughout Ray's whole project, from his reviews of the literature to data gathering and analyses, there is little reference at all to the idea that Islanders, as people, might have an influence on the grammar of their languages. Islander people only figure when identifiable elements of grammar require an owner. It is their speech, not their meanings, that is seen as the important part of the act of speaking. They are heard but not listened to; how the words are spoken is more important than what is being said. The speaker, it would seem, is irrelevant.

If the history of a language and its users is not factored into the theory as a primary standpoint, then any knowledge generated about that language is flawed. This is not to reject entirely what linguists have done, or are currently doing. It is to make the point that the grammarians' concentration on formal aspects of a language fundamentally separates the language from the people; it falsely separates the act of speaking from what is being spoken. Studies of this kind are content to describe and conclude with grammatical summations as if languages were floating in a vacuum, 'ready-made' within a system of phonetic, grammatical and lexical forms and divorced from the social context in which the speech is being uttered.

Considering the research of Ray and other linguists, Saussure (1959; 1972) was to find that little care had been taken to define what it was that grammarians were studying. It became increasingly obvious that a theoretical standpoint was needed to articulate a historical position about language that fundamentally links a language with its speakers. If it ever was to be a science, as Saussure contemplated at the beginning of the twentieth century, linguists first needed to clearly define what it was they were doing.

Saussure (1959; 1972) subsequently proposed that what linguistics of that century needed to be about was the linguistic sign. His (1959; 1972) linguistic sign was not about the literal word, for instance, formed by the letters 'm.a.n' but about the relational aspect of what and how the word meant. To Saussure, a word only provided a sign to a meaning that was always external to the word itself. But, as he added, meaning for each word, thus the sign, is achieved only in its relation to other signs. No word can stand on its own and have meaning only by reference to itself. For example, his argument was that the word formed by the letters 'm.a.n' on its own has no real significance unless the word 'man' has been assigned a meaning in its relation to what was known as the sign 'woman', and vice versa. Meanings for signs in these ways thus can only be relational. On their own words have no meaning but the sign and what is signed — signal and signification — does, and it was this which required primary consideration by linguists. With this position came Saussure's first principle, that 'the linguistic sign is arbitrary' (Saussure, 1972, p. 67).

Saussure contended that to approach the sign in these ways also enabled linguists to witness 'the fact' that relations between 'man' and 'woman' could be inscribed differently by different language communities — this would also help explain how they can be peculiar to a particular language community. Such relations and their patterns of coexistence with each other subsequently gave him reason to maintain that in every language community there would be a unique pre-given structure which groups of people have adopted to identify themselves and their lifeworlds. With this came his second principle: that the linguistic sign '(a) occupies a certain temporal space, and (b) this space is measured in just one dimension: it is a line' (1972, pp. 69–70). Others, in Saussure's eyes, neglected to consider these principal features of the linguistic sign and thus failed to see not only the pre-given structures but missed out on postulating a plausible measure for a psychological disposition of a language group. Structural linguistics thus requires that more complex psychological structures by which daily communication operates are taken into account, and not only the history of the language. The people's language and the history of its development in these ways however are still secondary in this theoretical standpoint — and they are still an ancillary consideration to the linguists' readings of how grammar determines meaning.

It is this inability of linguists to give primacy to language speakers and to the history of a language that remains a fundamental limitation of linguistic practice to this day. This shortcoming has come about because scholars have taken for granted an approach that single-mindedly submerges and subjugates the presence of people and their community. Such an approach affords little priority to language formation in its socio-historical context. In its most basic position, modern-day linguistics assumes some 'special kind of discontinuity between the history of language and the system of language (i.e., language in its ahistorical, synchronic dimension)' (Volosinov, 1973, p. 54). Indeed, Saussure is well known for his separation of *la langue* (language system) and *la parole* (speech act/utterance). It is well noted that he elected to prioritise in his theoretical proposition principles based not on the history of a language but on how words are strung together at any moment in time according to the peculiarities of language groups and their pre-given structures. As Matejka and Titunik indicated in their translation of Volosinov's 1929 *Marxism and the Philosophy of Language* (1973), there are serious implications in the way 'synchrony is separated from diachrony in the investigation of verbal communication' (p. 2). Indeed, Volosinov himself argued that the 'dualistic discontinuity is absolutely insurmountable' (1973, p. 54). As far as he was concerned, language in its synchronic dimension could not be spoken of outside its historical position and language in its diachronic dimension could not be spoken of as outside any communicative event. As he pointed out, 'the linguistic forms that comprise the system of language are mutually indispensable and complementary to one' (1973, p. 54).

The message to modern-day linguists, who continue to engage in synchronic dimensions of living languages, from social theorists, who have a view to a philosophy of language, is that

> the actual reality of language-speech is not the abstract system of linguistic forms, not the isolated monologic utterance, and not the psychophysiological act of its implementation, but the social event of verbal interaction implemented in an utterance on utterances. (Matejka, 1973, p. 164)

Obviously, it would be pointless to discount completely what linguists have achieved over the past century. By approaching languages solely in their synchronic dimension, modern linguists were able to document the grammatical structures and syntactical rules of many native languages across the globe. These have been very useful in the teaching of languages in formal settings.

Furthermore, structuralist positions of pre-given entities potentially enable Indigenous peoples a means to locate epistemological configurations of the history of people, space and time that can precede the impact of colonial institutions — and it allows them to identify their uniqueness as native to the land. When such fundamentals are omitted as they were in this early period of modern linguistics, it enables people like Ray to make very astute claims: 'The grammars now given, based upon oral communications and phrases taken down from native dictation, must therefore be regarded as superseding all that was formerly written on the structure of the languages. The vocabularies have also been corrected and extended' (1907, p. 5). There is little damage done even when grammatical structures are compared and declared in the following manner:

> 1. The Western language of Torres Strait is Australian.
> 2. The Eastern language of the Torres Strait is morphologically [similar grammatical forms] related to the Papuan of New Guinea.
> 3. There is no genealogical [community of origin] connection between the two languages of the Strait.
> 4. There is no evidence of an African, Andaman, Papuan, or Malay connection with the Australian languages. There are reasons for regarding the Australian as in a similar morphological stage to the Dravidian, but there is no genealogical relationship proved. (Ray, 1907, p. 529)

However, it is problematic when modern linguists make scientific statements to the effect that,

> [a]lthough a morphological likeness between the languages of Papuans or Andaman Islanders [the nearest 'black race' west of New Guinea, as Ray referred to them] cannot at present be satisfactorily demonstrated, it seems to be at least possible that as the two races are in practically the same stage of culture, the psychology of their languages may be found on closer knowledge to have some common features. (Ray, 1907, p. 525)

This is merely scientific speculation based on an assumption which presupposes that the grammatical structures of languages in different parts of the globe embody a pre-given set of features of a native language

3. Linguistic inscriptions of the language

group that could be used to identify where people are located in the evolutionary process. Grammarians like Ray and Saussure — having discounted people, histories and particularly the socio-historical positions of languages — simply do not have the basis, other than the grammatical arrangement of words, by which they can connect people or their culture in an evolving social world. We can see, for example, that the elected approach in their emerging discipline to focus solely on formal grammars as spoken in the past — the emphasis Ray took to documenting the traditional grammars and to eliminating the more contemporary ones — at once demonstrates the distance between the speakers and the language as well as the abandonment of the very means by which to identify stages of maturation of the language systems as they existed when he visited the islands.

Irrespective of the factors that motivated linguists like Ray or Saussure, later social theorists like Volosinov maintained that their form of the discipline still needed to be substantiated by a theoretical proposition that encompassed an interactive and dynamic sociohistorical trajectory. In other words, the early linguists needed to incorporate a political path to the speech event being described, and a presence that situates it fundamentally in an economy of negotiating social futures. To achieve this requires no less than a full consideration of the people and their connection to the land and seas, their histories, and their political position.

4

Psychological inscriptions of the mind

> ...the predominant attention of the savage to concrete things around him may act as an obstacle to higher mental development.
>
> (Rivers, 1901, p. 45)

The Cambridge project also involved an in-depth study of the physiological and psychological characteristics of Islanders from two of the many inhabited islands in the Torres Strait (Mer and Mabuiag Islands), which could provide a scientific basis for a comparative study of the 'physiology and psychology of primitive people' (Haddon, 1901, preface). This important task was entrusted to the trained psychologists Rivers, Myers and McDougall who were assisted by Seligmann. Rivers, however, held the primary role.

The Cambridge scientists regarded their work as standing apart from previous experimental psychological studies. The project would be, these scientists believed, revolutionary in scale and accuracy; more rigorous, more objective and more wide-reaching — a definitive study. Previous studies, the scientists contended, had been done quickly, with researchers often administering a series of tests within the space of an hour. Now these rudimentary findings were to be tested on a scale that would by far surpass anything that had been done before. In this expedition the tests administered to Islanders were to be painstakingly carried out over a period of several months, thus minimising the fatigue factors that could limit responses on both sides. The Cambridge project would also focus in more depth and experiment with 'a certain number of individuals...many times and in different subjects of investigation on different days' (Rivers, 1901, p. 5).

The compilation of data on the physiology and psychology of Islanders was published in Volume II of the report. It was presented in two parts. Part 1, which is the subject of this chapter, reported on the study of vision and involved in-depth reports about: the physical characteristics and diseases of the eyes; visual acuity; colour vision (colour nomenclature, derivation of colour names, colours of the rainbow, colour vision of the peripheral retina, colour contrast, after-images and preference for colour); and visual spatial perception (binocular vision, bisection of lines, dissection of lines into three or more equal parts, estimation of vertical and horizontal lines, and the Müller–Lyer and other illusion tests).

Part 2, which will be dealt with in the following section, reported on hearing abilities (pathological condition of the ears, auditory acuity, upper limit of hearing and smallest perceptible tone-difference); smell (olfactory acuity and discrimination of odour strengths, memory and discrimination of odours); taste and cutaneous sensations (delicacy of tactile discrimination, localisation of point of skin touched, temperature spots, and sensibility to pain); muscular sense (discrimination of small differences of weight, and degree of the size–weight illusion); variations of blood pressure; and reaction times.

The first task of this particular study was to counter claims that native people were closer to animals than they were to civilised people. Only after this was incontrovertibly established could these scientists proceed to show precisely how the savage mind interpreted the senses. How did the savage mind see, hear, smell, feel and taste the world in which 'it' lived? The logic behind the research was that if acuteness in the senses could be measured scientifically in native people and demonstrated to be similar — although obviously not the same — as results achieved by 'civilised' people, then it would follow that the idea that native people were closely related to animals would be proved to be false. Although 'these savages' were less socially developed than civilised people, the scientists were convinced that they were social beings nevertheless and, as such, could provide a window into the human history they wanted to define and understand.

The intent, without doubt, was a noble one. Yet there is no clearer example of the refusal of Islander people's intellectual capacities, historical position and cultural integrity than that which can be found in these reports, particularly in that of Rivers (1901). Intent aside, what these scientists did in the name of objective, tested, scientific observation requires a more detailed scrutiny.

Vision

Vision, of course, is not just a straightforward linkage between a concrete reality and the eye itself. It is much more complex than this to both Rivers and the science of his day.

In scientific terms the anatomy of the eye processes light rays which are then interpreted by the brain. The eye responds, for example, to differences in brightness and in colour. It interprets a stream of information and processes it into a meaningful illusion. There are two principal regions of the brain that process this information — the superior colliculus in the more primitive brain stem and the visual cortex in the lateral geniculate nucleus of the cerebral cortex. What we 'see' is an illusion or a cultural representation of reality limited by the physiological capacity of the visual system to interpret these signals. The brain takes the visual image and interprets it in reference to past experiences and present expectations. What we see therefore is an illusion that is at once limited by both physiological and psychological factors. A person's physiological responses are regulated by the senses, through which the mind conjures up an imagery that locates these experiences in memory (Rivers, 1901).

Rivers had been greatly influenced by John Hughlings Jackson, a British neurologist who had done intensive work on epilepsy and had developed sophisticated theories about the functioning of the brain and the nervous system. It was Jackson who had first theorised that there were different levels of brain function and that areas of the brain which had appeared more recently in the evolutionary scale dominate or suppress the lower or older centres. The cerebral cortex, he argued, has the prime function of 'refining and keeping control of, and inhibiting, the more primitive processes of the older mid-brain' (Whittle, 1997, p. 5). Psychology and anthropology, in this way, were considered by scientists like Jackson and Rivers to be intrinsically tied up with the biological sciences. The physiology and the psychology are part of the one process; racial superiority and racial difference can be seen in both biology and in culture. For this reason, Rivers and his colleagues needed to first examine the physiology of the Islanders before they could even begin to find out about native psychology.

Rivers' initial objective, however, was to draw a scientific outline of the physiological characteristics of the eyes, which would prove beyond reasonable doubt that these natives had the same visual equipment as civilised people; that they had at the very least the potential to see in a scientifically comparable way. To do this he first had to locate a standard by which comparatives could later be drawn. For if the physiological condition of the eyes showed no debilitating factor it could then be assumed that the starting points for Islanders would be the same as for those in civilised societies. Immediately, however, he ran into problems:

> On examining the eyes...I found a difficulty in getting an extensive view of the cornea and conjunctiva...it seemed to me that this was due to a greater narrowness of the palpebral fissure, but I have no direct measurements to show whether this was the case. (Rivers, 1901, p. 8)

Rivers' work is sprinkled throughout with apologies of this kind as time and time again he encountered insurmountable measurement problems which created serious limitations in his data and, as a result, in his findings — limitations which, he sometimes had to admit, effectively reduced the feasibility of conducting a comparative project at all. Even so, as we will see, this certainly did not prevent him from making a plethora of conjectures about the physiology and psychology of Islanders.

Rivers' examination of the condition of the cornea and conjunctiva found 'in nearly all cases [that] the conjunctiva was pigmented' (p. 8). That is, the types of pigmentation that modify the epidermis of the eye, a protective layer or membrane covering the eyes including the cornea and the inner side of the eyelid, were seen to range from irregular patches to an even distribution over the eye giving the eye a 'yellowish appearance' (p. 8). Other variations, he observed, included patches that 'existed together with the diffuse pigmentation; in other cases, especially in younger men and children, the rest of the conjunctiva was white and clear' (p. 8). Rivers found also that 'the cornea was immediately surrounded by a definite ring of pigment' (p. 8) and recalled this as something noted in his readings of the existing literature in Pergens' 1898 descriptions of the Congolese, as well as in Kotelmann's 1879 notes about 'a Negro' (cited in Rivers, 1901, p. 8). He also noted that 'a similar ring may be seen in many animals' (p. 8). In addition to this observation, Rivers witnessed cases of 'a definite arcus senilis' (p. 8) — a greyish fatty deposit in the cornea found in older people. This made the cornea appear hazy and gave the 'outer edge of the iris a bluish appearance' (p. 9). Opacities of the cornea were also observed by Rivers and were thought by him to be a possible factor that restricted visual acuity, especially in cases where the middle of the cornea was affected. He noted that people who lived on the south-eastern side of Murray Island where it was very windy and dusty, and who appeared 'less healthy in other ways' (p. 9), had 'the most marked corneal changes' (p. 9).

Rivers found no cases of people with a squint — strabismus — although conjunctivitis and cataracts were evident and pterygium and pinguicula were common. Pterygium and pinguicula resulted in the thickening of the conjunctiva that spreads over part of the cornea that can, at times, grow across the eyes: 'pinguicula forms one stage or part of one stage in the development of pterygium' (p. 9). He suspected that dust and smoke from within shelters, huts and houses were the primary irritants that caused pinguicula and its subsequent development into a pterygium. The youngest case he observed was in a boy aged 11 but the more marked cases were in men about 40 years of age. By contrast, the condition in older men was less marked, a fact which led him to surmise that pterygium occurs in the early years. Unfortunately he made insufficient observations of the condition in women, who in fact would have been those most affected by cooking fires and dusty interiors, an omission which inhibited his ability to make any definite statement on whether the condition could be differentiated by gender. Nevertheless, as the results of his visual acuity tests showed, the presence of a pterygium did not appear to affect the Islanders' sight (Rivers, 1901, p. 39).

Rivers observed that the Islanders' pupil size was generally smaller than in Europeans although, as he was to later regret, he 'did not make any measurements of the size of the pupils' (p. 11). Eccentricity of the pupils, on the other hand, he found to be not very different in the European people he tested. The few he observed were found to be on the nasal side, a finding which concurred with Kotelmann's findings of three Patagonians in Berlin: 'it is perhaps noteworthy in this connection that in such eccentricity as existed in Torres Strait, the displacement was also nasal' (Rivers, 1901, p. 11).

Visual acuity

Rivers started his analysis of his visual acuity data with the acknowledgment that it was the common view amongst travellers of the day in 'uncivilised parts of the world' (Rivers, 1901, p. 12), that 'savages can see objects and hear sounds which escape the most acute European' (p. 12). In his report Rivers pointed to the existence of an extensive scientific debate about this subject (see *Nature*, 1885, vol. XXXI, pp. 340, 359, 386, 407, 433, 457, 503, 552). Lord Rayleigh, for example, argued against those who were 'ascribing to savage and semi-civilised races a higher degree of acuteness of sense than is found in Europeans' (Rivers, 1901, p. 12). He suggested that 'on theoretical grounds there were necessary limits to the resolving power of the eye, and believed that the highly developed visual powers of the savage depended on his attention and practice in the interpretation of minute indications' (p. 13). This was Rivers' view as well and he hoped that his tests on Islanders would enable him to contribute the necessary scientific data to support his side of the debate, allowing him to speak with more authority about acuteness of the senses in the 'savage'. Unfortunately, his battery of validated scientific tests, which included the E method, Snellen's letter test types, No. LIV (tests using numbers), and Guillery's test-types (tests using black dots on white backgrounds), were to be beset, from the start, with unforeseen problems.

For example, the results from the E method suggested to him that of the 170 people tested from Murray Island, Mabuiag Island and Kiwai 8.8 per cent were below 'what is often supposed to be the normal European standard' (Rivers, 1901, p. 25). Looked at from another direction this meant, of course, that 91.2 per cent achieved normal or higher results (see Table I, Rivers, 1901, p. 25). This finding took Rivers very much by surprise so, in order to get some handle on this large discrepancy, he proceeded to question the supposed European standard, which, after all, had to be wrong to achieve such a result. If we were to compare the results of tests administered on army personnel by Seitz and Seggel in 1883 in Germany, Rivers countered, we would see 'no marked difference between the visual acuity of the average European and the Torres Strait Islander' (Rivers, 1901, p. 27). Moreover, he suggested, if we were to use statistics, and in particular average mean deviations, we will see similar results between Europeans and Islanders. For example, he continued, we may see from the average acuity rates from Cohn's (1896) tests on the European population in Heligoland, a small archipelago in the North Sea, that 'Heligolanders are distinctly inferior' (p. 28). But, he contended, if we were to consider the distribution below and above the average vision V=1, the 'difference...is not great and seems to show that European islanders living an outdoor, seafaring life do not differ very greatly in visual acuity from Papuan islanders whose life is also largely spent upon the sea' (p. 28). In this way Rivers was able to reason that if one chose a comparative schema wisely (for example, German army personnel or average mean deviations of Heligolanders), the Islanders' high visual acuity was actually of a lower status to what it might appear to be at first. Unfortunately, then he was left with the difficult problem of deciding what was to be the standard.

Rivers had other strings to his bow, and was hopeful that he would produce results from other tests that would come up trumps and produce sound statistical data. However, the results from Snellen's letter test-types also had to be abandoned because the Islander children's unfamiliarity with the English alphabet meant that, even with generous allowances for mistakes, it was hard to gain results that were in any way satisfactory. Apart from this, he also found that variations with the different letter shapes and sizes made it hard for him to gain any scientific consistency and thus any chance of the definitive scientific statement he needed. What little was achieved, however, was that, when compared with the results of the E tests, the Islander children rated considerably lower than European children — hardly a surprising result when the practicality of testing unlettered children is taken into account. Reluctantly Rivers had to conclude from these findings that Snellen's letter-type method was inadequate for measuring acuteness of vision and he later moved to declare that 'the method...[was] scientifically defective as a method of testing visual acuity' (Rivers, 1901, p. 31).

Delving into his test armoury Rivers then administered Snellen's No. LIV method, which had likewise been chosen because it was considered to be 'the most satisfactory of the methods which depend on counting' (Rivers, 1901, p. 33). On the basis of this test Rivers soon found that Islanders on Murray Island had a 'very poorly developed' (p. 33) counting method and a limited vocabulary. These Islanders, he explained, had 'words only for 1 (netat) and 2 (neis)' (p. 33). Numbers from 3 to 6 were described by compounding the words netat and neis while numbers beyond this were described using the joints of the fingers. Although the scientists still tried to use English numerals with modifications to limit the use of numbers in Islander responses, Rivers found the results to be so inconsistent and unreliable that he was forced to declare that Snellen's method in these situations was 'entirely worthless' (p. 33).

Similarly, Guillery's method, which Rivers had initially considered 'the most satisfactory method of testing visual acuity' (p. 34) also proved to be a problem in the field. This method involved using a black dot on a white background and gauging the distance 'at which a black dot of a certain size situated in a square space is no longer distinguished from the ground' (Rivers, 1901, p. 34). As this test required the use of effective communication skills in the subject's language — skills which Rivers and his party simply did not possess — he thought that he could get around this by modifying the test, giving each Islander he tested 'an empty square in which he had to mark the position of the dot in the same situation as occupied by that in the square to which...[Rivers] was pointing' (p. 34). No data is provided in the report to demonstrate what levels of visual acuity were actually measured by this method but once again Rivers was forced to insert an apologetic note to the effect that '[t]his method was necessarily laborious and I only made sufficient observations to satisfy myself that the method would be satisfactory if modified for ethnological purposes' (p. 34). Once again, it would seem, Rivers' scientific tests had effectively come up against a brick wall.

4. Psychological inscriptions of the mind

In this field research, Rivers attempted to target Islanders who had an 'abnormal refraction of the eye' (p. 35) — presumably he meant the 8.8 per cent who achieved low acuity levels from the E tests — and those 'who were found to have low visual acuity were tested for errors of refraction' (p. 35). However, with 'no ophthalmoscope or retinoscope' in his possession, he had to concede that 'it was not possible to determine the refraction' (p. 35). He added that apart from the fact that the task was very laborious — and presumably not only incomprehensible but also extremely boring to the subjects — '[t]he natives did not like being tested. They were always interested in anything in which they excelled', he suggested, 'but disliked having their inferiority in any respect shown, and consequently I had more difficulty with this than with any other of my observations' (Rivers, 1901, p. 35).

Having failed to implement reliable visual acuity tests to corroborate his position on the standard or his results from the E tests, Rivers was forced to resort to the literature on hypermetropia and myopia for a scientific explanation.

Hypermetropia, or long-distance vision, Rivers noted, has 'been described as the normal condition of the child and of the savage' (Rivers, 1901, p. 35). He supported this statement by citing results from other studies on children from the village of Schreiberhau in what is now Poland as well as children of Africa, and from studies of the 'Lapps, Patagonians, Nubians and Kalmuks...Sinhalese and Hindus...Chippeway Indians... Congolese' (pp. 35–36). Once again, to his vexation, his observations were thwarted because 'I had not with me a convex glass of less than one diopter, [but]...the fact that the vision of some was certainly not diminished, renders it probable that slight degrees of hypermetropia existed in Murray Island' (p. 36). In this way, with the absence of hard statistical data of his own, Rivers was reduced to making some general observations from his personal experience in the islands.

Myopia, or short-sightedness, was considered in the literature to be 'very rare among savage people' (p. 36). To support this view, Rivers was able to cite a number of other independent studies of Indigenous people: of the 17 Nubians tested, only one was found to be myopic; of the Kalmuks, Sinhalese, Hindus, Lapps and Congolese no case of myopia was found; of the 'Negro' children 2.6 per cent were myopic; of the American Indian children 2.4 per cent were myopic; of the 6163 children studied in Buenos Aries 4.2 per cent were myopic. On the other hand, Rivers pointed out, myopia is considered to be a common feature in Japan and Armenia, as well as in Georgia. This also was found to be the case with studies of children in Mexico who were 'attending superior schools [and] who were of European parentage' (p. 36); 19 per cent of these were found to be myopic. Although Rivers considered the results from Murray Island to be unsatisfactory and clearly insufficient to provide him with a 'percentage of myopia in Murray Island' (p. 37), he was, however, able to note in his report that from his observations 'the condition certainly existed, but only in slight degrees and in a few individuals' (p. 37). From these comparisons, he concluded that hypermetropia is a characteristic of people in uncivilised parts of the world and myopia, by contrast, a characteristic of more civilised people. Rivers was thus able to suggest that, although myopia certainly existed, the visual capacities of Islanders were hypermetropic like natives in other parts of the globe.

In order to give balance to a set of findings that seemingly pointed to Islanders having acute visual senses, Rivers considered cases on Murray Island of astigmatism, which is poor focus or poor vision in one eye. Studies cited by him supported the view that '[v]ery few cases' (p. 38) of astigmatism existed in native people but, as Rivers noted, several cases were found on Murray Island when Islanders were able to read the E in the vertical position, either the right way or backward, but not in the horizontal position, either up or down, when viewed from the same distance. He subsequently noted that astigmatism occurred in Islanders who had long-sighted vision as well as those who had short-sighted vision.

Rivers also wanted to investigate the theory that 'natives' (p. 39) were able to adapt their vision much faster in the dark than 'Europeans' (p. 39) and, as an objective scientist, he set out to test this theory scientifically. The test he devised was to measure the time it took, after someone had stuck their head in a dark chamber, to recognise a letter in the enclosed area. To perform this feat he selected three Islander boys and compared the results they achieved with those scored by himself and Haddon. The men, it transposed, took 13 and 15 minutes to guess the correct letter but were not really sure whether or not they were correct. In comparison, one of the boys took 2.30 minutes and another took 6.40 minutes, with results from the third child not mentioned in the data. Rivers challenged his own findings, however, suggesting that such a view of 'visual acuity in feeble illumination...may be misleading' (p. 39) because adaptations to poorly lit areas are subject, for example, to familiarity with contents in the Islander house and thus may 'suggest a greater power of vision than actually possessed' (p. 39). What he did learn from this test, however, was that 'the method was not good enough to allow any definite conclusions to be drawn' but they did, he felt 'support...[the held view] that the

4. Psychological inscriptions of the mind

eye of the Melanesian adjusts itself to the dark more quickly than that of the European' (p. 40). However, he concluded, the 'unsuitability of improvised apparatus' meant that no 'definitive results' could be claimed from this experiment.

Being unwilling, quite understandably, to come to no conclusion at all, Rivers hypothesised that 'increased sensitiveness of the dark-adapted eye depends on accumulation of visual purple in the rods of the retina. We know also that the formation of visual purple is closely connected with the pigment epithelium' (Rivers, 1901, p. 40). This information led him to conclude:

> In dark races there is reason to believe that the eye shares in the greater abundance of pigment, and it is quite possible that in deeply pigmented races visual purple may be formed more readily and more rapidly than in white races, and it is therefore quite conceivable that dark-adaptation should take place more readily. (Rivers, 1901, p. 40)

The qualifications used here — 'quite possible' and 'quite conceivable' — undermined the possibility of his reaching a scientific conclusion and he lamented this, 'regretting very much that...[he was not able to] contribute more positively to the problem' (Rivers, 1901, p. 40).

Clearly Rivers' attempt to test previously existing scientific observations was, in all these cases, not very successful and less than convincing even to himself. Nevertheless, data compiled on the comparative Table I (1901, p. 25), especially in the final column where it records 'percentages of those whose vision excelled what is often supposed to be the normal European standard' (p. 25), suggests that 88 per cent of people from Murray Island and 94.4 per cent from Mabuiag scored better than the European standard in this very subjective set of tests. Rivers played down these figures by saying that 'the visual acuity of savage and half-civilised people, though superior to that of the normal European, is not so in any marked degree' (p. 42) when compared with the visual acuity of German soldiers.

However, when Heligolanders were compared to Islanders they were found to be 'distinctly inferior' (p. 28). Fortunately he was able to explain this by using an interesting formula. As 'errors of refraction producing defect in vision, and especially myopia, are much more common among civilised people' (p. 42), he countered, these cases should be omitted from the count. The figures gathered this way 'do not exhibit that degree of superiority over the European in visual acuity proper' (p. 42). This result, in other words, could only be achieved by a rearrangement of the numbers. As a scientist, Rivers certainly recognised that the European norm presented him with a fundamental problem. His mind leant one way; his observations the other. To counter this, he searched through the literature, finding measurements from Germany that showed that the norm was underrated, corroborated by data from Heligoland that showed that the norm may well be correct if the numbers are rearranged. So, it follows, if there is nothing that can be relied upon as a standard then what can be stated about the Islander is also without basis.

Rivers' research at this stage exhibited a remarkable lack of precision, as stabs in the dark and elaborate circular arguments replaced scientific observation and testing. To salvage his research, he decided to deploy yet another test using Masson's Disc to measure 'sensibility to differences of brightness' (Rivers, 1901, p. 45). The results showed that some of the Islanders 'had a much higher degree of sensibility than had been previously recorded for European vision' (p. 46) — so high, in fact, that Rivers was moved to declare that the 'degree of sensibility seemed to be so greatly in excess of what has been recorded among Europeans that I was inclined to be incredulous' (p. 46).

This incredulity, it would seem, soon gave way to 'scientific' scepticism, for on his return to England he tested 23 subjects and was able to achieve results similar to Islander people. These findings overturned results previously gathered using European subjects. Certainly the test was just a little different at this time because he had modified Masson's Disc and administered the test in a different way. Thus vindicated, he reasoned that it was possible that 'previous observations have been made on laboratory workers whose visual powers are below average, or at any rate below that of many individuals' (p. 47). Whatever the case, as far as he was concerned, it was 'sufficient that the... [Islanders] tested have not shown any superiority over Europeans [when] tested by exactly the same method' (p. 47).

What gave Rivers some confidence here was that when the results of the visual acuity tests using the E method were compared with the Masson's Disc test there appeared to be corresponding trends for sensibilities to brightness as there were with visual acuity. The Islanders tested with both methods showed the same distribution patterns on each of the score charts. This was a very important result for Rivers because it confirmed both his findings and his theories. And the efficacy of these tests was important for another reason. The Masson's Disc test verified for him that, when carried out with English people, it proved the fallibility of what was often 'supposed to be the normal European standard' (p. 25). In other words, if the Islanders' achievements on the E test showed a corresponding pattern with the Islanders' achievements on Masson's Disc, and if the English people when tested with the Masson's Disc indicated that they can score just as well as the Islander, then it was conceivable that the supposed European norm based on the E test was itself questionable. In this way if the supposed norm was shown to be problematic, then the visual acuity scores of the Islanders could show no superiority over the British.

Visual powers

With his scientific method effectively in tatters, Rivers made another attempt to produce a credible scientific position from which to achieve his goals by putting together a theoretical case, which drew a distinction between the allegedly measurable levels of visual acuity and a different position he called 'visual powers'. He suggested that what he had actually done in his study so far was measure visual acuity proper wherein, he asserted, the 'Torres Strait Islander was not found to be in any way extraordinary' (Rivers, 1901, p. 42). By contrast, he contended, what has won the admiration of travellers in 'uncivilised parts of the world' (p. 12) was the appearance of visual powers — quite a different thing altogether. The special abilities of the natives to see things that are barely visible to Europeans — such as, for example, spotting birds high in the tree tops, or pointing out boats over great distances, even to 'describe its rig and in some cases know what boat it was' — were obviously 'of a kind in which special knowledge would be of enormous importance' (p. 42). He illustrated what he meant by relating a story in which he explained how he had discovered, while on a boat trip between islands, that the Islanders on board were able to make out a steamer in a harbour with only a little of its mast showing. At the time that they pointed it out to him, he explained, he was not able to locate the mast, let alone the ship. This, he suggested, was indeed the origin of the 'miraculous' (p. 43) visual powers observed by fellow travellers to other parts of the globe. In explanation, he pointed to a case in South America where Ranke in 1897, having learnt and practised looking for objects over great distances, had been able to increase his own visual powers, making them equally as good as that of the Indians, despite the fact that he was myopic. Once taught to identify the gait of a male deer, for instance, he was able to identify the sex of a deer at distances equivalent to the Indians who accompanied him. Visual powers, once understood as being informed by localised knowledge, were no longer a special characteristic attributable only to the native but were recognisable as being site-specific and could thus be attributable to people of all societies. Indeed, as Rivers explained, 'it is doubtful whether [the Islanders'] visual powers excel those of the European...There is little doubt that the most acute sighted savage transferred to a Scotch moor would, in the unfamiliar surroundings, be a very poor match for the gille' (p. 44).

Rivers provided a scientific explanation for his generalisation, hypothesising that 'correlation[s] between acuteness of vision and the development of accommodation' (Rivers, 1901, p. 44) should be considered in the interpretation of scientific data. He maintained that there was a limiting aspect to vision that had to be recognised. For instance, when one focused selectively on an individual object, only things surrounding the immediate area can be seen. The widely accepted view in scientific communities was that 'the amount of accommodation which takes place for distances greater than 6 metres [from the object being viewed] is negligible' (p. 44). For instance, if someone looks across a room through the window and focuses on one end of the house next door, they see that part of the house but not the other end. To see the other end, they have to move their eyes to that side of the house. Only by moving focus between the two ends can they arrive at some conclusive statement about whether there is a person on the full-length verandah. Rivers accepted that it was 'possible that delicate gradations of accommodation may take place which adjust the eye to much greater distances' (p. 44) but, as he qualified, there was not much evidence of this.

The most important point for Rivers was that this explanation enabled him to maintain that there were 'correlations between acuteness of vision and the development of accommodation' (p. 44). For instance,

> The frequency of hypermetropia in savage races may also have some importance in this connection. It is one of the consequences of hypermetropia that accommodation becomes necessary even for the most distant vision. In the hypermetrope the mechanism of accommodation is always more or less in action, and it seems quite possible that with the more extensive use of accommodation, there may be associated a higher degree of delicacy of adjustment than exists in the emmetropic eye, and that by practice this may become in the case of the savage one of the causes of his superiority over the European. (Rivers, 1901, p. 44)

That is, the more focused one's vision is on the object being viewed, the less can surrounding items be accommodated. As Rivers explained, '[t]here is no doubt that the savage is an extremely close observer of nature' (Rivers, 1901, p. 44) — so close, in fact, that '[n]early every detail of landscape and seascape had its special name and nearly every species which the zoologist or botanist would recognize as distinct was also differentiated. In the case of familiar plants, such as the yam or banana, there were many named varieties' (p. 44). However, focusing in depth on individual objects like this was, to Rivers, not actually a cultural strength. Indeed, it was an illustration of a cultural weakness because, Rivers argued, it demonstrated a lower level of intellectual development in the subject.

> Minute distinctions of this sort are only possible if the attention is predominantly devoted to objects of sense, and I think there can be little doubt that such exclusive attention is a distinct hindrance to higher mental development. We know that the growth of intellect depends on material which is furnished by the senses, and it therefore at first sight may appear strange that elaboration of the sensory side of mental life should be a hindrance to intellectual development. But on further consideration I think there is nothing unnatural in such a fact. If too much energy is expended on the sensory foundations, it is natural that the intellectual superstructure should suffer. It seems possible also that the over-development of the sensory side of mental life may help to account for another characteristic of the savage mind. (Rivers, 1901, pp. 44–45)

In this way Rivers traversed a huge theoretical distance by relating the hypothetical construct he called visual powers to a pre-existing theoretical schema, which allegedly illustrated mental development. Unhindered by this, Rivers allowed himself to make an enormous leap without scientifically substantiating a position on either of these elements. The Islanders' visual capacities may have allowed them to be vindicated as fully human because they were not demonstrably 'animal-like', but it was also clear from his theoretical position that Islanders were still savages at a lower scale of development. Proclaiming Islanders to be humans residing in a lower evolutionary position had, after all, always been the aim of the exercise.

From this theoretical vantage point, Rivers was able to observe and explain the phenomenon he needed to theorise while providing an explanation for the discrepancies even he could see existed in his data. Returning to the scientific literature, Rivers was again successful in finding material to corroborate his theories by once more citing Ranke's experiences as a European living with Indians in South America. After living with the Indians for a while, Rivers pointed out, Ranke had discovered that 'he had lost his capacity for the aesthetic enjoyment of scenery, he found that individual objects forced themselves upon his attention and prevented his enjoyment of the scenery as a whole...He also found that, owing to the fact that he was continually attending to details...he was unable to devote attention to the more serious problems of life' (p. 45) — problems that, presumably, lie outside everyday encounters on another plane of existence.

It was as if the comparative nature of his experiments had taken on a competitive status of its own which had little to do with either rationality or scientific observation. Skill had to be explained away by sleight of hand. Figures had to be rejigged to fit in with preconceived expectations. He lacked vital equipment; he misjudged the subjectivity and effectiveness of his chosen tests.

In his attempt to regain some intellectual ground he was continually reduced to postulations — for example, that although the yellow-eyed native of uncivilised parts of the world may, like the Islander, score higher on visual acuity tests and may be perceived to have outstanding visual powers, they are not 'animal-like'. However, using the same data, he was able to reaffirm the belief that Islanders were in no way as advanced as the more civilised people of Western societies. Islanders, to Rivers, simply had not yet developed the visual traditions needed to inform an appreciation for the aesthetic aspects of life. The savage mind interpreted the senses differently; it interpreted the senses from a lower stage of culture and development. To be a culturally developed people, he contended, there must be an appreciation of the aesthetics and, as he explained, '[t]here is, I think, little doubt that the uncivilized man does not take the same aesthetic interest in nature which is found among civilized people' (Rivers, 1901, p. 45).

Colour nomenclature

The indicator of the savage mind that Rivers felt would prove his theories about aesthetics was tied up in an elaborate evolutionary theory that divided the development of colour sense into intricate cultural stages. As people's colour sense — their appreciation of colours — developed over time, this theory asserted that the stages could be readily identified from the use of a naming system, which would in turn act as a clearly definable marker of progress made towards a civilised state. Working from the assumption that the colour nomenclature of people from the West was fully formed, anything short of this then would indicate an earlier stage in human development.

The theory of colour nomenclature had first been developed by Gladstone, based on his analysis of 'the epithets for colour used by

Homer' (cited in Rivers, 1901, p. 48). Gladstone's study had led him to conclude that in Homer's period little was known about the names of colours. What was found instead in these early written records were notions of brightness and of darkness. Building on this, Geiger undertook a much broader study of the literature and discovered what he interpreted as an evolutionary pattern to the emergence of colours. By the time the Cambridge project was in progress such a theoretical position had, at least for Rivers, apparently achieved the status of scientific fact. Rivers 'knew' that red was the first colour to be named and 'that the other colours had developed in the same order as that of the arrangement of the colours in the spectrum, the power of seeing blue and violet having been the latest to develop' (Rivers, 1901, p. 48). So, to position the Islanders along the evolutionary ladder laid down in this theoretical structure, Rivers painstakingly administered another series of exhaustive tests and proceeded to analyse the data. His aim, in this way, was to test the natives rather than the theory.

However, Rivers felt bound to acknowledge in his report that not all his learned colleagues had accepted this theory. A few, in fact, had summarily dismissed it, arguing that it was based on philological grounds and not on any physiological evidence. He cited Virchow, for instance, who had argued that Geiger's proposition was problematic as it assumed that deficiencies in colour nomenclature implied deficiencies in colour sense. Rivers, however, felt that this argument had been more than adequately refuted by other studies, such as, for example, that done by Magnus who had argued that developments in colour nomenclature could indeed be related to physiological developments. The debate disposed of in this circular manner, Rivers proceeded to test the Islanders.

He first tested his subjects for colour blindness to establish a baseline for comparing Islanders with people studied elsewhere. He examined 152 individuals from both the eastern and western islands of the Torres Strait, and Kiwai Island to the north. Participants were asked to match seven test wools: 'three test wools used by Holmgren for the diagnosis of red-green blindness were supplemented by four others' (Rivers, 1901, p. 49). Each attempt and all combinations using these coloured test-wools were noted. The Islanders matched the colours to Rivers' satisfaction and showed no evidence of red–green blindness because no Islander 'matched, or even transiently compared Holmgren's pink wool with blue or violet, the most frequent confusions which occur in red-green blindness' (p. 51). These findings matched other studies of colour blindness across the globe, allowing Rivers to argue that, 'It certainly seems…as if colour-blindness must be distinctly rarer in many races than it is among Caucasian and Semitic people' (p. 93).

Suspecting cases of yellow–blue blindness when some of the participants compared yellow and blue wools, and blues with browns, Rivers hypothesised that this was probably another potential characteristic of native people. Finding the persistence of these matches not evident in other combinations he suggested that the dullness of the yellow wools might explain the tendency for participants to associate blues with dull colours. It was possible that some of the Islanders, not fully comprehending what he was asking them to do, were comparing dull colours. Those who made these mistakes, he explained, were the same ones who did not fully understand what was expected of them in the experiment. The scientific literature had already isolated this phenomenon, with Scholer already reporting a case of a Nubian in Berlin who, as Rivers deduced, was 'probably yellow-blue blind' (Rivers, 1901, p. 51). The Nubian compared red and orange with purple; blue with yellow and grey; and yellow with blue and grey. Although the confusion was more marked in the Nubian, it was reason enough for Rivers to remain alert to any markers that could support Scholer's findings. 'The subject is one of great importance', he wrote, 'for it would be very remarkable if yellow-blue blindness, so rare among Europeans, should be present in other races' (p. 51).

At the conclusion of these tests Rivers felt himself able to claim that 'the number examined…[was] sufficiently large to justify one in saying that colour-blindness…[was] either absent in this race, or much rarer than among European populations' (pp. 52–53). He concluded that, as the people of these parts of the world could see all the colours, his task was now to see if they had developed the cultural ability to name them. To do this Rivers prompted them with coloured papers and coloured objects. The coloured papers had been purchased from Rothe of Leipzig and were considered at the time to be the standard used by experts who tested colour vision. Using the paper and object combination, Rivers felt, enabled him to check for variations between the naming of a colour and the naming of a coloured object.

From his preliminary work on Murray Island, Rivers observed a gradient that ran from children who hardly knew the names of the colours to older folk who knew them all. Women, he noted, did not know as many colours as men and, while the older men could recall and reproduce the colours of the rainbow using the coloured test wools, the younger men were not as good at doing this. Rivers felt this particular test demonstrated levels of memory retention. 'The observations are interesting in one way as showing the degree of accuracy with which the natives can give a description from memory of a natural phenomenon' (p. 70),

4. Psychological inscriptions of the mind

he wrote. He took this to signify that the older men were able to abstract a natural phenomenon and reproduce it from memory. Clearly, it could also have meant that the younger men on Murray Island were not really interested in reproducing rainbows but Rivers chose to argue instead that this demonstrated that 'the failure of the young men is only one among many instances of the loss of the powers of observation of nature which has accompanied contact with civilisation' (p. 70).

One of the most revealing issues in his findings so far, at least as far as Rivers was concerned, was the confirmation that, while there was a definiteness about a name for red in the islands, there was a demonstrable uncertainty about a name for blue. This, he felt, correlated with the philological evidence in the scientific literature that the name for red was the first to emerge and the first to become a universal term, and that subsequent names for colours developed in order of the colour spectrum with blues last. Rivers went as far as to speculate in his report that the definiteness of red in Islander schemas and the uncertainty about a name for blue could signal a prolonged primitive status. He was even more convinced from this shortfall in colour nomenclature that he would state conclusively that what he was dealing with here was a fundamental characteristic of the savage mind.

The two crucial elements he needed to catalogue were the derivatives of colour names and the definiteness or indefiniteness of colour names. Rivers documented the names of colours used in the Torres Strait and identified their derivatives, as well as noting qualifying terms used to describe shades of primary colours (colour shades were mostly reported as big, small, good, similar to, bad, dirty, etc.; see pp. 56, 60 & 61). He observed that the names of colours 'nearly all come into the lives of the people in some practical way, either as food, medicine, or as objects used in sorcery' (p. 63). Although there was some evidence to indicate that blues and greens were derived from names used for the sea as well as leaves, he found that the blood and bile names in red and green featured in more definite ways. The literature generally on results obtained in Melanesia showed that the use of the word blood in red is a very common one and the literature on Asiatic people showed that they, like the Islanders, had similar correspondences between the name for green and the name for bile and the gall bladder. While accepting that the English name for gall and yellow 'are [also] closely connected' (p. 63), Rivers still doggedly argued that it was more likely in native communities that '[o]bjects which might have attracted attention on account of their beauty seldom seem to form the basis of colour names' (p. 63). The savage mind, he asserted, was too rigidly practical to have developed any aesthetic sense. Apart from one case in Murray Island where a flower was the basis for a name for yellow, Rivers found that the names of flowers generally did not feature in the Islanders' colour vocabulary. This was, as he stated, very much unlike the British and their 'use of violet, pink, mauve, heliotrope, rose, etc., all derived from the names of flowers' (p. 64).

Fortified by the Western literature on native people, Rivers saw fit to argue that the association of the word for red with the name used for blood was a telling indicator of their savage status. There is no mention in his report of the findings by his colleagues, Haddon and Ray, that the Islander word *kulka* is used for red as well as blood, '[b]ut *kulka*, as Mr Ray was definitely informed, is used also for the dawn, as e.g. *ar kulka*, the dawn reddens: hence Kulkalaig means eastern people' (Haddon, 1904, p. 2). My family and the community I belong to are the Kulkalaig people being referred to here. People on a nearby island to us (my relatives) are known as Kulkalgal. We are literally the people to the east of Muralag, Badu and Mabuiag islands — the place where the sun rises. Despite this, I grew up with, and learned only to accept, the outsiders' reading of our place in the islands as meaning 'bloodthirsty' people.

Rivers felt that it was 'noteworthy that the sea, rather than the sky, should have been the source of the word blue' (p. 62). The variations in the colour of the sea range from aqua to black in the islands, and they change from week to week depending on the time of the year, the phase of the moon, the velocity of the wind, the strength of tidal surges, or the depth of the water. In these parts of the world, just south of the equator, there is, of course, no winter. The sky is almost always blue — even behind the clouds — and is black once the sun has gone. The fact that Islanders depend on the sea for staple foods means that much attention is paid to the changing ocean conditions — far more so than to the almost unchanging blue of the sky and the black of night.

However, his point was also to do with certainty or uncertainty about the names for colours (see table on p. 61).

Although Rivers did not quantify this data in comparative tables as he did with the visual acuity tests, he nevertheless felt able to arrive at the view that 'there was great definiteness and unanimity in the nomenclature for red, rather less so for orange and yellow, less so for green, and very great indefiniteness for blue and violet' (Rivers, 1901, pp. 54–55).

4. Psychological inscriptions of the mind

Colour Nomenclature

Colour	eastern Islanders	western Islanders
Red	'In Murray Island red was called mamamamam by all' (Rivers, 1901, p. 53).	'Red was called kuladgamulnga by nearly all' (Rivers, 1901, p. 57).
Purple and pink	The same Islander name, kebe mamamamam was used 'by many' (p. 54); three other names were in use.	The same Islander name kulkadgamulnga was used 'by most' (p. 57); several used three other names.
Orange	'Orange was called bambam by nearly all' (p. 54); three other names were used.	'Orange was called murdegamulnga...by the majority' (p. 57); four others were used.
Yellow	'Yellow was called bambam by most; siusiu by a good number, more rarely giazgiaz or zomkolberkolber and sunrsunur by one' (p. 54).	Yellow was called murdegamulnga by nearly all' (p. 57); three others were in use.
Green	'Green was called soskepusoskep by most' (p. 54); five others were in use.	'Green, maludgamulnga or ildegamulnga' (p. 57).
Blue	Blues were called by no less than eight different names.	'Blue was called maludgamuknga most frequently' (p. 57); six others were offered.
Violet	Violet was called by nine different names.	'Violet was called maludgamulnga by several... it was often called' (p. 57) by six other names.

The great definiteness about red was its consistent reference to blood. By contrast, the 'great indefiniteness for blue' resulted from the fact that some used terms from the sea; some used the same term used for green; and some used the term used for black. To Rivers this indicated that

Islander people had not yet resolved a common term for blue among themselves. As only red had been negotiated to fit one common term, it supported his view that he was indeed dealing with a group of primitive people who were in the early stages of their cultural development — a practical people with little appreciation of aesthetics.

It could also be argued that if Islanders offered more names for blue than they did for red this could be because blue was far more significant to them than red. In the islands there are very important reasons to have multiple names for blue. If we consider that Rivers noted that words and variations of words for blue were more reliant on the sea than the sky for practical reasons, then it is conceivable that close attention had to be paid by Islanders to the different shades and hues of the colour blue. This is particularly so if the success of diving, and the fishing, hunting and trapping of marine animals and mammals is contingent on particular tides, currents and changing seasons. There has to be concentrated attempts to make distinctions between the changing blue of the water: spring tides (green-white), neap tides (blue), deep water (blue-black), shallow water on grass (green-aqua-clear-yellow), shallow water on sand (turquoise), tides on reefs (clear-brown). Here, too, we need to consider that these colours are most evident when the sun is directly overhead. Even today, if asked, an Islander will offer a different name depending on the elements. It will depend mostly on where the Islander is positioned physically in relation to the area of water being referred to, on the presumption of a possible activity that could be conducted in that region, as well as on the intended time for a visit. Say, for example, if an Islander is asked whether diving for crayfish would be appropriate on a spring tide, and even though the water will be turquoise in colour, they will tell you 'no, dirty water', viz., poor visibility when diving. In other words, pointing to the water as an object and moving the arms around to indicate swimming movements and then asking the Islander, 'what colour is that?', there is every possibility that an answer will be 'dirty water'. It does not signify that the water is the colour of dirt. It signifies an element of cloudiness in the water that reduces visibility when diving. The actual colour is irrelevant in this designation. But the range of names is relevant to an entity, the sea, as more than just liquid mass.

Another prominent marker, that Rivers felt was crucial, was the Islanders' adoption of a corruption of the English word blue, as *bulu-bulu*. Here too there is a more simple explanation, if we consider that all blue items used as objects (e.g. coloured patches and glasses, personal adornment or clothing) in Rivers' study had to be referring to items introduced by those from the West, then it would follow that Islanders were mostly obliged to provide the English term used with the introduced items. That is, *bulu-bulu* is not necessarily a replacement term due to an absence of an Islander name for the coloured foreign object and thus a revealing factor to be considered as a corruption of an English word but, and more appropriately, the use of a term that rightfully belongs to the introduced items.

In this way, just as an argument can be made about the unanimity or certainty about the word for red as an indicator of development, a counter argument can also be made. Whichever truth one accepts, the central tenets suggested are that it is not the philological argument about colours that needs to be tested; it is the people who must prove or disprove themselves. On this cardhouse of theory, Rivers observed and tested his scientific truths.

Using these terms of reference Rivers determined that the colour nomenclature, especially at Mabuiag Island, was the most extensive system he had seen in the academic literature, even more extensive than the colour vocabulary of Murray Island. Islanders in the western parts of the Strait, according to him, had 'some natural object in mind to compare with every shade of colour shown to them' (p. 64). He reasoned that, 'the colour vocabulary illustrates very well the extensive knowledge which the savage possesses of the concrete things around him and the powers of observation which are associated with this knowledge' (p. 64). For Rivers, the intricate system of naming colours and every shade of colour with concrete objects indicated that cultural development was impaired because attention was devoted primarily to minute distinctions. It helped to explain the Islanders' perceived lack of interest in aesthetics, he believed. Building on this argument he proclaimed that the stage of development in the islands was 'but one indication of a characteristic feature of the savage mind i.e. a complete lack of any aesthetic interest in nature' (p. 64), and that 'this lack of aesthetic interest may be directly due to over-development of the sensory aspect of mental life' (p. 64).

On the basis of these painfully argued findings, therefore, Rivers attempted to construct an evolutionary map of the region by comparing the Islanders with other native people who lived nearby. Putting together data from the Fly River district to the north on the Papua New Guinean coastline, he built an elaborate continuum of practice between the three sites: Kiwai Island (located at the mouth of the Fly River), Murray Island and Mabuiag Island. His entire plan was primarily based around his data on names for the colour blue. 'As regards blue,' he argued, 'the three languages may be taken as representative of three stages in the evolution of a nomenclature for this colour' (p. 66).

Data from Kiwai Island, for instance, Rivers reported, showed no word for blue. This is a place at the mouth of one of the biggest river systems in a country (Papua New Guinea) with rainfalls measurable in metres. The rivers here start in very high mountains and travel to the coastline very quickly. The water is mostly filled with silt and debris. It is also the meeting place of fresh and salt water. For many months of the year, layers of fresh water sit on the surface of the waterways that look mostly brown. Kiwai Island is also more isolated geographically from major towns than the islands in the Torres Strait. Contact with the 'outside world' and their material objects was thus very limited. This may help explain why Rivers could find 'no word for blue' (p. 66). Most Kiwai people used the same term for green, 'black, dull or dirty' (p. 66) while *bulu-bulu* did not feature at all in their language.

Similarly, data from Murray Island indicated 'no proper name for blue' (p. 66). Most Murray Islanders, Rivers noted, used a modified version of the English word, *bulu-bulu*, and in its absence they use *suserisuseri* (blue and green) and occasionally *golegole* (black). Contrasting with Kiwai and Murray Islands, Rivers felt that the data from Mabuiag 'present[ed] a more developed stage in the existence of a word, *maludgamulnga*, which is used definitely for blue, but is also used for green' (Rivers, 1901, p. 67). The Mabuiag people, he noted, also had 'the tendency to confuse blue and black' (p. 67). He expressed surprise that Islanders would compare the colour blue with the dark of the night and was even more perplexed when 'these natives would compare a brilliant and saturated blue to the colour of dirty water' (p. 94).

The data Rivers had collected from Kiwai Island told him that the Kiwai people were in a much earlier stage of development than the Torres Strait Islanders, while data from Murray Island suggested that Murray Island people were not as developed as those on Mabuiag. He also learned from his colleague Ray that the colour nomenclature used by Aboriginal people on the Australian mainland was even 'less developed than that of the Kiwai' (p. 67). In this way the cultural status of divergent people over the entire region was determined mostly according to the preconceived configurations of the colour blue, creating an evolutionary path that began with Aboriginal people in the south, travelled north past Murray Island to the Kiwai people in the most north-eastern corner of the Torres Strait, then south to Murray Island almost a third the way back to the Aboriginal people, and then to the far west of the Torres Strait to Mabuiag. This data could simply have told Rivers that there were differences in colour nomenclature between Islanders, Aboriginal people in that part of Australia, Kiwai people and those in the West.

4. Psychological inscriptions of the mind

Instead, from deep within the impenetrable confines of his theoretical standpoint, he was able to make it do much, much more.

As a scientist Rivers needed to objectively check his findings so he made quantitative observations to measure any 'degree of insensitiveness to this colour, which makes a given blue a darker and a duller colour than it is to European vision, and may help to account for the confusion of the colour with black' (p. 70). To do this he used a Lovibond's Tintometer — a tube-like instrument one looks through to see three different coloured glasses passing over two square holes that allow the light in and enable the scientist 'to determine the threshold for each of the three colours' (p. 71) red, yellow and blue. Each of the three glasses was separate in colour and had the entire area covered with gradual stages of colour from clear to highly saturated. Rivers rotated a coloured wheel from its faintest point to the highest saturation point and then back down again. All the Islander had to do was peer into the tube and identify colour, or lack of colour, at the earliest possible moment as the glass passed over the square holes. The results of Rivers' experiments were such that he was able to 'show that the Murray Island natives distinguish red when very faint much more readily than blue, while, by the same method, to European vision there is little difference' (p. 95).

This directly contradicted his own later work on colour vision of the peripheral retina (pp. 75–80), which left Rivers in 'no doubt that the colour blue was recognized readily, even more readily than other colours' (p. 79). In this particular experiment Rivers got the Islanders to stare directly at him while he introduced colour patches gradually from either side to distinguish at what point, and at what angle, he thought they could determine colours. Rivers' explanation of the discrepancy was that 'the most ready way of reconciling the two observations is to suppose that the defective sensibility to blue is due chiefly, or altogether, to the influence of the macula lutea' (p. 79). His hypothesis was physiological and he referred to the literature to help his case. 'It is well known that owing to yellow-red pigmentation of the region of direct vision, blue and green rays are absorbed more strongly than in the extra-macular regions of the retina' (p. 79). 'It', unfortunately, was not referenced and was no more than an assertion, which he proceeded to back up with still more conjectures of his own:

> There is, so far as I know, no actual evidence that the yellow pigmentation of the macula is greater in black-skinned people than in the Caucasian races, but there is little doubt that this must be the case. If so, the absorption of green and blue rays would be greater than in

65

the European eye and may account for the relative insensitiveness to blue. (Rivers, 1901, pp. 79–80)

The convenient yet unconvincing nature of this proposition did not prevent Rivers from using it to reach his own logical conclusions. For Rivers, the colour patches fell entirely in the macular region with the tintometer tests while tests of the peripheral vision were distinguished in the extra-macular regions of the retina. It was then conceivable that 'the defective sensitivities for blue is to be regarded as a function of the pigmentation rather than of the primitiveness of the...visual organ' (p. 80). This was a credible position only in terms of its construction in the form of a logical argument and not one established by physiological science.

Rivers, having no further scientific apparatus on hand, sought to gain some idea of the colour sense among Islanders by simply asking them to pick out what they liked most from coloured papers. Some were asked to pick the three best colours while others were asked to arrange all colours in order of preference. One person, in fact, arranged the colours in the exact same order as Rivers had done when he was charting colour nomenclature. Not satisfied with the efficacy of this experiment, Rivers then asked Islanders to discuss their preferences and found 'in these cases that they never finished by agreeing with one another, but each gave his independent opinion' (p. 83). He found this to be the case also with married couples and their deliberations on colour preferences. The colours most popular with Islanders, he reported, were red, purple, indigo, black and yellow, with blue, green and violet being the least favoured. There was, however, a worrying element about this data that could not be easily explained away:

> I was inclined to regard the frequency of black among the papers chosen by the men as a very doubtful feature, and as indicating that they did not understand properly what was wanted, but when I found that black was so predominant in their personal adornment, it became no longer unsatisfactory, and may be taken as an indication of a real liking for this colour (or absence of colour). (Rivers, 1901, p. 83)

He believed that observations about what people wore to church on Sundays would add further confirmation to his scientific hypothesis. Black was most popular with the men, followed by red and green. Blue was the least popular. Women, by contrast, wore red mostly, with pink coming in second, then blue, and then yellow. There was, Rivers noted, a

4. Psychological inscriptions of the mind

notable absence of green colours amongst the women. The combination of colours worn by the Islanders suggested to him that there was a preference for yellow to be worn with blues, and reds with greens. Rivers described the red and yellow combinations worn by the Kiwai people as 'hideous' (Rivers, 1901, p. 84) and, when a father preferred yellow to be combined with blue and his daughter chose instead to combine yellow and scarlet, concluded that 'the man certainly seemed to have the better taste' (p. 84).

Thus demonstrating his possession of impeccable taste, Rivers was able to sum up his case:

> The bearing of this on the controversy mentioned at the beginning of this paper is obvious. In ancient literature, as among modern barbarous and savage races, it is the colour blue for which nomenclature is especially defective, and in Torres Strait this characteristic defect of nomenclature has been found to be associated with an appreciable degree of insensitiveness to this colour. The colour vision of the Torres Strait islander gives some support to the views of Gladstone, Geiger and Magnus that the defective colour language of ancient literature may have been associated with a defective colour sense. There can be very little doubt, however, that any physiological insensitiveness which may exist, can only be one of the factors determining the characteristic features of primitive colour nomenclature. (Rivers, 1901, p. 95)

Certainly there may be any number of explanations for this observed phenomenon. There is little to go on from Rivers' findings that could be used to construct either a scientific theory of colour nomenclature or one about the subjective matter of colour sense. What was never questioned, of course, was the acceptance of the proposition that there was a defect in colour sense in the first place.

Illusions

Rivers obviously felt that he had made substantial headway in his investigations in Torres Strait. However, what he needed to do now, he believed, was to uncover the essence of the illusions generated within the savage mind — to describe the way the Islanders' brains processed the stream of information and interpreted it into a meaningful illusion. Fundamentally, he wanted to amass data to collaborate his theories, derived from Jackson, about the different levels of brain function and the way areas of the brain which had appeared more recently in the evolutionary scale dominate or suppress the lower or older centres. The cerebral cortex, Jackson had already argued, has the prime function of refining and keeping control of, and inhibiting, the more primitive processes of the older mid-brain (Whittle, 1997). It is important to remember that, for Rivers, psychology and anthropology were intrinsically tied up with the biological sciences because physiology and psychology were part of the one process; racial superiority and racial difference could be demonstrated in both biology and in culture. He needed to demonstrate his belief 'that the illusion is primitive and deeply seated' and uncover whether 'its source is to be sought in some physiological condition, or if it is at present necessary to be content with a psychological explanation' (Rivers, 1901, pp. 116–17).

To do this Rivers proceeded to test the physiology of the Islander eye to see if there was anything that could affect the degree of illusion at different distances. Using Hering's fall experiment he initially tested whether or not Islanders had binocular vision. Islanders were asked to look through a cylindrical tube at a bead that was held up by very fine wire at a distance of 2 feet, and gauge whether objects dropped into view were 'nearer or farther from himself than the fixation point' (p. 97). As Rivers explained, '[t]hose with binocular vision are able, when using both eyes, to estimate the relative distances of such object even when quite close to the fixation point, while individuals without binocular vision are in the same position as normal individuals when only using one eye, and are unable to judge the relative distances of the falling objects even when much nearer or farther from the fixation point' (p. 97).

He found, from 17 Islanders tested, that when both eyes were in use nearly all were correct, while the results from the use of one eye were correct only half the time. Comparing these results with those from other tests on double images he was able to say that '[p]erhaps the main interest of these observations is to show that the Torres Strait people were certainly quite as good observers as the average European' (p. 99). This, of course, demonstrated that a common starting point to his tests could be assumed.

Some of the basic aspects Rivers sought to document when testing spatial perceptions were the accuracy of the contributions, the constancy of each attempt, and its comparative value when set against the overall results of the same group. Rivers was interested in the degree to which individuals were affected and how each person's scores corresponded to the rest of the group. Measurable degrees of variation of individual scores were charted and then compared with the overall degree of variation among all participants so that the results could figure as normative findings for the group as a whole. Data from these tests thus became the

4. Psychological inscriptions of the mind

scientific measure from which to identify the essential characteristics of particular groups of people. It was entirely on this basis that Rivers drew his comparisons between the civilised and savage minds.

Rivers also tested the Islanders' ability to estimate distances by asking four Islanders, aged between 40 and 60, to move a cursor along a ruler to show what they estimated to be a 'standard' of 80 mm and of 160 mm. He began by placing the cursor at the lower end of the ruler before asking Islanders to estimate the distances. Later it was placed at the top end. Rivers observed that there was 'a distinct tendency to make the variable length shorter than the standard' (p. 101) and that 'the variable was made larger when a long distance had to be shortened than when a short distance had to be lengthened' (p. 101). This was, as he patiently explained, something that was also done by Europeans and 'the same peculiarity [that] is also very marked in the observations on the Müller–Lyer illusion' (p. 101) experiments.

Rivers then asked 20 Islander men and 12 boys, all from Murray Island, to divide 100 mm lines into two or more equal parts. The Islanders tended, on average, to make the left longer than the right, although for the boys this tendency was not as constant as for the men (Table VII, p. 103). When compared with the achievements of 15 English psychology students and 12 village children (who were on average older than the Murray Island children) from Girton, near Cambridge, there was an opposite tendency to measure the right half bigger (Table VIII on p. 104). Rivers pointed out that not much can be made from this except that 'nearly all the Murray Island men had a constant error in one direction, while the English individuals had an error in the opposite direction' (Rivers 1901 p. 104). However, the average mean variation, Rivers argued, was worth noting (Table VIII, p. 104). For while the psychology students scored better with an average mean variation of 0.56, the Murray Island men and boys with averages of 1.31 and 1.77 respectively could only be compared with the English children's at 1.27. Interpreting this, Rivers concluded that '[t]he results given here show that the Murray Island man and boy are able to perform the simple operation of dividing a line into two equal halves with nearly as much accuracy and constancy as the English village child' (p. 104). It was, however, the constancy factor in achieving those results that Rivers believed separated them from the psychology students. By comparing the average mean variation of all attempts, he decided that the data showed the Islander men to be more erratic with their estimates than the psychology students, indeed to have a consistency level of a Girton village child.

In the tests he administered on dividing a 100 mm line into three or more parts, the average estimates of 8 Islander men and 6 boys from Murray Island were only compared with 12 Girton children, as the psychology students were left out of the comparison. Rivers noted that, comparatively speaking, the variation of the Murray Island children in bisecting lines into three or more parts was 'consistently smaller than for the adults, i.e., the accuracy of division was greater in the children' (p. 107) and that, when compared to the collective figures from Girton, the village children proved to be 'slightly smaller than those of Murray children' (p. 107). However, as he is at pains to point out, this does not necessarily equate with being 'inferior to the English child' (p. 107).

Except for one of the children tested, Rivers found that the Islanders mostly did not divide a line into four parts by bisecting the line into two equal parts first. He noted, as well, that the English village children divided lines from left to right as did the Islander children 'and there can be little doubt that this was due to the influence of their school education' (p. 108). By contrast, Rivers found that, of the 8 men tested on Murray Island, 4 started bisecting from the left, 3 started from the right, and 1 began from both ends. Rivers concluded that when taken 'into account the number of trials necessary before the lines could be divided successfully and the degree of accuracy as compared with the Girton children the Torres Strait natives were distinctly deficient in this operation' (p. 108). However, Rivers argues, when the language difficulties in undertaking such an experiment as well as 'their deficiencies in numeration' are taken into account, 'the results were surprisingly good' (p. 108).

Rivers also wanted to find out whether Islanders could draw a vertical line the same length as that given by a horizontal standard. In this test 20 men and 12 children from Murray Island were given three tasks. The first required them to draw a vertical line starting at the centre of a horizontal standard of 100 mm; the second required them to start at the end of the standard; and the third required them to draw a line that passed through the centre of the standard with equal distances on either side — as in a cross. Data from these tests were then compared with those of the 15 psychology students and 12 Girton village children.

Rivers found that both the Islander men and boys achieved an overall accuracy rate that improved over the tests. For instance, 'the average length of the vertical line in No. 1 was distinctly smaller than in No. 2, and in No. 2 than in No. 3' (p. 112). Comparatively, the boys were more accurate in their estimates of the standard and, as Rivers noted, there was a notable constancy factor — there was a consistency amongst the boys to estimate above 75 mm whereas the consistency factor for the men was to estimate below 75 mm. This told Rivers that 'the illusion was apparently less marked' (p. 112) for the boys. Data from 15 psychology students and the 12 Girton children (Table XIII, p. 113) also showed that all improved the accuracy of their estimates as they progressed through the tests. There was, Rivers noted, an interesting characteristic for all four groups in that all 'agree in making the vertical line shorter when drawn from the middle of the horizontal line than when drawn at one end, and shorter in the latter of the tests than when it is drawn so as to form a cross' (Rivers, 1901, p. 114). Notably, for Rivers, the psychology students were more accurate in the average scores than the Girton village children and the Islander children, and even more so than the Islander men.

However, the constancy factor was also important. As Rivers noted, when the mean deviation from the average is considered, it can be clearly seen that 'the illusion was most marked in the case of the Murray Island men…[and by contrast], [t]he illusion was least pronounced in the case of the psychology students' (p. 113). Rivers offered a few explanations for this, noting that some participants in England who had done the first test used a mode that divided the standard into two halves wherein they gained some correspondence for their vertical estimates. 'This observation illustrates very well one cause of difference between the results of the savage and the cultured measurements, for one may feel fairly confident that such an artificial method was not employed by the Murray Islander' (p. 114). Although the consistency with which the Islander men provided their estimates was, Rivers discovered, quite marked — 17 of the 20 men displayed the characteristic increases in their measures over the three tasks whereas only 8 of the 15 students did — his explanation was that 'I am inclined to ascribe this result to the influence of a factor, viz. Knowledge of the nature of the illusion, which is not present in the savage' (p. 115).

Rivers went on to consider the views of others and their explanations as to 'the cause of the erroneous estimation of vertical as compared with horizontal distances' (p. 116). Some, he noted, accepted the view that this was because of 'the curvature of the retina…[particularly when] the retina is more concave in one meridian than in the other' (p. 116). Others accepted the more popular view 'which refers the illusion to the influence of eye movements' (p. 116). This view was based on the idea that the muscles that control the vertical eye movements are greater than the ones that control the horizontal movements. Another view considered the oval shape of the field of vision people get from monocular vision and binocular vision. This view suggested that it is 'possible that a vertical distance may be overestimated as compared with an equal horizontal distance because it forms a larger proportion of the field of vision' (p. 116). To others, erratic estimations of vertical lines from a horizontal standard are caused by psychological tendencies because it is supposed by people like Lipps (1891), 'that we ascribe certain mechanical activities to geometrical figures and…that we ascribe activity more readily to vertical than to horizontal lines' (Lipps cited in Rivers, 1901, p. 116). Rivers, however, remains unconvinced, and is moved to suggest that

> [t]he pronounced character of the illusion in children and in people in the stage of mental culture of the Murray Islanders shows that the illusion is primitive and deeply seated, and that its source is to be sought in some physiological condition, or if it is at present necessary to be content with a psychological explanation, this must be of a simple and primitive character. (Rivers, 1901, pp. 116–17)

The Müller–Lyer Illusion test was another used by Rivers (Fig. 2, p. 117) to gauge visual spatial perceptions. The apparatus used in this test was a sliding rule. A standard length, 75 mm, was positioned on the sliding scale and the participant was then required to slide the scale the same length as the standard 75 mm by estimating how far to slide the measure. Participants were required to estimate the standard in two different ways by sliding the scale in to shorten the measure and by sliding it out to lengthen the measure. Rivers observed that the Islander men were definitely influenced by the direction the slide rule had to be moved. But he suggested they were 'influenced to a considerable extent by the position of the slide at the beginning' (p. 120). In addition, Rivers pointed out that the estimates were consistently longer when the rule was shortened (62.45 mm) and not as long (58.13 mm) when it was lengthened. He retried this test in reverse order to determine whether any change in order affected the trend. This was not found to be so and thus affirmed an Islander characteristic for Rivers.

The 10 Murray Island boys (aged 10 to 13 years), by contrast, achieved an overall average score slightly longer than the average of the 19 men. Two other boys, tested in reverse order to establish the characteristic trend, again reaffirmed a tendency to make the estimate longer when the rule was shortened and not as long when lengthened, but it was significant that results from 5 of the 12 boys did not correspond to the characteristic trend. The data from tests on 9 Islander girls aged between 10 and 14, by contrast, corresponded with each other uniformly and were characteristic of the overall trends. Moreover, they appeared to have

4. Psychological inscriptions of the mind

outscored the men as well as the boys. The girls, all from Murray Island, showed overall that they were more accurate with their estimates and the constancy factor was also superior. In regard to a measure of visual spatial perception, smaller variations equate to more constancy and the girls were, in this sense, the most accurate.

When the results were compared with those in the West, the Islanders were found to be more accurate with their estimates than their English counterparts. Rivers acknowledged that, at first glance, '[t]he illusion appears to be distinctly less marked to Murray Islanders than to the Europeans. This is shown not only by the average but by the maximum and minimum observations, and also by the median observations, which differ but slightly from the averages' (Rivers, 1901, p. 125). However, to Rivers, the constancy factors needed to be considered in more detail. While the Islanders scored with a greater accuracy than the English, it was significant that the English showed greater consistency in achieving their average scores. There was more of a disparity, Rivers noted, between the Islander men and a group of English students who were most familiar with the exercise. However, when all of the Islanders were compared with the English, 'Islanders show[ed] that they performed the operations involved in the test with a degree of constancy and accuracy, slightly inferior to an equal number of English people' (p. 125).

In light of this Rivers acknowledged that Islanders 'gave results which were more consistent with one another than those of an almost equal number of English people, and the group of Murray Island men varied from one another very much less than the group of practised English observers' (p. 127). This was difficult for him to explain but, as he suggested, perhaps

> [t]his is another example of the fact that in some respects the unpractised and wholly ignorant inhabitants of Murray Island give more consistent results than Europeans practised in psychological observation. In the introduction I suggested that the greater consistence of the Murray Islanders may have been due to their total ignorance and to the fact that they gave their whole minds to the special attention they had to perform, and were not influenced by speculations founded on knowledge, in this case on knowledge of the illusion. (Rivers, 1901, p. 127)

The 'success' of these Islanders in this way is again explained away by reference to those practised in psychological observation. In Table XVII, Rivers separated off 'students and others well acquainted with the illusion' (1901, p. 124) so that he could indeed make such comparisons between them and Islanders. From this, he found that it was 'the difference between the Murray Island men and the English group A (all practised observers) which make the average mean variation of the English observers superior to that of the [Islanders]' (p. 125).

What Rivers was struggling to explain in this ingenious fashion was simply the extent to which Islanders were more consistent with each other in their estimates than *all of the English* in achieving the combined average of both tests. In the context of his report it had become all important to explain away results which did not point in the desired direction. To this end Rivers speculated that 'it is possible that in the simpler mental features they [Islanders] may present more uniformity than is found among the members of a highly civilised community' (p. 127). From this he was able to conclude that

> [t]he very slight inferiority to the English observers in accuracy as shown by a comparison of the average mean variations (m.v.) and the remarkable correspondence of the three Murray Island groups with one another would have been impossible if the Murray Islanders had not applied their full attention to their tasks or if they had failed to understand what they were told to do. (1901, pp. 127–28)

There is little in any of this that delineates the psychological aspects of different groups of people. By quantifying the estimates offered by Islanders, Rivers had hoped to gain some measure of the psychological disposition of Islanders, comparing them with the normative positions of those in the West. Rivers should have been able to interpret and compare the range of tests 'both by the smallness of the mean variations and by the general consistency of the results' (p. 127) but he seemed to be unable to do this in a neutral way or in a way that recognised any positive Islander attributes at all. Instead, all findings were reinterpreted to reinforce, render and make consistent the inferior position of the 'savage'. After all, a notion of savages as remnants of a past people is what had currency in the broader intellectual spheres.

There is little substantive data in Rivers' study that could prove either inferiority or superiority, savage or civilised, or any of the theoretical positions he so desperately wanted to secure in statistics. Indeed it would be difficult to determine what objective measures could achieve such results or even attempt to measure such intangible concepts. In his report Rivers can be seen visibly struggling to provide something of substance about the physiology and psychology of the Islander; he twists and turns, making hopeful forays and doggedly backtracking to keep his destination in sight and yet, ultimately, all is to no avail. All his report can really suggest is that none of the tested Islanders possessed a discernible squint and that, from the one case found on Murray Island, it would appear that colour blindness was not a common feature of the Islanders' physiognomy; that the colour nomenclature for blue which had been developed along the lines valued in European aesthetics by the late nineteenth century had not developed in the same way in the Torres Strait islands; that Islanders seemed able to distinguish the particular contrasting colours selected by Rivers 'less readily than the average European' (p. 81); and that Islanders who showed more constancy and consistency on the latter tests were in fact 'unpractised and wholly ignorant inhabitants'. None of these conclusions tells us anything at all about the psychological capacities of the Islander people, let alone provides sufficient data to enable us to make a dubious comparison between Islanders and the minds of early twentieth-century Europeans. Quite frankly, it is not even particularly useful information and is really only interesting for what it says about the viewpoint of the scientist who developed it — a viewpoint which, as can be seen, it describes very well.

5
Physiological inscriptions of the senses

> ...the inferiority of the black races is due to the cessation of the growth of the brain at an earlier age than in the white races, and it may be that this is in part, or wholly, due to a less active response of the blood pressure to mental activity.
>
> (McDougall, 1903, p. 201)

While speech and vision were being intimately investigated by Ray and Rivers, it was mainly left to Myers, McDougall and, to a lesser extent, Seligmann to cover all the relevant aspects of the other senses by documenting the Islanders' hearing, smell, taste, touch, muscular sense, blood pressure, thresholds of pain and reaction times. Once again, the scientists' aim was to test as many aspects of the senses as possible to gain a blueprint of how the Islander mind functioned and to discover, on a comparative basis, how far the savage mind lagged behind the sensorily advanced, civilised European mind. In their reports they tried to distinguish between physiological and pathological differences; between racial and cultural differences. Myers' occasionally quite honest report (Myers, 1903) provides an interesting contrast to Rivers' and McDougall's attempts at scientific explanations.

Hearing

Like Rivers, Myers moved first to identify, in the Islanders he examined on Murray Island, any physiological or pathological conditions of the ears that could affect the Islanders' hearing capacity. The results showed that, although the Islanders were in good general health and that only one case of otorrhoea — or discharge from the ear — was identified, an outbreak of measles, which Myers found had occurred some years before, was suspected to be partially responsible for a degree of deafness he discovered in the community. However, another obvious reason for this deafness, he felt, would have been the extent of the diving depth required of their Islander labourers by the commercial marine industries.

> Until the recent legislation enacted by the Queensland Government, natives were induced to dive, without dress or helmet, into such deep water that deaths were of frequent occurrence. At the time of our visit, the hospital at Thursday Island contained several cases of paralysis, which had arisen from diving in excessively deep water. (Myers, 1903, p. 142)

Myers was soon left in no doubt about the extent of deafness that resulted from this kind of diving. After testing 18 divers he found that almost half had defective hearing in one ear, and a couple were found who had the same problem with both ears. Indeed, from all his tests on hearing, including those on children, he was 'forced to conclude that the general auditory acuity of islanders in the Torres Strait is inferior to that of the Europeans' (p. 148).

Myers was attempting to disprove the commonly held theory that primitive people, by being physiologically closer to animals than to civilised people, still possessed the remarkable ability to see, hear, taste, smell and feel at very acute levels — an ability which Rivers was, as we have seen, concurrently testing in great detail in relation to vision. Myers, like Rivers, did not believe that 'the remarkable capacity possessed by primitive people for distinguishing faint sound amid familiar surroundings' was an attribute of native physiology (Myers, 1903, p. 143). Myers' report pointed to two case studies in particular as references for this theoretical position in relation to hearing. First, Laszlo Magyar, who had visited the Kimbunda people in South Africa, had noted that the people possessed the remarkable capacity 'to distinguish very accurately sounds which are heard from a great distance, and at once recognize their nature and direction' (cited in Myers, 1903, p. 143). Second, P. Paulitschke, who had visited Somalia, had observed that the people there 'found the Somali hunters to have a very delicate sense of hearing, the slightest noise awakening their attention, its direction being recognized with certainty' (1903, p. 143). Once again this view was hotly contested in the literature, with its opponents arguing that all people hear and become accustomed to sounds just as well in their own environments. Generally, however, '[w]e need but imagine such an individual transported to the streets of a busy city, to obtain a complete reversal of the phenomena,' Myers suggested, with 'the primitive man heedlessly passing various noises which could be full of significance to his more civilized companion' (p. 143).

The theory, or more accurately the supposition, was not grounded in hard scientific data and, as such, it needed rigorous scientific testing to prove or disprove its foundations. Personally, Myers believed that the common opinions of fellow travellers had little scientific basis and he was ready and willing to give these ideas a much needed, and thoroughly rigorous, debunking. 'Savages', he and his colleagues were convinced were human, although differently human to civilised humans. As he could find only two experimental studies with definite tests — one by Giltschenko of Ossets in Caucasus and the other by Hyades of Fuegians on the island of Tierra del Fuego, which directly contradicted each other — he was undertaking ground-breaking work here. The first study had heralded the Ossets' extraordinary capabilities, while the second study had maintained Fuegians' capacities to be quite ordinary. There was, for this reason, no definitive scientific proof to be found in the literature. To test these common assumptions therefore, Myers undertook tests of his own to provide a rigorous measure of the auditory acuity, the upper limit of hearing and the smallest perceptible difference of two different tones by 'subjecting the ear to a definite test' (p. 143). Such work had the potential to enhance his already growing reputation in academe.

Myers had three methods of testing auditory acuity available to him at the time. The first was the most basic and very direct — to use a telescope into which, with the lens removed and the instrument placed in the vertical position, a small pith-ball could be dropped through the small opening onto a piece of felt fixed at the other end. As he says, '[t]he velocity of the fall of the ball, and hence the intensity of the sound produced by its impact against the felt-disc, could be varied at will by altering the height of the telescopic tube' (p. 144). The second was perhaps the more 'scientific' approach, involving the use of Politzer's Hormesser, an apparatus made up of a hollow steel cylinder and a hammer that falls from a fixed height. However, because of the noise of the surrounding environment, Myers chose not to use these particular instruments on Murray Island.

> Here the constant rustle of the palm-leaves and the beating of the surf on the sea-shore compelled me to lay aside my telescopic apparatus and Politzer's Hormesser in favour of a stop-watch. (p. 145)

Thus thwarted at one of his testing sites, he settled on the third available testing instrument, a Runne's clock, which is a particular kind of stopwatch 'which could be made to tick five times in a second, and could be easily stopped or set going at will' (p. 145).

To moderate the impact of external noise factors and to serve as a scientific control, Myers tested his colleagues alongside the Islanders on Murray Island, although it is not clear if he tested them at precisely the same time that the Islanders were being tested. Rivers had noted that there were some exceptionally quiet times at Mabuiag Island — times when there was, in fact, 'almost complete silence' (Myers, 1903, p. 147). At Mabuiag Myers was able to test 8 out of 13 Islanders — under unspecified conditions — using both a Runne's clock and Politzer's Hormesser (results in Table XX, Myers, 1903, p. 147).

In this way Myers set out to scientifically compare Islanders as a group with selected members of the Cambridge team, who became the de facto English or civilised control group. Quite simply, what was being investigated by Myers was the thresholds or limits of hearing of two small random groups, with the data being assembled to build a comparative study in a scientific report.

To do this the relevant scientific apparatus was first placed in the participant's range of hearing and progressively moved away at metre and half-metre intervals until it could no longer be heard. To check the findings the apparatus was then placed outside the range of the participant's hearing and progressively moved, using the same method, until it was heard once more. Myers assiduously tested the findings by making five subsequent trials between the two points to determine a threshold. These results were then listed as average scores and directly compared with each other. A point where Islander participants could or could not hear this scientific apparatus was, in this way, the basis on which comparative measures were made in relation to the scientists who were all too familiar with the tests being undertaken.

The results, Myers found, more than vindicated his belief that the commonly held theory was wrong. Myers reported that 7 of the 12 boys on Murray Island could not hear as far as he could, and 4 of the 5 adults could not hear as well as he did. How acute his own hearing was at the time was not specified in the report but it was clearly superior to that of Rivers for, by comparison, all of the girls on Murray Island could hear as far as, or better, than that gentleman. The reason for this is simple for unfortunately, as Myers observed, 'Dr Rivers…was certainly suffering from partial deafness when these estimations were made' (p. 148).

An examination of the standard-observer column in Table XIX (Myers, 1903, p. 146) of the findings provides a good example of the unscientific basis upon which the findings were made. In the first comparison, when 12 boys are compared with Myers (CSM) and Rivers (WHRR), 1 is 'not quite equal to CSM'; 2 are the 'same as CSM'; 1 is 'worse than CSM'; 1 is 'much worse than CSM'; 1 has the 'L.E. [left ear] of CSM'; 2 have the 'L.E. (left ears of both) CSM and WHRR'; and so on.

In Table XX (Myers, 1903, p. 147), the results of Mabuiag adults are compared with those achieved by Seligmann and Rivers. As Myers noted, '[n]ot one of the ten young Mabuiag adults [aged 17 to 35 years] with whom Mr Seligmann later compared himself, could hear as far as he could. Two others could not hear as far as Dr Rivers, whose auditory acuity even by this time had not much improved' (p. 148).

When recording his results Myers used a different method for Islanders from the control group of scientists. For Islanders he recorded separately the results for acuity in left and rights ears. The data clearly shows whether acuity is the same or different in an Islander's left and right ears.

For the scientists he records either the left ear only or one result for both ears (B.E.). In only two instances are results for the right ears recorded. We may deduce that this was shorthand for scientists who have the same levels of acuity in both ears. But where the results for only left ears are recorded, we are left to wonder about the acuity of the scientist's right ear.

Myers did question whether the auditory acuity of three scientists could be accepted 'as typical of Europeans generally' (p. 148). But his reservations related to a concern that their general health while conducting the tests was 'below par', and that he and Rivers were affected by temporary hearing loss. Myers also conceded that Islanders' lower auditory acuity was generally attributable to pathological conditions although nowhere in his conclusions does he discuss this as partial deafness or as an outcome of diving. Instead he concludes that

> as the children show a similar, although less marked, deficiency, one is forced to conclude that the general auditory acuity of the islanders in the Torres Strait is inferior to that of Europeans. (Myers, 1903, p. 148)

Thus while he implies that lower levels of auditory acuity are not innate, neither are they explained in the terms of partial deafness or state of general health afforded to the Europeans.

The rigour of these tests, the reliability of the comparisons and the interpretation of the data, as well as the validity of the test instruments, are all questionable. Comparisons made in these ways, with no actual measurement of auditory levels, are an extremely shaky foundation upon which to build a rigorous statistical data source and produce reliable scientific conclusions.

Myers went on to test the Islanders' upper limit of hearing. For this test, he used a Galton whistle — a tube-like instrument with a 1-millimetre bore — 'its length can be varied by sliding in or out the solid rod which closely fitted the tube of the whistle' (p. 149). Attached to this rod was a device that provided a measure, in millimetres, of any position in which the rod is placed along the whistle. The researcher began first by blowing the whistle with the rod fully extended and slowly slid it into the whistle until no audible whistle-note could be heard. He then blew again but this time he slid the rod out of the whistle until the first audible note could be heard. After five attempts like this an average was taken and this became a measure of the upper limit of hearing for that day. Unfortunately when Myers tested the same person on another day he found different averages.

Notwithstanding this, the results, when compared with similar tests done on a test group from Aberdeenshire in Scotland, indicated small differences between the two groups, with 'this small difference...[being] in favour of the latter' (p. 152). Myers also observed a distinct pattern in the data that suggested to him that 'children of both communities hear a higher tone than the adults, the upper limit of hearing becoming gradually lower with increase of years' (p. 154).

The first point that needs to be made here relates to the seven different groups of Islanders. Myers had formed these groups according to their relative experiences with diving:

> Class A comprises men who had not noticed any ill effects in the ear from diving. Those in whom diving had caused haemorrhagic or purulent discharge from one ear are grouped in Class B, a discharge from both ears in Class C, haemorrhage from the mouth and nose only in Class D...in Class E those whose hearing in one or both ears was defective from some other cause. The men who had never dived are in Class F. Those about whom I have no information are in Class G. (Myers, 1903, p. 152)

Rightly, Myers wished to take into account all possibilities that might impact on the overall relevance of the data he was collecting. Of note here, however, is the fact that the different categories used are determined by what Islanders could or could not recall from their diving experience and not, as Myers noted, by any physiological examination carried out by himself. The other significant feature to note is the comparative measures derived from Aberdeenshire. It would not be unreasonable to expect that Myers would be dividing the group in this way because he wanted to take into account, or at least acknowledge, the effects of diving on Islander ears.

Although Myers took care to categorise Islanders this way, he did not consider it in his conclusions. He briefly discussed the relevant literature that discussed whether 'affections of the middle ear' changed 'the appreciation of high tones' (p. 152) but he did not venture to draw conclusions about the effects of deep diving on middle and internal ears.

What he did was retabulate his data: 'If the Murray Island and Aberdeenshire adults be compared, irrespectively of any aural lesion or disease produced by diving or other causes, the following results are obtained' (p. 153). The two sets of results were of course almost identical. But even at this point Myers could not admit the meaninglessness of the comparison of these two groups.

The implications of diving on hearing loss of Islanders were not clear. His only measure of the hearing of the Scottish group was that they 'as far as I could judge; had normal hearing in one or both ears' (p. 154).

Despite these weaknesses and the general futility of the exercise, Myers speculated that 'possibly the small existing differences in favour of the latter [Aberdeenshire adults] would have been absent, had it been possible to take observations on a greater number of subjects' (p. 154).

In this study, as in others undertaken by the Cambridge group, there is continuing evidence of a tension which undermines the research as a whole. On the one hand, there is an earnest desire to accurately situate — or position — the Islanders in a human world by studying them intensively in their own environment. Yet on the other hand, all measures used to understand — or position — the Islanders make assumptions about the solidity of the instruments, methods and theories imported wholesale from academe.

From here, Myers widened both his instruments and his theoretical underpinnings to determine the smallest perceptible tone-difference that could be identified by the Islander '[f]or it be supposed that smaller intervals are employed by primitive than by civilized communities... we should expect them to show evidence of extremely high sensibility to minute differences of pitch' (p. 168). Two tuning forks were used in this experiment which was designed to ascertain the Islanders' ability to detect the smallest perceptible tone-difference between them. The first was of a fixed kind at 256 vibrations per second. The second was also of

5. Physiological inscriptions of the senses

the same pitch but had a sliding metal bar attached to one of its forks to vary the interval times. The Islanders, upon hearing the sounds of two selected forks, were to respond by indicating 'first one high, or second one high, or both all same' (p. 158). In all, 12 children and 21 adults were tested on Murray Island as they were in Aberdeenshire.

As regards some of the adult Islanders, Myers was left in 'no doubt that in these experiments their judgment of pitch differences was being exercised for the first time' (p. 159). The folk of Aberdeenshire on the other hand, 'belonged to a highly educated class. Six of them played a musical instrument, and of these three had had the valuable previous experience of tuning the violin, and one of the violoncello' (p. 159). But Myers thought he 'ought to add that at most only one or two could be termed highly musical' (p. 156).

Myers tested the participants over a six-week period and '[e]ach sitting lasted from twenty to thirty minutes' (p. 159). No doubt, each sitting involved many tedious encounters with the sounds produced by tuning forks and the number of participants tested shrank rapidly in number as the tests progressed over the six-week period. The results indicate that the Scots scored closer to the standard than did the Islanders. That is, as Myers concluded, the people of 'Aberdeenshire surpass the people of Murray Island in their power of distinguishing two tones of nearly identical pitch' (p. 167).

However, Myers did feel the necessity to make some clarifications about these results. The first alluded to the familiarity of the Scottish adults with their musical instruments and the fact that this was the Islanders' first encounter with a tuning fork. This suggested to Myers that, in a sense, perhaps only the children could be compared. However, the second clarification he made pointed to a large discrepancy in the number of tests taken by the Islander children in comparison with the Scottish children. He conceded, as a consequence of these problems with the tests, that it would be difficult 'to deduce a numerical measure of relative pitch-discriminability in the primitive and civilized races' (pp. 167–68).

To combat this, Myers thought that perhaps a view to 'existing difference may be gained, if we dismiss from consideration (i) the results given by those subjects, on whom the number of observations made at their first sitting did not exceed thirty, and (ii) the improved results, gained by telling the subject if his judgments were right or wrong' (p. 168). Thus huge differences could be deduced between the Islanders and the Scots. The comparative data, when re-configured, show the Murray Islanders in the first sitting had an average score of 15.4 and the Scots had a much better average of 7.6. In the second sitting, the new figures show them to be 12.5 as opposed to 4.7.

Myers interpreted his data to demonstrate that there was a stark difference between the Scots and the Murray Islanders. No matter what the real reason was for omitting from the overall analysis those participants who contributed below thirty measurements, the effect is certainly striking. The adjustment however does nothing to resolve the methodological problems of this research which, by adjusting an already flawed comparative score, only served to deplete Islander results even further against an already over-represented Scottish contingent. As can be seen from Table XXV (Myers, 1903, p. 161), 12 children from Murray Island in the first sitting made 424 measurements while their 12 counterparts from Aberdeenshire had made 616. The 21 adults from Murray Island made 857 while the 21 Scots made 929. By adjusting the figures as Myers did, the Islander overall numbers had to be reduced by a further 10 participants while the Scots had to be reduced by 3. This rebalancing act, though small, had a dramatic effect in the results. Despite the flawed comparative tables and the weaknesses in the methodology, Myers concluded that 'the weak discriminative sensibility of…[Murray Islanders] is probably due to their lack of familiarity with European musical notes, precise intervals and instruments' (p. 168).

Smell

Myers also tested the Islanders' sense of smell and compared the results with data from his Scottish experiments. Once more he was trying to debunk the idea that 'in the human species savage races have a characteristic fineness of smell in which they approach the animal world' (Ribot, cited by Myers, 1903, p. 169). Paulitschke held a similar view, noting in an 1896 publication, that the olfactory acuity of the Somalis 'equal[ed] that of the best sporting dogs. With dilated nostrils they scent[ed] the game' (cited in Myers, 1903, p. 169). Myers rejected the idea that this high sense of acuity had a physiological basis in that 'the wideness and flatness of the nostrils in the lower races' (p. 169) made this heightened sense of smell possible. Althaus, in fact, had suggested in an 1892 publication an even more scientific explanation for this, suggesting that

> the olfactory nerve is as highly useful to man in his natural condition as to beasts, and the peculiar pigment, which surrounds the endings of this nerve and appears to assist in an easier resorption of odorous substances, is even now better developed in the coloured races than

5. Physiological inscriptions of the senses

in the Caucasian, among whom the nerve itself appears attenuated.
(cited in Myers, 1903, p. 169)

Myers was also aware, however, that the little existing research that had been done at the time, in fact, suggested that the evidence contradicted this popular theory. Citing the work of Hyades amongst the Fuegians in 1891 and Lombroso and Carrara's work on the Sudanese Dinkas in 1897, Myers is adamant that they indicated no instance of animal-like instincts at all. These studies, the first attempts at measuring levels of olfactory acuity in Indigenous people, did flag many variables that inhibited any conclusive statements. In particular, they noted 'imperfections' (p. 169) of the language of Indigenous people as being a central issue. For this reason Myers resolved that his study would be 'directed rather to the discovery of suitable methods for future experiments than towards an estimation of the acuity of their smell-power' (p. 170). This, indeed, was so and all concluding statements he made were qualified by various imperfections in the tests. Nevertheless he devised tests to estimate the levels of acuity amongst Islanders, made some measurements, and reported his findings.

In particular, Myers made two measurements: the first experimenting with ways to estimate levels of acuity amongst Islanders and the second experimenting with different scents from 'Messrs Piesse and Lubin of New Bond Street, London' (p. 182) to test the Islanders' memory and discrimination of odours. Both of these experiments were to show that there were multiple variables at play that could complicate the identification of the sense of smell of Islanders as simply a racial characteristic.

Myers found from the first that the Islanders' olfactory acuity was slightly higher in the islands than in Aberdeenshire. His first series of tests, 'to determine the approximate threshold at which the dilute acid could be detected from water' (p. 177), involved the use of a solution of 5 minims of valerianic acid diluted in 15 ounces of water. This solution was then added to glass tubes in varying amounts, the first tube containing half a dram of the diluted solution; the next would contain 1 dram; the next 2 drams, and so forth. Four tubes containing the various measures were accompanied with four other tubes with corresponding measures of water from the local well. The tubes were arranged in the following order starting with the smaller measures: water (w4), diluted valerianic acid (v4), w3, v3, v2, w2, v1, and w1. Fourteen boys from Murray Island were asked whether 'they smelled water or something else in each tube?' (p. 173). They were then marked either as right or wrong and their results were recorded on Table XXIX (Myers, 1903, p. 173). From this, he found that half the boys failed to detect 'the weakest solution, a much smaller proportion with the next stronger solution, while all succeeded with the two strongest solutions' (p. 177).

The second series of tests were done in the reverse order to the first 'with a view to determining the differences brought about, when decreasing instead of increasing the strengths of the valerianic solutions' (p. 177). With no indication of the number of participants, Myers explained that the 'resulting judgments…were not sufficiently numerous to indicate more than an approximate equality in the results given by the island adults and children' (p. 174). No data were recorded and no comparative table constructed. For it would be 'impossible', he believed, to replicate this experiment elsewhere as there would be no comparable water sample due to the fact that '[i]n Murray Island everything had a smell' (p. 177).

The third series of tests involved 9 men and 8 children from Murray Island, and four glass tubes: two filled with 4 drams of water, and the other two containing 15 and 30 minims of 'filtered saturated aqueous solutions of camphor' (p. 174). The Islanders were first given a separate solution of camphor of unknown dilution to smell and then 'told that of the four tubes one or perhaps more than one tube had a camphor-like odour and that the others contained merely water' (p. 174). The Islanders had to pick out which ones contained the foreign odours, while Haddon (ACH in results table) and Rivers (WHRR in results table) did the same to represent the control group. This and the following tests gave Myers some confidence that the testing instrument would this time provide a 'greater promise of definite results than the preceding' (p. 174).

From this series of tests Myers discovered that

> [o]f nine islanders two had distinctly subnormal acuity, four were worse than, three were equal to two members of the expedition (WHRR and ACH), whose acuity was investigated at the same time. Of 8 island children, 1 had distinctly subnormal acuity, 5 were worse than, 2 were better than, the same 2 Europeans. (p. 177)

Unfortunately, despite the 'greater promise of definite results' no precise data from the tests was provided, the standard achieved by his colleagues was also unstated, and no similar experiment was repeated in Scotland. As a testing instrument, in short, it remained of little proven value.

The fourth series of tests involved 16 men from Murray Island, 16 men from Aberdeenshire, and four glass tubes, two of which contained 4 drams of rainwater, the other two containing 7.5 minims and 3.75

minims of the camphor solution. The numbers of right answers were then listed and compared (Table XXXI, Myers, 1903, p. 175), with the results showing the two groups to be almost the same. However, as Myers had already lamented, the water in the islands had a smell and this inhibiting factor had to be considered as a major variable in the comparison. For instance, Myers found that on Murray Island his colleague Rivers only obtained 4.5 right answers for the stronger solution and 3.5 right answers for the weaker solution, while in Scotland he was able to provide 'all ten answers invariably correct on three different occasions' (p. 178). However, Myers believed that there was a positive aspect to the difference in levels achieved by Rivers. For if Rivers had experienced both samples in the tests, his results could be used as the constant that allowed the making of comparisons between the Islanders and the Scots. He resolved thus that of 16 Islanders 'the olfactory acuity of three is decidedly defective, of seven is slightly worse than, and of six is better than his. Comparing the 16 Aberdeenshire adults...with the same standard observer, we find that the olfactory acuity of four is decidedly defective, of seven is slightly worse than, and of five equal to or better than his' (p. 178). The Islanders' levels of acuity were measured then against a standard of 4.5 and 3.5 achieved by Rivers in the islands while their Scottish counterparts were compared presumably with a standard achieved by this same colleague in Aberdeenshire that was said to be 'invariably correct' at all times.

In the final series of tests, Myers involved 6 men and 12 children from Murray Island, and 6 men and women and 12 children from Aberdeenshire, and six glass tubes. Each tube contained graduated amounts of camphor solutions: 7.5 minims, 15 minims, 30 minims, 1 dram, 2 drams and 4 drams. These were to test the participants' judgments on relative strengths of camphor solutions or, as Myers described it, 'to test the discrimination of odour-strengths' (p. 178). He listed all the right and wrong answers from these tests in Table XXXII (Myers, 1903, p. 176). However, in his summaries he elected for some reason only to display the frequency of wrong answers, which he then compared. He observed from these results that the Islander children 'made fewer erroneous judgments than the Aberdeenshire children... The Aberdeenshire adults were more successful than the Murray Island adults' (p. 178). But, as he hastened to add, 'the results show[ed] no remarkable differences in the behaviour of the two communities to the same experiment' (p. 178).

In his conclusion to the overall study Myers noted that the insufficient number of participants in the experiment limited what could be said about the data which, he admitted, was flawed from the outset because of two other qualifying factors. Firstly, of the 60 sets of observations made over the series of 5 tests, in

> no two of which are the experimental conditions the same. Secondly, in spite of these frequent modifications of experiment, I reached the close of my stay in Murray Island, as it will be seen, without having made use of a wholly satisfactory method. (Myers, 1903, p. 177)

Disappointingly for him, he had not been able to achieve the first part of his aims and find an adequate measure from which to build future evidence. Nevertheless, as he pointed out, '[t]here are, however, few experiments of which it can be said that they teach nothing' (p. 177), and he thus felt he was able to present a 'few general conclusions, which can be legitimately drawn concerning the comparative acuity of smell among Murray Islanders and among Europeans' (p. 177). For this reason Myers reported that

> [w]e may on the whole conclude, I think, that the average olfactory acuity is slightly higher in Murray Island...than in Aberdeenshire, a smaller proportion of the islanders having obtuse and a greater number having hyperacute smell-power. The average acuity of the children of both communities seems slightly higher than that of the adults. (Myers, 1903, p. 179)

The important goal of demonstrating that the Islanders' sense of smell was not entirely a racial characteristic was, for Myers at least, crucial for the success of the expedition as he saw it. Here, at least, he could not allow himself to fail. He therefore needed to construct a test that would demonstrate the Islanders' memory for, and discrimination of, odours. Father Guis, writing about his experiences in Papua New Guinea in 1898, had already reported that Islanders had a delicate sense of smell that enabled them

> to track a man down, some object belonging to him, preferably his garment, is procured if possible. They smell at it and then start off in pursuit of the individual, whom they will readily recognize among several others because of his odour. (cited by Myers, 1903, p. 180)

Myers himself had also observed his 'Malay boy' (p. 181) sorting out the washing of the expedition team by smelling the garments.

However, he also noted from the literature that Le Cat's experience with the South American Indians in 1740 was that, while they did have a fine sense of smell, 'Europeans would soon acquire this power of discrimination if they lived long among savage people, and that there is nothing strange in the matter at all' (cited by Myers, 1903, p. 180). Galton, for instance, was able to train himself 'to associate two whiffs of peppermint with one whiff of camphor, three of peppermint with one of carbolic acid, and so on' (cited by Myers, 1903, p. 181). Myers resolved that perhaps 'the mode of life led by primitive people and their general mental status combine to make them more aware of and attentive to the majority of external stimuli than we ourselves are' (p. 181). In other words there was a learned cultural aspect to what some had believed to be a purely racial characteristic. A smell that was culturally meaningful and significant was sure to command attention.

To test this theory Myers introduced 13 Islanders to a range of scents and other substances he had brought into the islands from London. Over a five-week period the tested Islanders sniffed the alien aromas of camphor, valerianic acid, thyme, sandal, benzaldehyde, jasmine, violet, verbena, heliotrope, vanilla, musk, asafoetida, caproic acid, civet, ocimum sanctum, linimentum terebinthae acetium, phenol and ammonia. With their noses thoroughly primed, they were then asked to identify what the various scents and substances smelt like, and to record whether they liked the scent or not. He found the Islanders were independent in their judgments and not influenced at all by any suggestions and that they gave responses with 'surprising readiness and assurance' (p. 184), readily evoking associations with the various scents and odours with a pace that exceeded any such experiences he had while testing Europeans.

This, he believed, fell into line with Rivers' findings and was 'yet another expression of the high degree to which the sensory side of mental life is elaborated among primitive people' (p. 185). Overall, however, '[s]o far…as these experiments go, they show that the people of the Torres Strait have much the same liking and disliking for various odours as obtains among ourselves' (p. 185). That Islanders had not yet developed a wider, more abstract, civilised mind was a product of their position on the human evolutionary ladder; that they could do so, with education and adequate guidance, was simply a matter of time and perseverance.

Taste

To test the intensity of the Islanders' ability to discern taste, Myers, Seligmann and McDougall undertook a number of experiments on

Murray Island and Mabuiag Island designed to sketch in the essentials of these otherwise scantily reported senses. This part of the report was obviously considered to be the least important and the research results are, at their best, haphazardly reported. At their worst, they are poorly done with a minimum of thought and care to detail. Myers and Seligmann were to concentrate their rapidly waning energies on the investigation of taste, leaving most of the planning and execution of the experiments on the other senses — except for reaction times, which Myers also tested — in the hands of McDougall.

Myers and Seligmann plied 7 adults on Murray Island with solutions of sugar, salt, acetic acid and quinine, while Seligmann simultaneously carried out the same test on Mabuiag Island. The solution was wiped onto the individual's tongue and he — those tested were all men — had to report on what was 'the nature of the taste' (1903, p. 186). They noted of both studies that '[s]weetness has the best defined taste word, saltness comes next. Acidity appears to have an even less definite name in Mabuiag than in Murray Island' (p. 187). Myers noted 'absence of a distinctive word for bitter [to describe the taste of quinine]...Several Aberdeenshire adults whom I tested had precisely the same difficulty as the Murray Islanders in giving a name to the taste of the bitter solution' (p. 188).

> It is...remarkable that there should often be no distinctive word for bitterness, the sensation of which is now regarded with such unanimity by physiologists as *sui generis*, differing from other taste-sensations as widely as the sensation of blue differs from that of red. A similar state of things has been already met with in the colour-vocabularies of primitive folk. (Myers, 1903, p. 188)

The Islanders were not alone in their inability to describe 'bitter' to the exactitude demanded by physiologists. Furthermore, while this may indeed have seemed to have been an important point for Myers and Seligmann at the time that they constructed their report — it was published in 1903 — it was directly contradicted by Ray's dictionary on the Islander languages, which was not published until 1907 but included an English index to the Mabuiag and Murray Island vocabularies (see Ray, 1907, p. 171). The index lists several Murray and Mabuiag Islander words that correspond with the English word 'bitter'. Nonetheless, the experiment, in short, did not reach any resounding conclusions which would shake the foundations of the scientific world and the scientists chose to do little with it except comment peripherally.

Reaction times

As part of his input into the team's study of feeling, while on Murray Island Myers also tested the reaction times of 53 Islanders. He compared them with 26 Englishmen and 26 people of Sarawak as well as 'five members of the expedition and...two Englishmen in Sarawak' (p. 205). There were three tests in all. The first tested the reaction times of Islander responses to an auditory stimulus, the second to a visual stimulus and the third to a choice-visual stimulus (this was one that required the Islander to respond to a visual stimulus but had to register a response by pressing morse keys and raising a hand to designate one colour being seen and the other hand for another colour).

Not surprisingly, Myers found that the older men of Murray Island were notably slower in their reaction times than the boys and this was mostly indicated in the results of the tests using the auditory stimulus. These results also showed that the boys scored just as well as the younger adults in the auditory tests. However, when the young adults of Murray Island were compared with adults of the same age group (16 to 35 years) from Sarawak and England — the English contingent were university students, graduates and laboratory assistants — new things could be observed. First, the Sarawak people outscored the others in both the auditory and the visual tests. Second, the English people did just as well as the Murray Island people in the auditory tests but were notably faster in the visual tests. The most outstanding feature was the reaction times of the Sarawak people in that they were half of those of the other groups in both tests.

Myers, however, interpreted these figures to demonstrate that the results were 'dependent on an arbitrary selection of one of many possible ways of arriving at the mean reaction-times' (p. 215). Indeed, he argued, if the average of the median was changed to 'either the median of the median columns...or the median of the "average of ten" columns' (p. 215) or, if we were 'to consider separately the individuals whose series contained no a- or b-reactions so that those who gave irregular reaction-times should no longer weigh upon the general mean' (p. 215), one could effectively form alternative figures, and thus new correspondences between them (Table XXXVIII, Myers, 1903, p. 215). In these ways, similar results could be achieved as before but with one notable exception, '[t]he visual reaction-time of the Sarawak natives...is almost identical with that of the English' (p. 216). In these ways as well, the results of the choice-visual tests could be further manipulated. For example, the results of the English people in this new formulation can now show that they were much faster than the Islanders were in their reaction times.

Quite appropriately Myers interpreted this as meaning 'that in a given time one people has adapted itself more readily than another so as to perform a prescribed reaction more rapidly' (p. 221) and, that '[t]he proportion of slow or irregular...[participants] (most of whom will react satisfactorily after adequate practice) must vary from community to community...[and] in this sense, reaction-times may be said to vary inter-racially' (p. 221). In his final summation, he suggested that

> [s]uch racial differences in reaction-times, if actually established by further research, may turn out to be merely the expression of racial differences in temperament. For it is easily conceivable that a highly strung, nervous people cannot develop the disposition, or assume the attitude, that is favourable to the most rapid and regular reactions with such readiness as can a relatively unemotional people. (Myers, 1903, p. 223)

The crucial word in this summation is the word 'if'. 'If' further evidence can be established, he suggests, then it would be possible to argue that racial differences may be little more than 'differences in temperament' — a theoretical position that Myers would have liked to prove. However, as he had no way of doing so he was left with the need to hypothesise and hope for future confirmation.

Touch

McDougall had no such illusions and no such goals. The way he saw things was clear, 'it was a principal object of our work to discover, if possible, racial characteristics' of the Islanders (McDougall, 1903, p. 189). So this was precisely what he set out to do. That he failed dismally was not from want of trying, as his experiments more than adequately demonstrate. If Myers' and Seligmann's work on taste was scantily done, McDougall's on sensory feeling — tactile discrimination and cutaneous sensations — was the most poorly conceived and executed in the whole project.

Four individual studies were done by McDougall to obtain a measure of cutaneous sensations. The first was a study on tactile discrimination; the second attempted to document whether Islanders could identify an area of skin touched by him; the third was an attempt to map temperature spots in the skin; and the fourth was designed to gauge the Islanders' sensibility to pain.

To test the delicacy of tactile discrimination, McDougall used a small pair of carpenter's dividers which had its points rounded and could measure the distance between them in millimetres. He began first by prodding the Islanders on the 'forearm...the nape of the neck...the palmar surface of the terminal phalanx of the thumb...and...the inner surface of the pulp of the second toe' (p. 191) but later limited his attentions to prodding the skin of the forearm and the nape of the neck, considering this limited application as sufficient for the purposes of his study. The dual point of the divider and its adjustable features enabled McDougall to find a threshold 'at which they yield a sensation perceptibly different from that yielded by a single point' (p. 190). The distance between the points of the divider was reduced successively by 20–30 per cent to the previous setting. In pragmatic terms, the threshold was determined thus: 'If in the series of ten double touches only one wrong answer was given I went on to the next step and usually found then a large proportion of wrong answers. The mean between the distances of the last two steps was then accepted as representing the threshold' (p. 190).

McDougall found from his study that the Islanders' threshold for identifying two points when the divider was at its closest was half that achieved by the working class English person — that is, the Islanders' 'power of discrimination is about double that of the Englishman' (p. 192). In other words, data from the 50 Islander men indicated that they could identify the two points of the divider when they were only 19.8 mm apart on the forearm and 11.6 mm apart when used on the nape of the neck. By the same method, McDougall was able to identify from 23 English men that they could identify the two points when used on the forearm at 44.6 mm apart. Data from the application to the nape of the neck suggest that 19 English men could identify two points when the distance between them was 20.8 mm.

In an attempt to resolve any uncertainty that might have been created by the fact that there was an unequal number of participants — with data from 50 Islander men being compared with data from 23 English men in one test and 19 in the other — McDougall attempted to compare his findings with data from other studies. He diligently cited Weber's study published in 1846 of an unknown number of Europeans, which found that their average on the forearm was 40.6 mm; and Landois' study published in 1885 — also of an unknown number of Europeans — which found that their average was 45.1 mm. However, as data from both these studies also showed that the average of 54.1 mm achieved from tests done by Weber and Landois on the neck was way over the 20.8 mm found by McDougall in his study, this raised some concern in his mind about whether he had actually reached an average for the English.

In any regard, the huge margin between the Europeans and the Islanders did nothing to change his view on the general trends. Indeed, he went on to remark that it was 'noteworthy that, while among 23 Englishmen only three gave thresholds for the skin of the forearm of less than 10 mm…among 50 Murray men 7 gave thresholds of less than 10 mm' (p. 192). This may have been a revealing issue for McDougall but the actual percentage of men who achieved this was relatively the same: 3 of 23 English equates to 13.04 per cent of them achieving less than 10 mm; 7 of 50 Islanders equates to 14 per cent who achieved less than 10 mm.

The final twist came when McDougall suggested that the Islanders be compared further with 10 Sea-Dayaks or Ibans of Sarawak. The people of Sarawak had achieved an average of 35 mm when the divider was applied to the forearm but, as McDougall remarked, the more telling story lay within the top ten thresholds of both groups. If the highest thresholds were considered from the top ten people from Murray Island and compared with the top ten of Sarawak, then the Islanders would still maintain a lower average. It was this final element that enabled McDougall to conclude in his report 'that this delicacy of tactile discrimination constitutes a racial characteristic' (p. 193). In other words, it was not that Islanders were able to distinguish two points of a divider when they were prodded on the forearm and the nape of their neck that counted but how these sensibilities weighed up with the existing literature and the expectation of the result.

From this investigative vantage point McDougall then went on to test the Islanders' 'power of localization of a point on the skin' (p. 193) after it had been touched. In this experiment 20 Islanders, with their eyes closed, held a pointing rod in the right hand while McDougall touched a point along the left forearm — laid at rest with the palm side up — with a similar rod. The Islanders would then open their eyes and, using the rod in his or her right hand, identify the point of skin that had been touched. Although each Islander went through the procedure no less than thirty times, the results of his experiment, says McDougall, served no 'especial interest and do not lend themselves to tabular statements' (p. 193). As a result no data was provided, although he did later use the experiment to make some observations of the tendencies of errors that 'were preponderantly in the direction of the long axis of the arm, either upward or downward, and in most the accuracy was greatest in the region just above the wrist' (p. 193). The experiment yielded 'no certainly recognizable correlation between the accuracy of tactile localization and the delicacy of tactile discrimination' (p. 193).

McDougall also attempted to identify temperature spots in the Islander's skin but he was unable to make a full assessment of these either. Four individuals, who were tested to his satisfaction for cold spots, showed that the distribution 'over an area of four square centimetres... presented no peculiar features and the spots seemed entirely similar in every way to those of English subjects' (p. 194). This was another investigative dead end.

Thresholds of pain

McDougall attempted in his fourth and final experiment to chart cutaneous sensations — to measure the Islanders' sensibility to pain to test the widely held perception that 'savages in general are less susceptible to pain than white men' (p. 194). To obtain a measure of this, McDougall used an algometer 'devised by Prof. Cattell' (p. 194), which involved pushing an ebonite rod, with a flattened point 9 mm in diameter, through the middle of the instrument which is pressured by springs so when downward pressure is made onto the skin surface one can obtain readings in kilograms.

His initial attempts involved

> a single application to the nail of either thumb, of either forefinger, and of either great toe, and to the skin of the small hollow just above the patella of either knees…and two applications to the forehead on adjoining spots in the middle line just above the glabella [the area between the eyebrows] and two to the sternum [breastbone] in the middle line' (McDougall, 1903, p. 194).

He found that thresholds were much the same from the different areas and subsequently moved to concentrate his examinations 'to the nails of the thumbs and forefingers and to the forehead. (p. 194)

McDougall's results showed that 47 men from Murray Island yelled out stop after an average of 6.7 kgs was applied to the thumb nails; 5.5 kgs to the forefinger nail; and 6.2 kgs to the forehead. Similarly, 18 boys (aged 10 to 14 years) of Murray Island yelled stop after an average of 3.8 kgs was applied to the thumb nails, and 3.3 kgs to the forefinger nails. No reading was provided for the tests on the boys' foreheads; perhaps McDougall thought this was going a bit far. By contrast, the 23 English men yelled stop earlier after an average of 3.8 kgs was applied to the thumb nails, 3.6 kgs to the forefinger nails, and 3.8 kgs to the forehead. Similarly, the English boys (aged 13 to 14 years) similarly were less inclined to the pressures and succumbed after an average of

2.9 kgs was applied to the thumb nails and 2.4 kgs to the forefinger nails. Again no results are given on tests to the forehead. When McDougall compared the men from England and the Torres Strait he concluded that,

> while their [Islanders'] average threshold of tactile discrimination is only about half as high, their average threshold for skin pain...is nearly double that of the Englishmen; or expressing the difference in other words and more loosely, we may say of these Murray men that their sense of touch is twice as delicate as that of the Englishmen, while their susceptibility to pain is hardly half as great. (McDougall, 1903, p. 195)

McDougall made no further comment on these results. There was no attempt to interpret their significance as characteristics of savages although the tests had been conducted 'in view of the oft-repeated statement that savages in general are less susceptible to pain than white men' (p. 194). He made no general reflections as to why these differences may occur or whether they were racially based.

Size–weight illusions

McDougall set about a rudimentary study of muscular sense to determine thresholds for the discrimination of small weight differences. This involved Islanders estimating the weight in tin cans of the same size. There were eleven tin cans in all and each had their weight graduated by 10 grams. The Islanders were given the heaviest and lightest cans first and then asked to say which was the heavier. In each of the subsequent steps, the weight differences of each can were reduced until the least perceptible difference in weight could be determined. As the participant neared his or her limit, McDougall determined that the proportion of right and wrong answers would become his gauge for measuring the participant's ability to discriminate between small differences in weight. He admitted that this was a somewhat arbitrary device but argued that it could be relied on nevertheless.

A difference evoking five correct answers and one wrong was held to be a difference above the threshold, i.e. greater than the least perceptible difference. Five right and two wrong answers were held to indicate the threshold, and if the proportion of wrong answers was larger than this, the difference was held to be below the threshold, and the mean of this difference and that of the preceding step was chosen to represent the value of the threshold.

5. Physiological inscriptions of the senses

The Islanders' ability to tell differences of weight in the cans were thus measured by an arbitrary reading of when right answers merged into wrong ones. This was the device that enabled McDougall to compare Islanders with the English. Although no data were provided from the actual tests, McDougall felt himself able to draw firm scientific conclusions.

> Of 19 boys and 45 men the average least perceptible difference was almost exactly the same in the two groups. I therefore put them together and give the average least perceptible difference of 64 Murray Islanders, namely 27.2 gms. (median 25 gms., extremes 10 and 55 gms.). If then we take 850 gms. as the mean value of the weights compared, the average least perceptible difference equals 3.2% of the total weight.
>
> For comparison with this result I give the corresponding average least perceptible difference of 30 Englishmen, namely 33.3 gms. (median 35 gms., extremes 10 and 50 gms.) which is 3.9% of the total weight. (McDougall, 1903, p. 198)

The above comparison was based entirely on what McDougall gives as the sum total of the two groups and the possibility that the results of 64 Islanders were directly comparable to the results of 30 English men. Indeed, even before both these considerations were taken into account, he assumed the efficacy of his device for locating the thresholds which, he believed, clearly showed that the English did better than the Islanders.

In another experiment, McDougall tested 21 men, 21 boys, and 13 women and girls on the effects of size–weight illusion. Two series of tests were made. In the first, there was a large tin 10 cm in diameter and 16 cm in height and a set of smaller tins, which measured 7 cm in diameter and 11 cm in height. The large tin was used as the constant and weighed 32 ounces. The smaller ones had their weight varied. One was set at 32 ounces and the others were reduced in steps of 2 ounces.

The test began with the large tin being presented along with a smaller one of the same weight, whereupon McDougall found Islanders to say consistently that the smaller tin was the heavier of the two. Subsequent comparisons were made with the smaller tins reducing in weight each time by 2 ounces, and continued until Islanders determined that the smaller tin was no longer heavier than the large tin. This experiment was to give McDougall some measure of the visual as well as the kinaesthetic influence on their judgments.

The second test involved the same cans and the same procedures. However, the difference was that the Islanders had to lift the can by a piece of string. To McDougall this allowed him to gain some measure of the effects of the illusion through sight and without the kinaesthetic aid of his grasp. McDougall then had to devise a normative position by which he could gain a measure of the judgments.

> When the subject pronounced the smaller tin to be equal to the larger or was undecided, the difference of weight between the large tin and that smaller one was taken as measure of the extent of the illusion produced in him. When the subject pronounced one small tin to be heavier than the large tin and the small tin next in descending order to be lighter, the mean of the weights of these two small tins was subtracted from that of the large tin and the difference was taken as the measure of the extent of the illusion. (1903, p. 199)

McDougall found from these two tests that, although the results corresponded in much the same way, the illusion was 'greater by both sight and by grasp than when by sight alone' (p. 199). And the overall result showed that '[t]he illusion affected the judgment of weight of the Murray men almost twice the amount that it affected that of the English men, and the Murray women shewed themselves still more markedly subject to it' (p. 199).

However, while interpreting these results, McDougall was relying on Müller-Schumann's theory of 1889 that it was normal for the body to adjust itself physiologically when encountering the sight and feel of objects. What he was trying to prove was that the human body had reflexes that went beyond any conscious deliberations — that is, that there was a certain degree to which muscles of the body were responding to impulses automatically. To what degree this occurred remained unstated but, as McDougall maintained, we cannot altogether omit the influence of suggestion. As far as he was concerned then, it followed that the Islander men, 'although they exhibit a greater nicety in the discrimination of small differences of weight, are yet subject to the size-weight illusion to a very much greater degree than the English men' (p. 200).

Blood pressure

McDougall then moved on to measure the Islanders' blood pressure to test the theory 'that the inferiority of the black races is due to the cessation of the growth of the brain at an earlier age than in the white races, and it may be that this is in part, or wholly, due to a less active response of the blood pressure to mental activity' (p. 201). His final contribution to the documentation of racial characteristics was thus premised on the following idea:

> ...since the effective working of the brain is so intimately dependent on a rapid circulation of the blood through it, and since that circulation is so largely determined by the state of the arterial pressure throughout the body, the power of mental activity to raise the general blood-pressure must be of great importance in promoting the vigour and effectiveness of mental processes. And it may be that this power is an element of fundamental importance in determining the superiority of the higher races. (1903, p. 201)

McDougall set for himself the task of studying 'to discover, if possible, some correlation between the activity of mental processes and the response of the blood pressure' (p. 201). He used a Hill-Barnard sphygmometer to measure the Islanders' blood pressure when at rest, during muscular work and in the course of mental work. This was all done in one sitting. To gain a measure of the Islander when at rest, McDougall 'engaged the subject in conversation for some minutes in order to allow any exciting effect of the application of the band to his arm to subside' (p. 201) before taking five to ten readings. The same Islander was then required to squeeze a dynamometer at 50 per cent of his maximum capacity and a reading taken 15–20 seconds after he began squeezing. Five to ten readings were taken in these ways.

In the next test, the Islander was given a maze drawn on a card and was required to trace his or her path to the centre, apparently in an effort to mimic mental stimulation. A series of readings were taken during and after this activity and, in a few cases, readings were made when an algometer was applied to 'the hypothenar eminence' (p. 202) with such force as to cause slight pain in the Islander. However, Table XXXIII (Myers, 1903, pp. 203–4) recorded the details of readings taken only at rest and during muscular and mental work. Unfortunately, while McDougall gave the details of every measure taken of the Islanders, he did not provide details of the English data — the report simply states their overall averages. Again, no heed is paid to the disparity in the number of participants in each test.

Like Myers, McDougall's consistency in not providing documentation of the European results in an equivalent way to the statistical data given for the Islanders was a recurring problem throughout his report, although it was a handy device in terms of interpretation. For what it allowed him to do was concede, whenever he needed to, that differences between the men of the islands and Europeans could not be contemplated due to 'the numbers of individuals [being] too few and the difficulty of the observations too great' (p. 202). In Table XXXIII he provided all his data on 'touch and weight discrimination, sensitivity to pain, size-weight illusion and blood pressure' (1903, p. 202) of Islander participants, with no corresponding information on the English. He came to no conclusions himself but simply used the table to close the chapter on the touch senses of Islanders. His deliberations, it would appear, were complete.

With their investigations of the different senses complete, Myers, Seligmann and McDougall finalised their part of Volume II of the Cambridge Report. They had intensively charted the physiology of the Islanders, measuring what they saw as their capacities to hear, smell, taste and feel. They had tested their own scientific theories and reached the widest conclusions they felt they were able to reach. As a result of all their work they believed they had a measure of their subjects — and it would allow them and their peers to assess and theorise upon the workings of the savage mind for years to come.

6

Anthropological inscriptions of the community

> Fortunate is the Country that has no history; and Mer, and the other islands of the Torres Strait, have very little.
>
> (Raven-Hart, 1949, p. 58)

Haddon had been fascinated by the culture he observed during his first visit to the Torres Strait as a marine zoologist in 1888. He and his assistant Wilkin, together with his colleagues Rivers and Seligmann, believed their research on the Cambridge expedition would be capable of salvaging a comprehensive picture of the culture of the people living in the Torres Strait, before it disappeared forever. To the best of their ability, Haddon and his colleagues documented all the things they saw as pertinent to this end: the Islanders' birth and childhood practices; their puberty rites; their toilet habits; their spiritual beliefs; social organisational schema; and burial rituals. The data contained in the Cambridge team's reports (1904, 1908 & 1912) is impressively extensive and detailed. The product of a lengthy intellectual gestation, it was not to be published in its entirety as a general ethnography of the Torres Strait until 1935, decades after the studies were carried out. As noted earlier, this report is increasingly regarded by both Islanders and non-Islanders as a valuable source of data on Islander beliefs and traditions and, by definition, of Islander people. Yet, despite the wealth of detail, these remain little more than random snapshots. In fact, they can never be more than this no matter how carefully they are reinterpreted or filtered simply because the viewpoint from which they were framed was, from the beginning, constrained both historically and intellectually. Ethnology and early anthropological theory once again informed practice in a way that not only framed the snapshot but also provided a background against which Islander society itself became in reality little more than an offstage presence imagined into being by a scientific audience.

Haddon and his colleagues felt that it was important to describe in detail the way in which a society with no written historical knowledge and no apparent formal structures — including law and order — could apparently function quite efficiently based on the myths, folktales, totems, taboos and intricate kinship systems which regulated an otherwise ungoverned society; a primitive society, which had not yet developed the sophisticated formal structures which typified more civilised societies. If there had been relatively little written about the people of the Torres Strait Islands in 1898 when the Cambridge team first landed, there were plenty of theoretical frameworks into which to mount the images they were collecting.

The team were looking for that core of something to which the people adhered; the psychic unity which they believed all primitive people used to guide their communal lifestyles; that primitive something which fulfilled a similar function to historical knowledge, social etiquette, and formal concepts of government and religion within civilised societies such as late Victorian England. Their starting point was simple, for these Cambridge scientists believed that to understand even the most primitive of societies the anthropologist must first understand their history. They must be able to position such societies with a certain amount of scientific precision on a socially evolutionary continuum. Yet how could this be done without written records and without any validated form of ancestral memory to serve as historical markers?

The collecting of myths and folktales as a window into a pre-industrial and fundamentally oral culture had become something of a preoccupation of European academics during the course of the nineteenth century. In the early years of that century the Brothers Grimm, influenced by the Romantic movement and its desire to document and capture what they saw as constituting the spiritual essence of the German people, had collected together several hundred stories which they felt formed part of an important oral tradition that was rapidly disintegrating under the impact of industrialisation, urbanisation and a growing literate population. The 'stories', they believed, told them a lot about the roots of German civilisation as they laid bare the mindset of a people who were rapidly becoming anachronistic under the onslaught of a rampantly developing modernity. As linguists, the Brothers Grimm had already compared different Germanic and other European languages to construct a theory of language development. The result, known as 'Grimm's Law', was based around a set of sound correspondences — a law which became

6. Anthropological inscriptions of the community

fundamental to the later development of comparative linguistics. Here, in the building blocks of the language and the lived experience of a people, they felt lay the blueprint of German cultural history, as, indeed, it would in any society similarly studied. The authentic 'voice' of a people was being 'rediscovered' across Europe by a newly urbanised 'middle class', a class that was reinterpreting and restructuring folk culture as a 'traditional' prop upon which to build a new society and found a new culture.

Cultural anthropologists, such as Haddon, transferred this preoccupation to other cultures, believing that these studies would uncover the distant roots of civilisation itself; their subjects included those 'savages' and 'primitive cultures' which still existed intact outside the realm of the civilised world. These folktales, in short, would provide the scientists with clear indicators of cultural shifts and their spread throughout the Torres Strait region. To this end Haddon meticulously documented sixty-nine folktales and analysed their meanings minutely.

A fly in the ointment, however, was Haddon's limited understanding of the languages. Nevertheless, he did not see this as posing too much of a problem.

> In collecting these folk-tales I could not take down the actual native words, having limited time and insufficient knowledge of the language, but I have given a faithful rendering of the tales as told to me in broken English. I have nowhere embellished the accounts, and I have given most of the conversations and remarks of people in the very words my informants used; thus preserving, as far as possible, the freshness and quaintness of the original narrative. I believe that in many cases the native idiom was bodily translated into the 'Pigeon English'. (Haddon, 1904, p. 9)

Engaging middle-aged men as his informants, Haddon asked them to recollect stories in the exact way that they had been related to them by the old men of the community. This, he felt, allowed him to 'confidently claim that this collection of tales really represents the traditional folk-lore of the last generation and the stories therefore may be of any age previous to the influence of Europeans and South Sea men' (1904, p. 9). Once collected, he proceeded to collate the tales into what the existing literature interpreted to be significant categories: nature myths, culture myths, totem myths, religious myths, tales about Dogais (devil spirits), tales about people and comic tales. He provided a synopsis of their plots and interpreted their anthropological relevance using a universal schema which, although necessarily translated into English, he believed would be 'sufficiently representative of native thought and expression' (p. 1). This rendering and distilling becomes all the more important because it constituted the basis upon which he rested his argument that a folklore society existed in the Torres Strait islands.

In this way, Haddon equated his documentation of myths and folktales with an accurate representation of the tradition of Islanders. In other words, he confused his own intellectual schema, which he used to translate the myths and folktales he collected into a culturally recognisable form, with actually existing Islander ideas; he simply conflated the one with the other. He assumed that what he had heard and, as he put it, 'faithfully' rendered into English was actually synonymous with what had been intended to be said. He assumed that the exact meaning was accurately and 'faithfully' passed intact between the storyteller and the listener — all this despite his ready admission that he could do little more than sketch the bare bones of the story linguistically and to say nothing of the fact that the 'stories' were part of a totally alien culture from his point of view. In doing all this he assumed far too much.

Apart from all of this, his assumption that the tales came out in a pristine state was shared by all his Cambridge colleagues. He believed the tales to be unblemished by any external influences; they belonged to this region and were the spontaneous products of it; they were the unchanged traditions of a timeless and motionless people. As we have already seen, the Cambridge team continually assumed that, prior to the arrival of missionaries, pearlers and the Queensland government, the Islander cultures had been 'unaffected' (p. 411) by their contact with early voyagers from Europe, Asia or any other place. Haddon, in fact, was quite confident about this, saying: 'it is safe to assert that thirty-five years ago there was no intelligent intercourse with white men; this period may practically be reduced to twenty-five years, and in some islands to even less' (1904, p. 9). From these sources he surmised cultural movements from west to east, with 'the journey of Auken and Terer from Murray Island to Boigu in the west' the only 'apparent exception, as this was merely the route taken by the spirits of the dead' (1908, pp. 128, 131–3). Once the marvellous and the exaggerated had been isolated, he believed he was quite able to accurately detect the traditional aspects in these tales — the 'anthropological incidents' (1904, p. 10) that lay bare the cultural evolution of the people. He boldly made an assessment of the cultural spread in the region, even though he admitted that a relative chronology of the evolution of culture in the region was not in itself possible.

6. Anthropological inscriptions of the community

> The earliest people were simple hunters and collectors, but the introduced art of the cultivation of the soil improved their mode of life. The natives of Muralug and the neighbouring islands never really attained this second stage, and even in Murray Island three folk-tales (vi, pp. 6, 9, 11) refer to the cooking of aroids for food, which now are eaten only in times of scarcity; this may be a remembrance of a time anterior to the cultivation of yams. The story of Yarwar shows that some of the inhabitants of Badu were then extremely incompetent gardeners.
>
> The introduction of new kinds of cultivated plants or better varieties of yams and the like is accredited in the eastern islands, or at all events in Murray Island, to named persons who came either from the western islands or from New Guinea.
>
> We may guess, but we do not know, what other elements of culture were used or practised at this period. (Haddon, 1935, pp. 412–13)

Haddon also incorporated the bare bones of Islander history; a history which, he asserted, was not adequately comprehended by the Islanders themselves.

> The folk-tales state that the original inhabitants of Daudai were in an extremely low state of culture from which they were raised by cultural influences coming from the north.
>
> The earliest western islanders were doubtless in a state of culture similar to that of the Aboriginal people of Daudai, but the same cultural influences from the north spread into the islands — when or what length of time this took we have no means of knowing.
>
> The migration to the eastern islands may have been about the same period. (Haddon, 1935, pp. 412–13)

Here, then, was the historical background to the region. As a scientific account, it could replace the old reliance on folktales and myths.

A concept of history was not the only element missing from Islander knowledge, for the Cambridge team could not find any recognisable conceptualisation of a formal system of government, or state, in the islands either. This was hardly surprising because 'savages', according to their understanding, always structured their societies using other, less formal, structures. Nevertheless, Haddon surmised that in the eastern islands, prior to the arrival of the missionaries and the Queensland government's presence in the region, 'the method of governments…was probably by the elders, who followed traditional custom in coming to their decisions' (1908, p. 178). He suggested that thirty-five years prior to their own arrival there had existed in the western islands 'a simple form of government, which may be described as a limited democracy, or an oligarchy of elders' (1904, p. 264). In short, what he believed to have been in place in the Strait all those years before their arrival was a system of hereditary chieftainship (1908, p. 178).

Haddon was struggling to identify something from which he could paint a historical picture of the past regulation of public life in the islands. He was looking for something that could be represented as an organisational structure or state; common rules for example and, in particular, some, probably amorphous, central authority that held it all together. His brief sketch of periods prior to his arrival in the islands began with an appeal to the genealogical records of western Islander families as 'the social duties of life were relegated by custom to definite members of the community as will be seen on a perusal of our accounts of Kinship...Little appears to have been left to chance or to private initiative or enterprise' (Haddon, 1904, p. 263). Having established a view about some basic structures in the community he was able to construct a notion of hierarchy, division and thus conflict as a basis for political interaction in Islander lifeworlds. He did this to establish a mechanism that could illuminate some form of authority. To make his case, Haddon outlined the organisational needs of traditional ceremonies, for here, surely, he would find the authority structures he sought.

> The time for the performance of certain ceremonies was fixed by the appearance of particular stars, but these ceremonies had to be prepared for and various details had to be arranged, and this necessitated an executive of some sort that would command respect and obedience...Disputes of various kinds must always have arisen in each community and some form of arbitration was necessary. (Haddon, 1904, p. 263)

Haddon believed that if he focused on a study of ceremonies he would find an event that required some supervisory person — hopefully even a group of such authority figures. The ceremonies and feasts he observed involved whole communities and oftentimes several communities. Many people needed to be coordinated to catch and kill numbers of animals and fish, to crop gardens, to prepare the earth ovens and to process the large amounts of food required for the enormous feasts, often catering for hundreds of people at a time. Clearly, these kinds of events required special people to carry out the formal organisational aspects. To Haddon, who was unfamiliar with these spectacles, it seemed obvious that in the past '[t]here must have been many occasions for argument and misunderstanding in the inter-relations of a community however minutely its affairs may have been ordered by custom. To meet all these exigencies some form of government…[must have been] necessary' (p. 263).

Once this formerly 'unknown' history of a society and its informal structures had been illuminated, the scientists could now turn their attention towards comprehending the ideological structures that made this primitive society hang together. The Islanders might have had no readily recognisable formal structures of government and religious institutions but there were, as Haddon and his colleagues had seen elsewhere, very active informal structures which kept this primitive group together; structures which could now be used to pinpoint Islander society in terms of a broader social continuum. For although the twin pillars of church and state were as yet 'unformed', their primitive roots were clearly visible and could be exposed through an analysis of ceremonies, totems, taboos and kinship patterns. To this end, Haddon and his colleagues set about investigating the ideas which created a legal, spiritual and moral cosmos for this savage mind.

Observing the way in which taboos operated as a form of regulation — for the community as a whole as well as for the individual in Islander communities — Haddon tried to determine what gave the communal lifestyle a degree of social cohesion. Some form of law and order, he knew, must have been developed in Islander society to correspond with the place filled by the legal system and its enforcement agencies within civilised societies. Both Haddon and Seligmann were convinced that Islander society was ruled by taboos — that primitive set of prohibitions and injunctions enforced either by the individual or by public opinion. Haddon theorised that 'there was merely the customary usage or the orally transmitted law. There was no legal machinery by means of which these could be enforced, but it is probable these regulations were well kept on the whole as they had behind them the weight of public opinion' (p. 269).

Taboos had already been widely theorised in the existing academic literature and their role was well known. A taboo, explained Haddon, generally operated tacitly throughout the community and was understood by all its members. There were taboos that could be placed on items that prohibited anyone else from owning them — for example when property, crops and other possessions were marked as taboo to prevent people from infringing on designated areas, houses and trees. Other aspects of the taboo involved injunctions placed on the consumption of certain foods or the performance of certain acts at specified times. Sexual taboos, Seligmann reported, constrained the Islanders from sexual intercourse before a fishing or hunting expedition as it was believed that this would 'spoil' the chances of success. In the case of warfare, he was told, it meant that bad luck would accompany the warrior, who risked an acquired infection, which would attract the missiles of the opponents rather than weakening the warrior's ability to attack. This, Seligmann noted, could be likened to menstrual taboos as practised in other societies and he documented cases where men or women had sexual intercourse before sacred rituals with disastrous results — the Islander man would 'spoil the food' and the woman, it was said, 'would be shamed'. Chastity at such times, reported Seligmann, was to be 'recommended…[and] it was generally found expedient to abstain' (p. 271).

Taboos, if broken, could bring a severe reprimand from the person who was offended, from the magic man, from the elders or from the community in general. This could take many forms, for taboos had a restraining influence as well. For example, knowledge of a violation could bring about illness or even death in the transgressor. The fear of some physical deformity, Haddon was told, was usually enough to ward off the most determined person. In other words, fear of retribution acted as a strong deterrent. Rivers, obviously in a similar quandary, tried a different approach, observing that in the eastern islands it was 'very difficult to understand…the social organisation of the Miriam people… The most definite feature…is the existence of a system of exogamy in which the village is the social unit, but there also exist other groupings of the people which are of social significance' (Rivers, 1908, p. 169). While Haddon searched for some mechanism within the ceremonial activities to demonstrate structure and control by some higher authority, Rivers turned his attention to the order of things in the community to show that there were some elements that were at the basis of the social organisation of the community.

On Murray Island, Rivers identified four possible ways of grouping social units: 'firstly, a grouping in villages, of especial importance in connection with marriage; secondly, a grouping in districts; thirdly a dual division into two groups, called the *Beizam Le* and the *Zagareb Le*; and lastly, a grouping of people who are named after certain animals' (p. 169). Such groupings, he believed, had some political influence that determined day-to-day existence.

6. Anthropological inscriptions of the community

The genealogies of the people of the Torres Strait fascinated Rivers (1904, pp. 121–28; 1908, pp. 64–92), so much so that collecting them became a lifetime passion for him (Whittle, 1997). He was, in fact, to become a pioneer in the analysis of kinship patterns, developing a method that allowed him to construct kinship diagrams of such complexity that he was held in high regard in anthropological circles for years to come. Reminiscing, Frederick Charles Bartlett, who succeeded Rivers as head of the Institute of Industrial Psychology in London, spoke of Rivers' enthusiasm for this work:

> The method, as I crudely understand it, consisted of asking every informant to name as many of his or her relatives as possible, stating the relationship. This allowed to him to place every member of the community...on a vast grid of relationships. It provided internal checks on the reliability of informants, because each relationship is described by more than one person. You can see it would appeal to an experimental psychologist. It is quantifying culture, or at any rate social organisation. Its attraction diminishes slightly when one reflects that it was all carried out through an interpreter, and that the meanings of the relationship terms were the end product, not the start. (cited in Whittle, 1997, p. 8)

Rivers was struck by what he saw as the amazing complexity of the kinship system he uncovered in the western islands, remarking on how much a child needed to know to operate effectively in such a system. Even in such a primitive society, it would seem to his surprise, the average child had a very steep learning curve. He began by explaining that the child 'learns to give to each individual person his special term of kinship just as he learns to give a special name to other objects around him. There seemed to be little doubt [to Rivers at least] that the child used terms of kinship as commonly as, or more commonly than personal names' (p. 140). The complexity, Rivers explained, was compounded when the child heard how others were related to each other. For instance, Rivers pointed out, those older folk whom the 'father or mother call *tati* or *wadwam* will be his *atei* or *babat*, and that all whom they call *apu* or *ngaibat* will be his *kaiad* or *aka*' (p. 141). As the children grew up and married they learnt new terms for wife, husband, in-laws, children and so on, and this added to the dimension of a very complex system underpinning the social organisation of a people.

Obviously the use of traditional names heightened the complexities of the alien kinship system Rivers was struggling to understand. In hindsight, however, there really was nothing very complicated about any of this. Today in English-speaking countries, for instance, there are sons, daughters, fathers, mothers, aunts, uncles, grandfathers, grandmothers, great-uncles, great-aunts, first cousins, second cousins, third cousins, wives, husbands, in-laws, nephews, nieces, grandsons, grand-daughters, and so on. As children grow up in Western societies they hear and learn very quickly who is who by centring themselves and adopting terms that refer to them. They also hear people referring to others in a different way to what they are used to but this is not confusing because what matters is that they use the terms that relate to them. For example, children who hear their mother referring to 'mum' and 'dad' will learn that they are known as their grandmother and grandfather. They also learn that those their father calls mum and dad are also grandmother and grandfather and when the grandparents refer to the child's parents as son and daughter the child learns that they are his dad and mum — and so on with aunts, uncles, nieces, great aunts and uncles. There are also vocative and ordinary forms used today: 'Here is my grandmother'; and, 'Hello granny'; 'That person is my mother'; and 'Meet my mum'. This is not to dispute the complexity of what Rivers observed but merely to point out that what he found confusing was not particularly unusual.

Rivers was extremely interested in the way in which people related to each other. For instance, he noted there were kin relationships that determined how people could be approached, how they should be addressed and who could not be approached directly. Indeed, if the social etiquette was violated they would shame themselves. One example noted by Rivers constrained a man from using the personal names of his in-laws, allowing him only to communicate with his in-laws indirectly through his wife. If direct contact was necessary between the father-in-law and the son-in-law, for example, the son-in-law would be 'very subdued and…he would suffer more or less from shame' (p. 143). Rivers hastened to add that these were not 'strict regulations against every kind of intercourse between a man and the relatives of his wife, but there seemed to be a certain amount of mutual avoidance of each other' (p. 143). He recalled an incident during an interview when this social etiquette was clearly becoming lax and this suggested to him that such traditions were being eroded by the presence of foreigners in the region. In short, he argued that the former orderly — to his belief, rigid — organisation of the community through kinship systems, which regulated all social interactions, was in the process of breaking down. The necessity of change, as a primitive unchanging society met headlong with the advance troops of civilisation, made the kinship system less effective as social determinants.

Clearly a lot of this so-called complexity revolves around the fact that the observer, while scientific, was, quite simply, unfamiliar with the society he was categorising. The protocols of Rivers' own society seem extraordinary to us, should we be inclined to study them.

To Rivers, the Islanders' kinship system 'was a means of regulating social etiquette, but it was much more than this' (p. 144). He identified within this system 'very definite duties and privileges attached to certain bonds of kinship' (p. 144). For example, Rivers found that 'the special guardianship of a man at the most important period of his life was entrusted, not to his father but to the brother of his mother…[and] this bind between nephew and uncle becomes especially close after initiation' (p. 147). In all instances, this was to do with the uncle overseeing his responsibilities to his sister. According to Rivers, there were clear duties and privileges for the male members in the Islander community in other ways: 'The essential feature of the various customs connected with the relationship of brother-in-law…is that an individual could demand certain services of anyone who stood to him in this relation' (p. 149). He would, as Rivers was told, organise and take charge of a hunt, procure what he needed for the hunt including other people's boats, take charge of the sharing of the catch, and throughout maintain a subdued but senior role in providing and keeping the family harmonious. While the owner had the charge of steering his boat, as Rivers pointed out, his brother-in-law had a place in the front of the canoe designated especially for him and would direct the activities on fishing trips. Although he did all the labouring tasks during the trip, he also took charge of the hunt, giving directions to the owner on how to prepare for the hunt, which tides or areas to work, when to go, when to anchor, and so on. Rivers' view of all this was that it was a deeply seated practice: 'The whole group of customs is strongly suggestive of a survival of a condition of society in which a man was closely associated with and had to render service to the family of his wife' (Rivers, 1904, p. 149).

Rivers observed that as times were rapidly changing such usage was also in the process of rapid change. The maternal uncle might have had right of way in Mabuiag in the old days but, at the time of Rivers' visit, 'there seemed to be little doubt that the duties of *imi* were reciprocal and that a man could demand service of his sister's husband, while the latter could in return demand service of the former' (p. 150). He reiterated that at one time there was clear right of way given to the maternal uncle but 'by a process of generalisation, these duties have now come to be regarded as pertaining to the relationship of *imi* in general' (p. 150). This, he claimed, has caused confusion in the expectant roles of the male members of the community, and particularly about who was supposed to do what. Combined with his hypothetical sketch of the 'confused child', Rivers' explanation is that this was because there was 'a tendency to confuse together things possessing the same name' (p. 150). Moreover, this was a tendency he likened with the confusion of colour names in the islands: 'I think there can be little doubt that the influence of nomenclature in the case of kinship has been a cause which has led to the confusion of duties originally distinct' (p. 150).

While there is little that can be regarded as complex or confusing about the nomenclature of kin, Rivers, in his role of the cognitive psychologist studying 'the pedigree of a people of low culture' (Rivers, 1904, p. 64), claimed that 'the close relations between a man and his mother's brother which exist in Mabuiag may similarly be regarded as a survival of a state of society which has now disappeared' (p. 150); a state which had not, in Rivers' eyes, simply moved on but was, in contrast, rapidly disintegrating. The team's other observations had already pointed to a picture of social decline and collapse and the evidence Rivers was collecting on kinship patterns, he felt, provided further evidence to fuel these theories. Confusing change with collapse, he could draw the outline of a society in crisis. The problem, of course, is inherent in the tendency to view any society as static; to equate currently existing custom with fixity; and to fail to see the flexibility which is always clearly visible in the interstices of custom and tradition.

In terms of totems, both Haddon and Rivers found plenty to interest them; evidence which provided them with the means to confirm the validity of their theoretical perspective. A totem they defined simply as 'a class of objects that is reverenced by a body of men and women who acknowledge a definite relationship to that class of objects' (p. 153). Starting from this point they were able to identify further clear divisions within the Islanders, and clan groups also had social obligations that bound their members together. They observed that a totem was spoken of in the islands as *Augud*, and that *Auguds* were represented 'usually [by] a single species, of animals' (p. 153), which was common practice in the literature concerning primitive people, but that on Saibai Island they also observed representations of 'the *Daibau*, a tuber like a sweet potato, the *Kokwam* or hibiscus, and *Goba*, a stone that was used for making stone-headed clubs' (p. 153). Other totems took the form of 'legendary heroes' (p. 154), some the form of a star, *Titui,* and the first and last quarter moon phases, *Kutibu* and *Giribu*. In the case of *Kutibu* and *Giribu*, two crescent-shaped turtle shell objects that belonged to the hero *Kwoiam*, later achieved sacred significance and were elevated to *Augud* status.

To Haddon and Rivers, the most important function of the totemic system was its management of marriages, although they admitted that at the time of their visit marriages were organised along kinship lines. As they recalled, marriages regulated by the totemic system were not allowed between clan members. Sexual intercourse, they added, was likewise prohibited. In the few cases evident in the genealogical records where this had broken down, the marriage partners were found to be from the same clan groups but from different islands. In other cases they were found to be traditionally of the same totem but belonged to different clans and were, presumably, of a different generation. In one case, where a man married his sister, the man was simply listed as 'unbalanced'.

Haddon and Rivers also documented the magical and religious aspects of totemism, stating at the outset that this was not to be confused with the concept of religion that had been developed by civilised people. Instead, Islanders 'regard[ed] as religious those totemic regulations and practices that have reference more directly to the non-practical side of human life' (p. 182). Like Sir James Frazer, the scientists saw magic, in contrast to religion, as 'a pantomimic or symbolic action on the part of the human members of a clan which is designed to have a direct effect upon the non-human members of the clan' (p. 182). In short, the Islanders had not yet evolved in Frazer's continuum from magic to the stage of religion but still engaged at a level of symbolic ritual employing pantomimes that used animals or parts of animals to invoke, for instance, good or bad seasons. Much of the report details the magical ceremonies used by Islanders; ceremonies, for example, that were connected with dugongs and turtles. In the terms of already developed theories, they saw these rituals as providing vital evidence about the way in which magic acted as an important regulatory element in the social world of the Islanders.

Haddon and Rivers observed that the mystic affinity between clans and totems was 'deeply ingrained and…[was] evidently of fundamental importance' (p. 184). Moreover, they went on to add, there was an expectation that clan members would adopt the characters of their totems. For instance, the cassowary, explained Haddon and Rivers, was a violent creature 'of very uncertain temper and can kick with extreme violence' (p. 184). The cassowary clan — and similarly the crocodile clan, the shark clan and the hammer-head shark clan — were thus described by Haddon and Rivers as fighting clans. By contrast, they documented clans with totems representing the skate, the ray and the sucker-fish as being peaceable clans. Such alliances with their totems, they contended, provided a ready disposition, if not the means, for members to measure their characters.

In addition to these mechanisms for social organisation and regulation of Islander societies a substantial part of the research of the Cambridge expedition was directed towards documenting the spiritual constitution of the people in the Torres Strait, and Haddon, Seligmann, Wilkin and Myers all spent large amounts of time observing 'some of the religious conceptions and rules of conduct and avoidance' (p. 241). Once again the importance of this research was dictated by the existing literature which provided the scientists with an important theoretical framework with which to analyse the collected material.

> The term 'religious' is applied in this memoir to those actions which depend for their efficacy upon appeal to, or reliance upon, something which is extrinsic to the performers or to the objects employed…This non-human influence is usually of a more or less personal nature, and is approached by means of words or ceremonies, and operates through a ceremony or object, or directly on the petitioner of those in whom he is interested, or it accomplishes those aims which he desires. The extrinsic influence can also act of its own initiative. Usually an emotional relation is established with this extrinsic influence or power. (Haddon, 1908, p. 241)

True to their expectations, the Cambridge team discerned nothing that corresponded to 'anything like an All-father or Supreme Being' (p. 316), confirming for them the fact that the Islanders had not yet developed past the first stage of magic as it was accepted in the literature and defined in the report:

> Magic, or sorcery, is the constraint of nature by man through the action of the spoken or written word, or through some deed in connection with an object, or by a pantomimic ceremony, or in some analogous manner. (Haddon, 1908, p. 320)

Religion, on the other hand, was defined both in the literature and the report as 'a belief in the existence of a personal or impersonal being or beings with powers transcending those of mere mortals and the actions that result from such a belief' (p. 320). Using the accepted definitions they were able to establish a clear distinction between the magical world

6. Anthropological inscriptions of the community

of the savage and the world of the enlightened civilised man before he, too, developed past religion to the world of scientific knowledge. By their definition,

> if a man, who requires something specific, recites a formula or performs a mimetic action, he is doing a magical act, but if he requests some power to assist him to obtain that of which he has need, he is performing a religious action. (Haddon, 1908, p. 320)

In these terms magic, as opposed to religion, requires reciting a formula or performing a mime rather than requesting the assistance of the Almighty to intervene on their behalf.

Haddon should have been aware that it was not always strictly easy to separate what was proto-religious and what was magical, as there were many places where the concepts, although very rigidly drawn, would have overlapped. Even in civilised Britain there were still pockets of superstition, especially in the countryside away from the modernising influence of the cities. The line between pagan festivals and the Church of England — for example the link between Easter and the old fertility rites — had not entirely disappeared.

Haddon stressed that he had 'not attempted to make a definite classification of the observances dealt with in this section' (p. 320) and instead 'thought it desirable to bring together all I could find on the subject of magic' (p. 320). His observations included: 'The Training of a Magician' (p. 321). By documenting the training of a magician, he could vividly show the gulf that stretched between Islander society and the civilised world of the Christian ministry or priesthood. The scientists had been told that any 'man' could become a magician — obviously no vocation or calling was necessary — although, they observed, few chose to do so because this involved an unpleasant initiation process.

> He was taken into the bush by the instructor and the first operation consisted in the old man defecating into an alup shell filled with water; when the mixture was well stirred the novice had to drink it all up, and in order that he might have the benefit of it, he was enjoined to keep his eyes open whilst drinking…if the eyes watered during the process of training the novice would not make a good maidelaig [magic person]. (Haddon & Seligmann, 1904, p. 321)

In another example, 'he had to eat the decomposing flesh of a dead man which was full of maggots, the effect of this revolting diet was to make the throat bad' (p. 321). Magicians in the islands, in this way, clearly had more in common with sorcerers than civilised churchmen. Reportedly they 'understood all kinds of magical and medical lore…[and] could cause disease and death and could cure illness. He could lure dugong, turtle and fish by charms or he could strike and kill animals with unerring aim, and he knew furthermore the virtues of animal and vegetable products' (p. 321). After three years of training the graduate would be deemed a magician, who was able to kill, to place a curse, to injure, to lure, to cure, and to set rituals and performances as well as incantations that had to be followed closely. To carry out these rituals and performances they had a large armoury of implements including stone-headed clubs and spears (p. 324), human effigies (p. 324), a vine called *kuman* (p. 325), and a crocodile's tooth (p. 326).

The team was obviously disappointed that they found no evidence of the 'voodoo dolls' they had expected but they made clear that this by no means meant that they ruled out the possibility of their existence. Instead, they preferred to leave the possibility open, saying '[w]e have no information whether the *maidelaig* operated through objects belonging to the victim or intimately associated with him such as hair, nails or the like' (1904, p. 324). The high position of magicians in the society was noted — little wonder, as the *maidelaig* could do deeds which were well beyond any mortal being — but it was intimated that this had more to do with the potential to wield power than it had to do with the 'acceptance of superiority' granted by the 'acceptance of a true calling'.

This magician's world, nevertheless, played an important social function as it was seen to ensure 'a sympathetic relation between human beings and between people and animals' (p. 327). The team cited, for example, that 'at parturition a woman would get a good-looking man to come and sit behind her so that the child might take after him' (p. 327); they cited mothers who adorned themselves in fish bones to ensure their children would become beautiful; they cited the case of a particular tree at Mabuiag Island that was so significant to the men that if the leaves were burnt it would mean some of them would die in their next encounter with enemies. Various implements were used in carrying out ceremonies; bull-roarers, throwing sticks, the bark of a particular tree and boar's tusks were used to increase prospects on animal hunts, bring on stronger winds or to assist Islanders in warfare encounters (see Haddon and Seligmann, 1904, pp. 328–29). Haddon and Seligmann claimed that, like the specialist practices of the *maidelaig*, in the old days the magical acts involved 'an expressed wish or command, or the utterance of a formula of some kind or another' (p. 329).

6. Anthropological inscriptions of the community

However, Haddon and Seligmann stressed there was no evidence to show that the Islanders were in the process of moving from magic to religion and the recognition of a supreme being. Neither, it was asserted, should an account by MacGillivray in 1852 which alleged that Islanders believed in the 'transmigration of souls' (cited in Haddon & Seligmann, 1904, p. 354) be taken as evidence that Islanders could perhaps be conceptualising the soul in the same way as the Christian soul or even the Buddhist concept of reincarnation. MacGillivray's account conveyed the notion that Islanders believed that 'immediately after death they… [would be] changed into white people or Europeans' (p. 354). However, Haddon and Seligmann insisted, there was another reading of this in 'that instead of a return of the deceased native's actual body after death in the form of a European, the meaning intended to be conveyed was that the vital principle (spirit, etc.) is re-incarnated in the white man' (1904, p. 355).

Haddon and Seligmann noted that it 'was extremely difficult, indeed practically impossible, to get any very definite information respecting the belief of the people as regards spirits generally' (p. 355), although there were clear signs that a belief in spirits existed. According to Ray, there was a distinction made between a ghost (*markai*) and a spirit (*mari*) — *markai* was the ghost of a dead person and *mari* was a 'disembodied spirit' (cited in Haddon & Seligmann, 1904, p. 356). Haddon and Seligmann maintained that Islanders held a belief that 'the soul, or ghost, *mari*, of a person…left the body at death' (p. 355) in that it was, in one telling, in the corpse and, in another, it was wandering nearby. Others, they claimed, told them of spirits who may leave the island to go to an unknown place in the west but could also come back. That is, at the time of death the '*mari*…is a very intangible sort of thing' (p. 356) and is said to travel west, always to the west, where upon arrival at 'spirit-land' (p. 356) he or she is met and taught how to be a '*markai*'. To verify this belief Haddon and Seligmann cited a case where an Islander pointed out that '[w]hen the friends at home see a water-spout they weep and say, '[t]hey are now teaching him, he is now a proper *markai* and will forget us all'. They also cry at a new moon as the *mari* is then killed and converted into a true *markai*' (p. 356).

On the issue of the possibility that the Islanders practised ancestor worship, Haddon and Seligmann contended that '[t]he ghosts of the dead were neither regarded as demons nor divinities, nor do I think it can be said that they were actually worshipped' (p. 364). While the skulls of revered individuals and family members were kept in houses and, at times, carried as charms on various voyages, Haddon and Seligmann theorised that 'the preservation of skulls of relatives in the houses was due to the sentiment of affection and to keep the dead in remembrance' (p. 364). They were adamant that they could find no evidence to support the view that ancestor worship was implicated in any of the Islanders' ceremonies.

Similarly, confirming the idea that Islanders could, in fact, be practising hero worship instead, Haddon contended that '[t]he invocation of dead heroes...is part of the hero cult; they were prayed to solely as heroes and I did not find any indication that they had any existing human kin other than the totemic kinship. We cannot then regard the hero-cult as an ancestor-worship in the strict sense of the term' (p. 365). MacGillivray's account, like those from missionaries, also supported this view and rejected the possibility that anything higher was being intimated, saying, '[n]either at Cape York, nor in any of the islands of Torres Strait...do the Aboriginal people appear to have formed an idea of the existence of a Supreme Being' (cited by Haddon & Wilkin, 1904, p. 378). The point they were emphasising here was an important one in their schema, for hero worshipping in the islands cannot be regarded in the same league as worshipping a supreme God: 'I think it can be definitely stated that the western Islanders had no deities and certainly they had no conception of a Supreme God' (Haddon & Wilkin, 1904, p. 378). In Volume VI of the Cambridge reports Haddon concluded, '[n]othing is more difficult than an attempt to discover and interpret the religious ideas of an undeveloped people, and I cannot profess to have succeeded in my efforts in this direction among the Miriam' (Haddon, 1908, p. 241). One thing was certain, however. The elements that Haddon associated with a supreme God were missing. Haddon considered four main icons worshipped by the Islanders: *Lu babat*, *Ad*, *Zogo*, and *Agud*. *Lu babat* was listed by him as the worship of items belonging to some ancestor. *Ad* was said to be 'something old and traditional with the idea of a sanctity that is associated with ancient wont, thus certain folk-tales are *ad*' (p. 242). So too were tales of legendary characters or items of a sacred nature like 'magical stones' (p. 242). *Zogo*, on the other hand, was considered to be an array of objects like rain, effigies, shrine, birds, plants, totems, etc. Haddon claimed it was even more distant from religion because it could also be the term for the whole rite associated with some form of worship. *Agud*, or *Augud* as it was known in the western regions was, according to Haddon, a name used for the *Zogo* that superseded all *Zogos* and all totems. Nowhere in Haddon's account is there any notion entertained that one of these icons bears any relation to a human being with spiritual powers like Jesus Christ. What is represented are those things worshipped in the islands like stones, plants, animals, legendary heroes and so on.

However, Haddon allowed, the ways people engaged with their icons were 'distinctly religious' (p. 245) and such practices, and in particular those to do with 'Bomai-Malu *zogo* were collectively a socialising religious factor in the life of the people' (pp. 242–43). Predictably, not much was found that could be equated with the formal religious institutions existing in the West. What the team detected was a representation of the people's spiritual and moral conscious as embodied in rules of avoidance and rules of conduct — taboos. What they dwelt on were descriptions of taboos associated with places, gardens and produce, names and food as a demonstration of how such things function as rules of avoidance. Anything of religious value in the Strait was thus equated with the simple forms of taboos. Finally, in closing the chapter on mythical beings, Haddon was able to write:

> I am inclined to believe that neither among the western nor the eastern Islanders has the idea of a definite god been evolved. They have, I admit, come very close to the conception, but do not appear to have taken the final step, and I am tempted to connect this omission with the absence of a definite and powerful chieftainship… hence there was no autocratic social type upon which the incipient demigods could be modelled and thereby be transformed into actual deities. (Haddon, 1908, p. 316)

Not only was a concept of religion — and the institution of the church — missing from Islander society but the Cambridge team could not find coherent moral or ethical codes corresponding to those which operated in civilised societies; that is, codes which gave the grounds for self-regulation as opposed to social regulation. This was not to say that the Islanders were immoral. Far from it. In the 'old days', Haddon suggested, a 'definite system of morals was inculcated to the lads during the period of initiation…and…it was an excellent code' (Haddon, 1904, p. 273). At these initiations, the younger generations learned that

> [t]he injunctions were: remembrance of admonitions, reticence, thoughtfulness, respectful behaviour, prompt obedience, generosity, diligence, kindness to parents and other relatives in deed and word, truthfulness, manliness, direction in dealings with women, quiet temper. The prohibitions were against: theft, borrowing without leave, shirking duty, talkativeness, swearing, talking scandal, marriage or connection with certain individuals. (Haddon, 1904, p. 273)

Furthermore, Haddon could find 'no reason to suspect any trace of missionary influence' (Haddon, 1904, p. 273) in the building of these injunctions. Constructed in the 'old days', these were identifiable forms of social morality that provided the basis on which the Islanders lived their everyday private lives. However, while Haddon believed it was 'fairly evident that the obligations of the social life were at the basis of the morality of the Torres Strait islanders, indeed it would be scarcely incorrect to speak of it as social morality', he had significant reservations about this. 'On the other hand' he said, 'individual morality had scarcely emerged' (Haddon, 1904, p. 272).

Haddon was making a clear distinction here between what he saw as social morality and what he saw as individual morality. He characterised the former as forms of morality that were codified in terms of an understanding of what constitutes acceptable behaviour in a community; behaviour which was designed, regulated and enforced by a members of a community in the same way as secular law was created and enforced in civilised societies. Individual morality, on the other hand, Haddon defined as that law which comprised those forms enshrined in important articles — such as the Ten Commandments — which laid down personal moral codes which should not be broken for personal reasons. This differed from social morality in that the concepts had been laid down and were individually enforced through the power of an authority higher than the community itself — and far higher than the authority which created the secular laws of a society. The Islanders were still operating from a position of 'magic' on the evolutionary scale, so this higher form of morality could have no meaning for them. Instead, social regulation alone constructed Islander morality which operated on the basis of the avoidance of direct consequences and retribution, placating nature rather than obeying the moral commandments of the deity.

At the time of his visit, Haddon said, things had already changed somewhat in this regard due to the influence of missionaries, 'together with the contact with other white and coloured men' (p. 272). This influence, he said, 'has undoubtedly brought about altered moral conceptions. The clearest example of this is to be found in their attitude towards the wearing of clothes and the idea of modesty' (p. 272) — an idea he apparently saw both as civilised and moral, a virtue rather than a convention. 'Thirty years ago,' he exclaimed, these people were 'absolutely naked and unashamed' (p. 272). Now he was able to cite an incident when his team members had found it difficult to get an Islander to strip off his clothes and to pose in the fashion of a dying legendary hero so that the Cambridge team could photograph him — he had, in fact, become 'prudish' (p. 272). Haddon's comment is interesting. His intention was to illustrate the emergence of an elevated consciousness of the self as laid down by moral codes set down by some 'external authority outside of the community' (p. 272) and he took pains to show that this was an import. It could also be said, however, that this Islander simply might not have felt compelled to strip off his clothes and to pose in the fashion of a dying legendary hero for reasons which may have had nothing to do with being prudish.

Haddon also commented on what he called 'commercial morality' (p. 276) and expressed the opinion that in commercial transactions, particularly in cases where canoes were purchased on the basis of an 'instalment system' (p. 276), there would have been some 'utilitarian foundation' (p. 276) by which credit was established between two people. He contended that there was not only such a system in place but that there was an accompanying moral code by which Islanders were bound, although his source for this is very elusive and it is impossible to see on what evidence his opinion is based and whether or not he saw this code as a recent development or one of long standing. Anyway, Haddon added, it would have been senseless to violate any agreement when one's livelihood was swinging in the balance. As one Islander told him, if we do not observe such conventions 'how we get fish, or turtle, or dugong' (p. 276)? It was rarely the case that anyone would have been dishonest, he remarked. Again, the implication is that the Islander was operating from a desire to avoid retribution rather than from a moral sense of 'decency'.

Haddon had already deduced from his study of folktales that there had been extensive trading between the western Islanders and mainlanders from Papua New Guinea and Australia for a long time. Now, of course, there was trade with 'white men' as well (p. 293) — the exchanges mostly taking the form of bartering goods like crafts, dance masks and drums, foods, plants, sea shells, turtle shells, tools, bows and arrows, iron (from shipwrecks), canoes, feathers and plumes of birds, tobacco pipes, and so on. He mentioned, in particular, that there had long been an extensive network for the trade of canoes, one that spanned the breadth of the Torres Strait region and involved many middle men and their contacts. For this reason the protocols in negotiating the exchange (sale or purchase) of a canoe, as well as the art of testing the soundness of the material and craftsmanship, and buying on credit, would have been quite extensive. By contrast, in the eastern islands there appeared to be only two trade routes to Papua New Guinea and none to the Australian mainland — the Miriam were practically debarred from intercourse with Australia' although now there was also trade with foreign sailing vessels (Haddon, 1908, p. 185). The people of Murray Island exported crafted shell ornaments and imported ornaments crafted from cassowary feathers, bird-of-paradise feathers, dogs' teeth, boars' tusks, leaves of sago palms, pandanus leaves, and items such as canoes, drums, mats, stone clubs, etc. Many of these were bartered for iron, knives and axes. They were clearly not isolated outposts of 'savagery' unconnected to the outside world. However, Haddon and his colleagues consistently remained blind to this fact despite their in-depth investigations into Islander culture.

In a further attempt to elucidate the Islanders' moral constitution, Haddon commented on 'domestic morality' (p. 274), saying that, while he could not learn much about the position of women before contact with the West, he did 'believe that on the whole the wives had not much to complain about' (p. 274). He rejected MacGillivray's accusation that Islander men were 'wife-bashers' (p. 274), suggesting that MacGillivray must have said this because the group he observed was 'less advanced than the other islanders' (p. 274). Or, perhaps 'the lack of gardens and the hunting and collecting nomad habits of the men would tend to make them less considerate to their wives' (p. 274). In regard to sexual morality, Haddon reported that incest was considered by the Islanders to be the most reprehensible act. Sexual morality, he explained, was also a very good determinant of who could marry whom but importantly, he said, this was 'an example of a social convention which was probably of fundamental biological importance to the community' (p. 274). His other 'impression is that chastity before marriage was formerly practically unknown' (p. 275) and, 'there was no term for fornication or adultery' (p. 274).

He says, however, there was a word for theft, *puru*, and in this way Haddon pensively suggested that adulterous acts by Islanders could be termed 'stealing' (p. 275). If caught 'stealing', he went on to say, there was an expectation that the guilty couple should marry 'to make them honest folks' (p. 275). If they were not shamed into getting married, physical markings were made on their bodies as posters for public humiliation. Wilkin had already observed that a very complicated inheritance pattern of land ownership existed in the region — ownership that seemed to him to favour men — and had concluded that '[t]he sense of property is very well developed' in the islands (Wilkin, 1904, p. 168).

However, Haddon is contradicted by his colleague, the linguist Ray. In his English-to-Islander languages dictionary, Ray listed two terms for adultery in the language of the western Islanders — namely *kupa-kuasar*

6. Anthropological inscriptions of the community

and *kuasar-kupa*; and two terms for adultery in the language of the eastern Islanders, namely *kogem* and *kosekerlam* (Ray, 1907, p. 170).

Interestingly, there is a marked shift in the use of emotive language when Haddon and his colleagues describe Islander temperament and what they see as savage practices such as cannibalism and infanticide. For this is language without parallel anywhere else in the six volumes of materials collected by the expedition. Once more the Western preoccupation with blood and gore in savage people — cannibalism, warfare and cruelty towards others, especially innocent children — is trotted out, with all supporting evidence about the alleged barbaric acts drawn either from Wemyss' story of the two survivors of the shipwreck *Charles Eaton* on an eastern Island reef, or from unverified accounts collected from a multitude of other sources. All the incidents mentioned are allowed to cover every corner of the Torres Strait and give the impression that such practices were rife throughout the area in the earlier periods and that all this 'evidence' can be scientifically verified. In short, this gives a measure of scientific credence to material which cannot, at any level, be verified and is, on the contrary, extremely suspect. For not one of the events described in the report was founded on scientific observations made by the Cambridge group. It is also interesting to note that Haddon had already observed elsewhere that anthropophagy, or cannibalism, was *not* a practice found in the islands.

One example, from Wilkin, is a narrative given in great detail:

> At Pulu they cut the heads from ear to ear across the scalp and slit them from back to front even to the end of the nose and down to the teeth...The small boys they constrained to eat the cheeks and eyebrows and the balls of the eyes, and those that were unwilling they beat, for unless a man do this in his youth he will remain a woman or a child all his life long. Moreover when he has taken such a head for himself in battle he is to be accounted fit for marriage. (Wilkin, 1904, pp. 313–14)

The relentless repetition of tales of feuds, warfare, head hunting, and massacre — which include earlier claims made by Haddon (1890) and MacGillivray (1852) that the Islanders were killers of their infants, in particular, female infants — need not be duplicated here as such stories have already been touched upon in an earlier chapter. What is noteworthy, however, is that Haddon, albeit only in his footnotes, tried to qualify this quote by stressing the need to treat such material with scepticism. He warned that 'the narratives give a vivid picture of native warfare, and we may regard them as being as accurate as most historical records which are narrated by the conquering side. These are accounts of historical events, but it is not difficult to imagine how these could easily be transformed into hero-tales and so become folktales' (p. 308). In other words Haddon knew that the accounts provided to colleagues such as Wilkin needed to be viewed with scientific caution but, unfortunately, he hid this caution away in a footnote, presumably not wanting to eliminate much of the cultural colour from the final report.

Fortunately, although much is made of the Islanders' much vaunted predilection for infanticide as a population checking device, this is offset by the many instances also cited in the report which indicated that Islanders possessed a strong sense of kin relations and that there were close bonds between parents and their children. Seligmann had cited two stories to indicate the closeness of the parent–child relationship: 'The story of Siwi shows spoilt children were not unknown, and Amipuru tried to catch a pelican in order to give it to his child' (Seligmann, 1904, p. 199). He later commented that the older kinfolk not only provided care but also organised celebrations for girls during puberty customs and for boys during their initiation which recognises a time and role of younger generations to create new generations (1904, pp. 201–21). Haddon, too, commented on the strength of the bond between Islander parent and child, saying: '[w]hen the wife is pregnant a *waiwi* is paid, presents are given when the child is born, when he is named, a small present is given when he first stands up, again when he begins to talk and also when he kills his first bird or catches his first fish' (Haddon, 1904, p. 232). Rivers also observed that 'Divorce appears to have been rare' (Rivers, 1904, p. 246), the main reason for its occurrence being that the couple was childless. Haddon emphasised that he had no reason to believe that 'devoted fathers' (Haddon, 1904, p. 229) were not there in the past: 'I have never heard of a parent ill-treating a child' (p. 274). He later cited old folktales to support this position.

However, this did not deter Seligmann from including these earlier accounts about infanticide in order to write something into the section on the treatment of children:

> Although foeticide and infanticide were formerly practised the desire for children is now manifest by the frequency of adoption and by the readiness with which the charge of orphan children is assumed by their relatives…At the present time parents treat their children with kindness and indeed they may be regarded as indulgent towards them. (Seligmann, 1904, p. 199)

Not one of the scholars involved in writing these accounts had witnessed any such event; nor did they explain how many infant deaths it took to constitute 'a practice'. Furthermore, their superficial understanding of Islander ways might have led them to make a gross error here. The Islanders had (and to a certain extent still continue to have) a belief that when someone dies it is because another has had a hand in the death — that is, they have a ready disposition to view deaths as the result of the wrath of a devious other. For instance, in describing funeral ceremonies, Haddon noted that, on announcement of the dead, 'the brother of the dead man "got wild" and took his bow and arrow and wished to kill the *maidelaig* (sorcerer) who had caused the death' (1904, p. 248). His footnote on this stated: 'According to native belief all sickness and death were due to sorcery' (p. 248). The point to be made here is that if an Islander was asked how a baby died there was always a ready disposition to blame and name someone. In other words, when one asked about the death of a child, an Islander was likely to attribute it to foul play by someone, even if they had died from particular illnesses like small pox or natural causes following birth.

Haddon also reported elsewhere that '[a]lthough foeticide and infanticide were commonly practised, the desire for children is manifested in the frequency of adoption and the readiness with which the charge of orphan children is assumed by their relatives' (1908, p. 110). Again on the following page, he pointed out that the 'fondness of the parents for their children, own and adopted, was very obvious, and one frequently sees a father nursing young children. It is evident from the fearlessness of the children of all ages and the way in which they mix with their elders that they are uniformly well treated' (p. 111). However, the point of such accounts was not to counter perceived practices of infanticide but rather to note that such practices amongst primitive folks had, through contact with the West, changed in favour of Christian values.

It is easy to understand from Haddon's compilation of other people's writings that, because of a limited food supply in the islands, there was a custom to control population numbers so as 'to avoid the toil of having to provide food for them' (Reverend Gill cited in Haddon, 1908, p. 108). This explanation provides the basis of understanding why families were restricted to two (Reverend Gill) or three (Reverend Murray) children. Once the reason and the need for infanticide is articulated in this way it follows that it may have been an 'unwritten rule' which said it was undesirable to rear more than three children and that one should kill illegitimate children and, in particular, kill female babies at birth if there were too many children.

Interestingly enough, there were some statistical data gathered on the expedition on Islander families, put together from genealogies documented on Murray Island, which could have halted such speculations. This showed the average number of children in Islander families: '2.6 is the average number excluding marriages in which there are no children, and 3.6 excluding also those in which there is only one child' (1908, p. 108). The data showed that in the present generation — at the turn of the nineteenth century — 138 families had a total of 264 children, an average of 1.84 children per family. In the second generation, the data showed 160 families had 409 children, with an average of 2.55 children per family; in the third generation, 56 families had 209 children, with an average of 3.73 children per family; in the fourth generation, 9 families had 27 children with an average of 3 children per family; and in the fifth generation, there were 2 families, with 5 children in one and 1 in the other.

Haddon suggested that if we take 'the second and third generations only, so as to eliminate missionary influence, we find that the average numbers in the families of above three children were respectively 4.8 and 5.7. Ignoring families of 0 [children] or 1 [child], there is an average of 3.41 in the second generation and 4.18 in the third' (p. 108). These are respectable figures for a growing population. In real terms, and by their own accounts, there was no statistical evidence to support any claim that could amount to a particular 'practice' of foeticide or infanticide in the islands. Furthermore, there was no evidence to support the claim that female babies were killed in preference for males, for 'out of a total of 915 children, 489 or 53.4% are boys, and 426 or 46.5% are girls, thus female infanticide does not appear to have produced a very marked effect upon the relative proportion of the sexes' (p. 108). This data could have raised questions about the information provided by the authors on infanticide and foeticide if Haddon was so disposed. Instead, he concluded, 'these figures tend to show that while foeticide and infanticide doubtless were prevalent, their practice did not seriously tend to affect the actual population of the island of Mer, though they prevented overpopulation' (p. 108).

Embedded in the analytic terms of this scientific expedition, with its high-minded goals about ethnographic observation enriching academic knowledge through precision and objectivity, is the idea that in temperament and disposition these people were still uncivilised; people with savage minds only capable of expressing basic desires. They were primitive and childlike, the victims of undeveloped sensibilities and intellects; responding spontaneously to their emotions. For example,

6. Anthropological inscriptions of the community

in the eastern islands, Haddon observed, 'there is no doubt that their vain-glorious excitable temperament led to frequent squabbles, but they expended most of their energy in words' (Haddon, 1908, p. 190). To illustrate this foible, he provided one account of a quarrel amongst Murray Islanders and one against the South-Sea men living at Dauar. From the latter account, Haddon pointed out that, 'although they were great braggarts, the natives were unskilled in fighting, probably owing to lack of practice on account of their isolation' (p. 191). In the western islands, however, Haddon (1904) identified three distinguishable kinds of fighting. They were 'blood feuds' (p. 298), 'head-hunting' (p. 298) and 'ceremonial fights' (pp. 298–99). It was the condition of Islander people in the old days, according to Haddon, that a 'life for a life was the recognised doctrine' (p. 298) and blood feuds thus were enacted as 'reprisals for injuries' (p. 298). In contrast to this, head hunting was 'to gain glory and the approbation of their women' (p. 298), and ceremonial fights were for 'settling quarrels when there were more than two people concerned, and assumed quite the character of a duel upon a large scale' (p. 299).

Rivers, who was to become a friend and confidante of the poet Siegfried Sassoon while studying the effects of shell shock for the British High Command in 1915 (Whittle, 1997), along with his colleagues Myers, Seligmann and McDougall, must surely have looked at the wreckage of these men and had doubts about the concept of civilised as opposed to savage behaviour. The missionaries certainly did. Clearly it would seem apparent that the Europeans — and especially their leaders — also possessed a 'vain-glorious excitable temperament [which] led to frequent squabbles', although Haddon never saw the obvious parallel.

By dislocating Islanders from their own historical context as they went about their studies, scientific scholars sutured over — and rendered invisible through this process — the selective nature of the production of their reports. They did this from the assumption that the whole context of their activity was devoid of any politics, and the position of Islanders in this process was ostensibly as a people from the past. It is, in this way, that the activities of scientific knowledge construction, as exemplified in these reports, might now appear to be logical, objective and benign products in terms of their effects on Islanders. However, as I have tried to show here, the scientists' activities were far from detached, a far cry from being merely descriptions of the state of Islanders at the time. They were part of a much wider web of activities on the part of the researchers who, through denying Islanders their own historical context and suturing over the selective nature of their position, could then easily view and represent their own position in apolitical ways and in relation to an entirely different order of things. In this process the Islanders' own world view simply disappeared, having been rendered invisible and unintelligible. The position of Islanders is then rewritten into another set of relations, namely in relation to Europeans and their world views. The legacy of this practice is still evident in social science disciplines (Foucault, 1970). We tend to view the intellectual practices of these scientists as belonging to a long-gone historical context rather than see them as belonging to the intellectual and scientific disciplines in which current practice is still embedded. We tend to think that the practices of these scientists went home with them when they left the islands of Torres Strait. But these practices are still with us and in this sense, like the missionaries, the scientists have never left. Islanders, likewise, have not been returned to their own historical context and understood from that position.

7

Disciplining and regulating the body

> The islanders have not yet reached the state when they are competent to think and provide for themselves; they are really overgrown children, and can best be managed, for their own welfare, as a prudent parent would discipline his family.
> (Queensland State Government Protector's Report 1915, cited in Ganter 1994, p. 83)

This final chapter of Part One turns to focus on what the assumptions and premises of outsiders meant for the 'disciplining' of Islander bodies. Islanders were not only inscribed into the textual world beyond them; Islanders' bodies were also regulated and disciplined by an array of bureaucratic, regulatory and discursive mechanisms associated with government, church and commercial interests which was premised on and circumscribed by particular ways of thinking about 'natives'. A new order at the beginning of the twentieth century, discursively drawn through legislation, policies, regulations and official directives was enacted on Islander bodies, setting new limits and boundaries in relation to the way they were to work, organise their domestic lives, determine where they could go, who they could associate with and so forth.

The question in my mind as I engaged the disciplinary constructions of Islanders was personal, political and intellectual. When it came to the regulation of our lives as enacted on our bodies, I was interested in the 'what' of others' thinking and how that conditioned the possibilities in the everyday world where Islanders were active and had a long historical trajectory of independence and political autonomy. As these ways of thinking about us have changed over time, I wondered, are Islanders in any better position to assess and assert our position within the array of regulations, policies, discourses, arguments, rationales and choices placed before us, than we were in earlier times? How are Islanders to get underneath the surface of these things emerging in our lives and use this knowledge to position ourselves more effectively within what are essentially knowledge and power relations (Foucault, 1972). And what might all this mean for our pursuit of 'better' education? It was these questions that drove my interest in more recent historical writings.

To understand our colonial history there are now a significant number of serious accounts of various phases and aspects of the colonisation of Torres Strait Islanders (for example, Beckett, 1987; Sharp, 1993; Ganter, 1994; Williamson, 1994; Mullins, 1995; Osborne, 1997) and a range of accounts from those who have lived there, visited or been the agents of colonisation (MacFarlane, 1888; Douglas, 1899–1900; White, 1917; Barrett, 1946; Mollison, 1949; Raven-Hart, 1949; Bleakley, 1961; Singe, 1989). Together these build towards a fuller account of Torres Strait colonial history. In earlier accounts the events of the early period of colonisation are considered within the paradigms of now bygone thinking, elevating the good intentions of administrations, patronising Islanders and downplaying the harsh realities of our position. However, in more recent accounts authored since 1987, the position of Islanders has begun to be politicised, allowing the emergence of analyses that focus on the array of external forces and factors that led governments to impose extreme measures of control over the entire population of Torres Strait Islanders. These later accounts allow for some reconsideration of Islander agency and perspectives.

It needs to be established at the outset for those unfamiliar with Torres Strait history that the story of colonisation in the Torres Strait is not one of dispossession, dispersal or removal, although Islanders did lose title over islands and seas and some were subject to acts of considerable violence, forced removal and relocation. Ours is a story of infiltration and the closely supervised imposition of a new order — what Noni Sharp (1993) has called 'soft violence' — of intrusive surveillance, of confinement and suppression, of boundaries and restrictions and of collective deprivations and diminishment. It is the story of Islanders whose lifeworld was encircled in the intersections of administrative regulation by the state, moral regulation by the church and economic exploitation of them and their marine resources for global markets and commercial profit.

The colonial history of the Torres Strait was characterised by three overlapping phases of administration style within the century from 1880 until the 1980s (Sharp 1993, p. 130). Until 1904, Islanders were managed through a form of indirect rule. This involved a code of regulations with certain powers of implementation and enforcement delegated to a *mamus* or island leader who could choose his own assistants, known as 'Island police'. The *mamus* was directly responsible to the Government Resident on Thursday Island. This gave the government a direct avenue for influencing and directing Islanders (in the absence of enough personnel) that sat alongside and, when need be, could override the considerable authority of the London Missionary Society (LMS) in the supervision of daily life. It also gave Islanders a nominal mechanism for making representations to government, though the effective influence of the Islanders to work in their own interests was close to zero.

The next phase lasted from 1904 until the 1980s and was characterised by paternalist exclusion. In this form of separate development, Islanders were kept apart from other Australians and from each other and closely supervised by the 'singular eye' of the Queensland government, although the church provided some moral representations on behalf of Islanders at critical points. The *mamus* system was effectively disempowered by the transfer of most powers to the government teacher-supervisors until the Maritime Strike of 1936, when Islanders refused to man government boats until a list of accumulated grievances were addressed. The government and teachers continued to work through an Island Council system to variously influence, seek co-operation, coerce and force Islanders to follow government direction and its changing demands. Government practices involved control of labour, finances and freedom of movement, and restrictions on consorting with others. Lest readers think this was benign control, there were harsh punishments for small transgressions, although variations between Islands depended to a large extent on the personalities of the government teacher-supervisors. One 16-year-old was jailed for four months with hard labour for accompanying a white woman (at her request) on the way back from running an errand (Sharp, 1993, p. 143). Until 1936, head shaving and the use of stocks for public shaming was common practice, for a period a nightly curfew was installed, and the only contact with the outside world was via the Department of Native Affairs and its antecedents and successors.

Following the Second World War until the early 1980s a period of controlled integration began where Islanders were allowed to move away to fill labour needs elsewhere in Australia. Nonetheless, Islanders still required permission to move to the mainland and permission to leave the Torres Strait still depended on labour needs of the local marine industry. And even when shifts in national policy officially recognised Islanders as equal and free citizens, the Queensland government retained its surveillance mechanisms through its well-honed knowledge of Islanders and well-grooved channels of influence. The 'channel' was the old Island Council system, where elected Islanders represented Islander interests directly to governments and where governments expertly persuaded, coerced, threatened, rewarded and manipulated as always.

However, colonial experience is also the story of Islanders surviving, reconstituting their social and economic practices and identities, of maintaining continuity with old traditions, of participating, co-operating, ignoring, resisting, asserting, and generally standing up and pushing through the disruptions, intrusions, rewards and injustices of rapid change. It is also a story of diverse Islander responses across the islands and regions of the Torres Strait. These responses were engendered in local specificities and circumstances associated with traditional practices and thinking, the degree of influence of missionaries and Pacific Island pastors, the degree of participation in the marine industry, the isolation of communities from each other, and the effects of key individuals and personalities (Beckett, 1987; Sharp, 1993; Ganter, 1994; Mullins, 1995). Only at points of crisis did Torres Strait Islanders really solidify around a unitary collective political position.

As well, the historical experience of Torres Strait Islanders is the story of changing external discourses about Islanders: from savages to equal human beings; from mentally inferior to culturally different; from dependent 'children' in need of protection to pseudo self-managers with a recognisable case for regional autonomy and self-government. The continuing story also suggests what does not change for Islanders. The discursive and material imprints of earlier times are legacies which continue to shape Islanders' minds, bodies and souls.

The reader is encouraged to approach this chapter with a disposition to understand how an underlying epistemological configuration — the systems of thought, logic and knowledge that are employed to construct ways of knowing Islanders — shaped the possibilities that could be imagined and therefore enacted for us and on us.

Positioning Islanders at the peripheries of another political economy

What happened to Islanders during the first century or so of intrusive activity from the 1860s to the late 1970s was not the result of any grand plan. As Alan Williamson (1994, p. 56) points out, policy was often made by government officials as they assessed and responded to changing circumstances rather than by governments with any particular vision or goal for Islanders. Colonial practice was the result of coincidences of interests, conflicts of interests, struggles over economic resources, the psychology, interpretations and actions of individual personalities, the vagaries of global markets and events, political pragmatism and expediency, absence of public accountability to Islanders and to the wider Australian public, and the serendipity that often determines a particular flow of events. What happened to Islanders was also premised on understandings of who Islanders were and what they were capable of. These understandings were deployed by industry, individuals and governments primarily to bolster arguments that variously served the interests of commerce, government and, to a lesser extent, the church. Such understandings conditioned the possibilities that were available for Islanders in the changing order of things.

From the beginning, arguments to support labour needs for the marine industry tagged racial characteristics to skills and capacities and these helped shape legislation, policy and practice. For example, in arguments to circumvent legislation being proposed in Queensland (the *Pearl-Shell and Beche-de-Mer Fisheries Act 1881*), pearl-shellers submitted in 1879 that it was unnecessary to include Pacific Islanders because

> the class of [imported] Polynesian labourers so employed in the Fisheries are mostly seamen who have served in the trade for many years, and who being in a high state of civilization are thoroughly acquainted with, and accustomed to, and satisfied with the conditions of their service...Moreover, the services rendered by them [are] in most cases...of a skilled nature, for which they are specially adapted. (Petition, *QVP* 1879 cited in Ganter, 1994, p. 37)

This argument kept Pacific Islanders in the Torres Strait outside of legislation that pertained to Pacific Islanders recruited for the cane industry, allowed many of them to remain in the Torres Strait when others were being repatriated from Queensland, and until 1934 enabled them to remain outside the terms of the major protective legislation for Aboriginal people and Torres Strait Islanders, the *Aborigines Protection and Prevention of the Sale of Opium Act 1897–1901*, despite their intermarriage with Torres Strait Islanders.

In turn, their Melanesian origin, their reputation as warriors and traders, and the influence of Pacific Island missionaries, seamen and intermarriage on their cultural and social practices enabled the deployment of arguments to differentiate Torres Strait Islanders from Aboriginal people. These arguments had kept Islanders outside the terms of the *Aborigines Protection and Prevention of the Sale of Opium Act 1897–1901* until 1904 and determined the different conditions for their participation in the marine industry throughout the period. The under-lying reasons for this were less about racial differences and more about the labour needs of the marine industry and the overwhelming degradations being endured by Aboriginal people in North Queensland. Nevertheless, racial characterisation underpinned the arguments for Islander exemption and led to a workforce hierarchy on grounds that linked skills and capacities to particular racial groups. This hierarchy was reflected in wage differentials for different racial groups. As Regina Ganter (1994) comments, what was more comprehensible to Europeans was more respected, with very real material outcomes for the people under discussion.

The influence of particular individuals and their arguments about the relative intelligence of Islanders was what determined Islander exemption from such restrictive legislation. John Douglas, a former Premier of Queensland and the Government Resident on Thursday Island from 1885 until his death in 1904, regarded Islanders as 'capable of exercising all the rights of British citizens'. He argued that 'they ought to be regarded as such. They are a growing and intelligent people, and they want to be educated' (Douglas, 1899–1900, p. 35).

In this way, relegating Islanders to the peripheries of the new order depended on struggles for control over the bodies, labour and minds of Islanders based on European perceptions of their intelligence in relation to others and the evidence of its demonstration. The fragility of Islanders within the new order of things was demonstrated after Douglas' death when they immediately came under the terms of the 1897–1901 Act. No explanation was given for the termination of the Islanders' exemption but in his account John William Bleakley, a former Chief Protector (1961) simply asserts that, although some Islanders were managing their affairs well, many were not able to take care of themselves.

However, it was not just how Islanders were inscribed differentially within legislation or the arguments that could be put to exempt them from legislation that determined their position in the new order. It depended as well on the interpretation of local conditions by various individuals and/or their methods of implementation. The distance of the Torres Strait from the centre of government in the Queensland capital of Brisbane meant that much power was invested in those individual agents of the government who resided in the Strait such as local protectors and teacher-supervisors. The importance of individual personalities and their perceptions of Islanders also underscored the fragility of the Islander position in this hierarchy and the entitlements it brought.

An example of the different perceptions of Islanders is evidenced in the different approaches to co-operative lugger schemes. In 1904, the Reverend Fred Walker, a former LMS missionary had established

Papuan Industries Limited (PIL), a philanthropic trading venture that established copra plantations and stores in competition with commercial enterprises for trading cash crops and goods. Walker's scheme allowed Islanders to work for themselves and to buy boats on credit using the sale of what they collected and delivered to PIL to pay off debts at rates of 5 per cent interest. In 1903, the Queensland government took up this idea and instituted a parallel system of similar advances, albeit at interest rates of 10 per cent. These boats came to be known as 'company boats'.

Although these parallel schemes appeared to work in similar ways, initially they rested on different perceptions of Islanders. Ganter explains that

> The PIL regarded [Islanders] as fully autonomous entrepreneurs with property rights over the luggers, which they bought on the time-payment system. It sought to secure the trade from these luggers for its Badu store by contractual relationship. The local Protector opposed this contractual arrangement. For the Protector, the 'natives' were wards of the state, not the fully responsible legal entities of a business relationship…When [Protector] Costin was asked 'When a boat has been paid for, to whom does it then belong?' he replied that 'it is vested in the Protector as trustee for the natives'. (Ganter, 1994, pp. 76–77)

Once boats were paid off Islanders tended to use them for travel or community activity — and for work, if cash was needed. In most instances Islanders would work hard to pay the debt, often seeing it out in a couple of seasons. For many there was pride in the mere fact of ownership. When the independence of the Islanders to work the boats as they wished once they were paid for was asserted, the Protector considered the scheme a failure, arguing, '[b]ut here the predominating characteristic of the aboriginal race asserts itself, and immediately they know the vessel is no longer in debt, all incentive to work is gone...' (Costin cited in Ganter, 1994, p. 75).

Over time, the two schemes ran on increasingly similar lines and in 1930 they merged; PIL became the Aboriginal Industries Board and then in 1939, the Island Industries Board. By this point the management of Islanders was effectively the management of boats, labour, wages and movement. The alternate possibility for Islanders to independently engage in the new economy, as had been envisioned by the PIL, was gone.

The closing off of other possibilities occurred in increments between 1912 and 1936. As early as 1912, arguments against Islanders working for themselves to manage the tension between subsistence and cash economies had been deployed by government and commercial entrepreneurs. For example, pearl-shellers, keen to wrest back labour from company boats agreed with government agents that Islanders should work for wages, 'because they would earn higher wages, and because "all coloured men do better with a little supervision. They work better"' (Mitchell cited in Ganter, 1994, p. 79).

In its desire to access the lucrative profits of pearl-shelling as a means to underwrite government administration expenses, the government refused to concede that Islanders' continuity with subsistence practices would enable a continuing degree of independence from government support. Rather, they chose to pursue the economic opportunity within the shell industry as a means for Islanders to obtain the cash to fund the costs of their administration. Within this reasoning, Islanders' ability to be self-sufficient could only be achieved if others managed for them the somewhat fluid space between subsistence and cash economies. This fluidity emerged in times of low shell prices and poor seasons which limited the crop production that Islanders traditionally depended on. The mechanism for managing this space was to coerce men to work, generally in the form of directives communicated via teacher-supervisors. Sometimes a community would be ordered to make gardens, while a different community would be forced to go to sea to collect shell. In proportion to its earnings, each Island had to contribute to an Island Fund to provide for the infrastructure of communities, such as it was, and for emergency circumstances, such as crop failure or seasonal variations in catches and prices.

From 1912 deductions between 20 and 50 per cent (Ganter, 1994, p. 78) of all earnings were put into an Island Fund to ensure that such contingencies were covered. However, it was impossible for Islanders to know how much sat in the Fund and the purposes for which it was used, or if their money was being handled honestly.

As well, the government controlled the disbursement of remaining wages to individual men. This was often dispensed 'according to intelligence' (Chief Protector Howard, 1908, cited in Ganter, 1994, p. 78). For the most part, general living expenses came to be paid in the form of credit in the government-controlled local store. Although Islanders had 'passbooks', they had to apply to withdraw monies from their accounts at the local Department of Native Affairs (DNA) office and were often refused. Remuneration for labour, then, was not according to how hard individual Islanders worked, or in line with what they actually earned but by what individual government agents deemed they needed for their own purposes, after collective needs were provided (Ganter, 1994, p. 82). Any semblance of a balance between effort and reward did not exist, as unclear amounts of deduction, uncertainty about the calculations related to the amount and price of shell being paid them, and uncertainty about how much was in their accounts prevailed.

This had the paradoxical — indeed self-fulfilling — effect of making Islanders dependent on the state firstly by reducing their traditional independence, and secondly by denying them the chance to develop the necessary skills to operate independently and understand the financial systems of the cash economy. It also caused resentment as 'tension between cash economy and subsistence economy was exacerbated by an administration which encouraged wage labour on the one hand and clung to a restrictive paternalism on the other' (Ganter, 1994, p. 83). The government felt justified in its policy and positioned Islanders as unreasonable, if they objected.

> As we are endeavouring to gradually raise a strong healthy race to a higher plane, it is the duty of these people to take the utmost advantage of the facilities provided for them…I am convinced that persuasive methods have failed to produce the desired results, and the only alternative is legislative authority to insist upon every able-bodied man doing a fair day's work. In some quarters this procedure would be termed 'slavery', but any person who possesses an intimate knowledge of the people and the subject will think otherwise. (Protectors Report, 1915, cited in Ganter 1994, p. 83)

'Intimate knowledge of the people' led the Queensland government in 1918 to place the relevant department 'alongside the other sub-departments of Home Affairs: prison, benevolent asylums, chronic diseases, inebriate institutions and institutions for the blind. They were all inmates' (Sharp, 1993, p. 129).

Control of bodies to support this regime was quite literal. An important aspect of colonial practice was confinement and restriction. Many teacher-supervisors restricted inter-Island travel and some required Islanders to apply for a 'pass' to do so. The system of company boats meant many Islanders only worked with other Islanders. Isolation meant they rarely interacted with Europeans other than teachers, clergy or Protectors, all of whom were in positions of authority. Ostensibly so they could not get liquor, Islanders were not allowed on Thursday Island. Regulations made sexual relations between Islanders and others an offence, marriages needed approval. Eventually there was a nine o'clock curfew on all Islands.

To achieve political and economic control, personal autonomy also had to be reduced. Dependency was orchestrated and helplessness conditioned through the withdrawal of rewards and public punishment. These regulations were coded in 'Island Law' and administered through teacher-supervisors and Island 'policemen'.

The great paradox of this period and style of management is not simply that government created the 'welfare' dependency of Islanders on the state by denying them other possibilities such as the freedom to manage the tensions between traditional subsistence practices and the new opportunities emerging around them. Nor does the paradox lie simply in the government's failure to take the opportunity to educate and skill Islanders to manage in this new order, so they could eventually be 'independent' once again. Perhaps the greatest paradox is that the government instituted collective and communal modes of 'wealth' distribution amongst Islanders, which did not equate individual effort to reward. In this they went entirely against the principles of capitalist democracies that provided the motivation to and organisation of work. In the process, the government ensured the Islanders collective identification of, and unity against, uniformly felt state oppression as the singular source of their diminishment. Thus, while government agents could manipulate the traditional rivalry between Islander communities to their own ends, and while they could keep Island communities relatively separate and ignorant of the ways of the wider world, in a period of escalating discontent they could not avoid the Islanders' analysis that the government was the singular source of their predicament (Beckett, 1987, Sharp, 1993, Ganter, 1994).

In 1936, Islanders united against the government's treatment of them and refused to sign on to the 'company' boats. The government official, Cornelius O'Leary, charged with resolving the Maritime Strike of 1936 and reining in Islander 'insubordination,' instituted a shift in thinking to underpin a less coercive but more insidious form of control over Islanders. According to Sharp:

> He saw Islanders as people with some knowledge of unionist principles, rejecting the belief that 'these people are possessed of a child mind to be moulded on accordance with the whim of the government...': the 'suggestion that the Islander is a child subject to dictation of his father, the Government, is wrong and any policy for his protection based on this assumption must be fatal to its sponsors' (Report 19). Nevertheless 'appreciating their intelligences' did not preclude inducement and manipulation into accepting their lot as non-citizens in a continuing paternalist relationship: '...it should be

the policy by sympathetic treatment of the aboriginals to induce them to recognise the benefit which they can obtain from the measures designed for their protection and assistance' (Report 28, 1936, cited in Sharp pp. 203–04)

The basic democratic principles on which the government of other Australians rested were still not in evidence. The style of management that ensued was still firmly in place when I was growing up in the Torres Strait Islands in the 1960s and 1970s. 'Surveillance under the guise of informality' (Sharp, 1993, p. 217) became the key to a new disciplinary control. A sophisticated and not so subtle system emerged that depended on the Protector (or Managers as they became known) using direct personal contact and knowledge of each Islander family alongside 'a highly visible system of unequal rewards' (1993, p. 217). Personal attention and the granting of concessions or assistance to Islanders as the 'personal favours' of the Manager because he deemed you or your family worthy of his intervention became the operational norm. The responsibilities, the accountabilities, the workings of government and the rights of Islanders were rendered as invisible and irrelevant to actual governance as they ever had been.

This style of management remained firmly in place until the early 1980s despite the changing discursive field that circumscribed Islanders in the post-war period.

Isolation for Islander males ended abruptly with the advent of the Pacific chapter of the Second World War in 1942. Throughout the war, Torres Strait Islanders worked alongside white army men of equal rank and quickly saw their unequal treatment and relative disadvantage. Following the declaration of peace in 1945, an international discourse of human rights emerged and began to underpin global decolonisation struggles. The Queensland government came to quick conclusions as the Department of Native Affairs (DNA) report of 1947 reveals. Policies of assimilation ensued, although this did not mean the end of separate development for Torres Strait Islanders.

> Complete conversion to the white races must come, and all concerned should realize the implications of such a transition and be ready to deal with any eventuality that may arise. The change has come rapidly, and to prevent disillusionment a carefully thought out plan for education must be instituted. (Beckett, 1987, p. 66)

In 1950, Federal Minister Paul Hasluck gave the following address to the House of Representatives

> The Commonwealth parliament is the custodian of the national reputation in the world at large. Our record of native administration will not stand scrutiny at the standard of our own professions, publicly made in the forums of the world, of a high concern for human welfare. We should be condemned out of our own mouths if those professions were measured by the standard of native administration accepted in Australia today. When we enter into international discussions, and raise our voice, as we should raise it, in defence of human rights and the protection of human welfare, our very words are mocked by the thousands of degraded and depressed people who crouch on rubbish heaps through the whole of this continent. (Hasluck, 1950, cited in Beckett, p. 173)

Even so, as Islanders were attempting to claim their 'citizen' rights, the former Protector Bleakley commented,

> It would be a sorry day for their happiness as a race if the franchise were extended to them and they were subjected to the disturbing influence of political partisanship, which actually could have little meaning and interest for them…[but they are] shrewd enough to know they would have nothing to gain by trying to take the tiller of their own canoe. (1961, p. 299)

In the early 1970s the Commonwealth government entered into Islander Affairs in the Torres Strait. The first report of the Whitlam government's new Department of Aboriginal Affairs (DAA) for 1972–74 articulates a further change occurring in policy discourse for Islander and Aboriginal affairs. Amidst growing Australian Indigenous activism, Commonwealth government policy now made integration the new aim 'based on recognition of the value of the minority culture and of the right of Aboriginals to retain their languages and customs and maintain their own distinct communities' (Department of Aboriginal Affairs, 1975, cited in Beckett, p. 172).

This ushered in a new era of self-management and community development, which has run through to the present. Characteristics of Australian Indigenous people, once seen so problematic and in need of changing through the 'civilising' influences of separate development, and then assimilation into Australian society, were now deployed differently.

> Elements in the traditional Aboriginal culture and system of values may 'impede' programs aimed at changing Aboriginals, but if the aim is rather to help Aboriginals achieve their own goals as individuals

and communities, such elements cease to be seen as obstacles and can be seen rather as factors for influencing the choices. (Department of Aboriginal Affairs, 1975, cited in Beckett, p. 175)

With the entry of the Commonwealth government into the arena of Aboriginal and Islander affairs, the Queensland government was slowly forced to relinquish its tight web of authority over Islanders. But its methods continued. Sharp (1993) refers to the style of the then Queensland Premier, Sir Joh Bjelke-Petersen, to illustrate the continuing influence and surveillance exercised over Torres Strait Islanders in the 1970s and 1980s in these changing times: '"We know them; you can't tell us anything about the Islanders"…"He knows me"'(Sharp, 1993, p. 217–18).

I had my own experience of Bjelke-Petersen in the lead-up to the 1986 State election. In a meeting with my grandfather and other members of the family about the possible renegotiation of a lease for our family's islands, Bjelke-Petersen said in a conspiratorial but authoritative way, 'You know, it's a funny thing but when you are the Premier of Queensland you can do anything.' As if we didn't know. Why else would we seek a meeting but to circumvent and fast-track his own bureaucrats? Yes, 'we knew him' and 'we knew them'. Although voting for his party was suggested, I think I can confidently say that any polite nods were not translated into votes for the National Party at the ballot box by any of my grandfather's family.

Islanders at the centre of their own changing world

If the government and others 'knew Islanders' then it must be strongly asserted that Islanders also had the measure of government and other 'outsiders' and that this measure began to be taken from the beginning. Sharp, a contemporary historian, acknowledges that 'a "standpoint", unwritten, developed from which Islanders judged Kole [white men]… In the language of Kole, something not unlike a "reverse anthropology" developed within Islander networks' (Sharp, 1993, p.14).

For Sharp, this recognition stemmed from her interviews with Murray Islanders, which, to her, articulated notions of Islanders as people who experienced 'change in continuity/continuity in change' (1993, p. 13). This connection of continuity with change recognises that Islanders were active in their own worlds and in their engagements with outsiders. It is important, in my view, that those who seek to understand Islanders acknowledge that the great loss to Islanders was of political and personal autonomy, of independence, control, honour and dignity. By isolating Islanders and determining the conditions of their participation in the new order, 'Islanders were cut off from learning and having the "new"; they were then ridiculed for their ignorance' (Sharp, 1993, p. 147). Colonial practice was premised on a total refusal and disrespect for our intelligence, capacity and humanity. It has been fashionable in the last few decades to rewrite this loss in terms of cultural loss and to see cultural renewal as a primary mechanism for strengthening politically diminished peoples.

The loss of cultural traditions that accompanied the changes in the Torres Strait was often not of our making. But in many cases traditional practices were remade by us in response to changes and in efforts to reconstruct the meanings attached to our social practices as the context and content of life changed. Jeremy Beckett (1987) and Sharp (1993) provide accounts of how Islanders managed to express continuity with former traditions in new practices. These strengthened an understanding of ourselves as 'in the present' and not 'from the past' as scientific and commonsense deliberations about our perceived lower stage of development had suggested at the time. Scattered throughout the historical accounts is the evidence of Islanders taking a measure of those who were encircling them in a new order. This measure was not couched in singular moments but filtered through and across events and down over time and generations to constitute the 'standpoint' expressed through my own family history and in more recent historical analyses such as Sharp's. This standpoint is fundamentally political. Perhaps what emerges to be named a cultural standpoint is what is visible and given voice: 'this is who we are'. Perhaps cultural distinctiveness is what is able to be evidenced by those who look in from the outside at the contemporary expressions of traditional practices, practices that distinguish us from others. But the Islander struggle is fundamentally a political struggle to refashion and reinstate political autonomy in changing times and the standpoint forged from within Islanders' analysis of their colonial predicament is a political, rather than a cultural one. (I will take this up again in Chapters 10 and 11.) When Islanders talk of 'custom', of 'our way', we talk on the surface of things of the particularities of culture, of the way we do things. Those practices do rest on deeper meaning systems that form an entire cultural system. But the meaning systems of Islanders engaged in 'the present' of their everyday worlds necessarily required, and still do, the incorporation of other sets of meanings anchored elsewhere in other knowledge systems. Islander understanding as it evolves is grounded in past traditions but forged through continuity and change. In order to maintain ourselves in changing times we need to position ourselves more powerfully within the political and economic systems that give form and structure to our daily world, systems that are always in flux. It is not enough to 'know them', the individuals who represent those systems. We need to understand 'thinking' systems, how they position us — materially, discursively and subjectively — and work to understand our position in ways that will allow us to forge political effectiveness in the interests of future generations of Islanders.

The accounts of Beckett (1987), Ganter (1994) and Sharp (1993) provide insights into how Islanders struggled to make sense of the new order emerging around them, how they attempted to negotiate and reconstruct different sets of meanings from within their own traditions and those of the new order, on their own terms.

Sharp (1993, pp. 177–8) identifies five singular events that stand out as special times of Islanders 'taking stock' of themselves in relation to others': the 1936 Maritime Strike; the experience of the Second World War, 1942–1946; the Australian–Papua New Guinea border issue in the 1970s (when a proposal was floated to divide Torres Strait Islanders between the two countries); and political sovereignty and land rights in the 1980s, culminating in the 1992 Mabo judgment (which overturned the concept of terra nullius in Australia). These do indeed standout and represent definitive moments of collective focus and action.

But Islander standpoints were also built on and forged in the everyday accommodation of the new as well as the relentlessness of injustice and unfairness. Islander standpoint developed like a stalagmite forming slowly under the constant drip of water. In historical accounts there is plenty of evidence of Islanders attempting to negotiate the terms of their participation, complaining about unfairness, refusing to co-operate, and demonstrating ambivalence towards the new order. And in the memories of Islanders who lived through some of those periods are the analyses forged in shared reflection and carried down through time. Even where there is no 'evidence', there was and is in private Islander 'talk' the continuing themes of equality and independence from the control of others and ongoing debate about the best way to achieve that goal. In the historical accounts we merely obtain glimpses of this standpoint.

For example, we may consider the Islander protocols of demonstrating deference to white authorities who visited their Islands. This could be viewed as a mixture of common human decency, generous hospitality and consideration for others rooted in Islander traditions of reciprocal exchange. It was no doubt done according to Islander sensibilities for treating others on terms of equal exchange and yet the irony was not lost on Islanders who were at the same time denied and refused respectful treatment through the unequal balance of power wielded by white authorities in the colonial relationship. Deference it clearly was, but with both awareness of positioning and some irony as the following statements reveal.

> Well, I was listening to this government officer who was right in the middle and he was pointing to himself: 'Me bigfeller government', introducing himself to the people in the court-house and 'this man, Mr Guillemot' [government teacher], on his right, 'him smallfeller government'. And no notice was taken of *mamus*. (Islander cited in Sharp, 1993, p. 131)

> We always think that when visitors come to the island we respect them. But when we go to Thursday Island they always look one side. And most of them, you'll find they won't take coloured people into their home. (Islander cited in Beckett, 1987, p. 105)

> The Islanders used to carry them [white authorities] across the shallows to the shore before: with the Bishop and the government people too. I said, 'No more! Finish, finish!' I called out to the man who had the job of carrying him ashore, 'You Ailanman, you stop here, you nothing lesser than him'. I said, 'You might as well go put a bloody saddle on your back and go ride em ashore'. (Islander cited in Sharp, 1993, p. 168)

Or we may compare official assessments of the effects of the Second World War on Islanders with those of Islanders themselves:

> The serious disruption occasioned by the advent of war to the long accustomed mode of life practised by the Torres Strait Islanders has had a profound effect on both the economic and psychological aspects of their make up. From a cultural point of view the war contact was disastrous, in that it was swift and all-enveloping. In its aftermath came various degrees of bewilderment, for the rehabilitation of these people embodied not a return to pre-war conditions but a return to conditions forever changed by the wave of unprecedented prosperity that has swept over the entire area. (Department of Native Affairs, 1947, cited in Beckett, 1987, p. 66)

Most accounts of this experience recognise that the war provided Islander men a wider view of the world through their contact with white army men. Many of these men were older unionised men who were sympathetic to the Islanders' situation and respectful of their capacities. In that Islanders gained knowledge from the outside world

7. Disciplining and regulating the body

and skills previously denied them, wartime experience left Islanders with affirmation of their worth and 'the means to construct an alternative to their present situation' (Beckett, 1987, p. 63). That alternative was initially conceived to be the Commonwealth government. Contact with white men also gave the Islander a new language through which to express continuing grievances and craft demands. In 1944, a Murray Islander Councillor petitioned the Governor of Queensland with the following demands:

> Torres Strait Councillors Application.
> To his excellency – Sir
> Torres Strait Islanders be self-controlled by the people with the aid of the Commonwealth Government. When Japan declared war against Australia all our European leaders of Torres Strait were escaped for their lives and leave us helpless there was no word of evacuation, we were left as precious bait for the enemy. And the Governor is now asked that Torres Strait be self controlled by the aid of the Commonwealth Government for that purpose. Torres Strait had volunteered in this present war therefore its people must be on same position as the European. That is to say have full Citizen Rights. To have full Trade of Union. To have full European wages for all employment and Labour condition and to have a higher standard of University Education. (cited in Beckett, 1987, p. 62)

Islanders had been pressing for more rights since the 1936 Maritime strike. Six days before the 1937 Councillors Conference, Murray Islanders demanded home rule and full citizenship rights (Sharp, 1993). Resolutions put forward at the Conference requested the Commonwealth pay maternity allowances to Islanders as they did for other Australians. The establishment of a secondary school, the need for better hospitals in the islands and greater control over Island affairs were also matters raised with the Federal Minister (Sharp, 1993).

The 1949 Department of Native Affairs report provides evidence of further demands that continued to be denied. According to the report, Councillor's resolutions conveyed

> ...the desire of the people to obtain a greater recognition as citizens of the state. The councillors were unanimous in their request that civil rights as applicable to white citizens should be granted them as tax payers of the nation. Already social service benefits, to an even greater extent than applies to Aboriginals, are enjoyed by the Islanders. But these people have not yet attained their desire for the franchise. (cited in Beckett, 1987, p. 74)

Oral testimonies of Islanders also provide evidence of Islander efforts to re-position themselves vis-à-vis the state.

> All the older blokes belonged to the movement and talked about freedom and getting out of bondage…All this group representatives thing was born out of the work of one South Sea man. He came and talked a lot about citizen rights and freedom in the Torres Strait and Murray and Darnley Island Councils wanted to meet with the Director [DNA] with him as their spokesman to get out of the house of bondage. (Sharp, 1993, p. 169)

One of the primary themes running through Islander analysis is a recognition of the need to know about the 'other side' of things. How could Islanders gauge how to participate in the new order if the meaning of its symbols and the working of its institutions were never fully revealed and were continually denied both through state-provided education and in the practice of daily life and work? Over time, Islander analysis gave them a sense, not only of injustice but of the opportunities that had been lost.

> A Boigu man told me that they got a white man's boat off the reef. When that white man come to pay, Mr Walker (PIL) said, 'They don't know about money, their reward is in heaven'. So he took the money for Papuan Industries. That Boigu man said, 'If we got that money today, we might be alright. We never know that time, money cover the world'. (Islander cited in Beckett, 1987, p. 99)

> For a long time the money was controlled by them. 'Yet the money was ours; we battled to get it. We used to crawl on our knees and say, please, please, I would like more… If she said "no" that was it. If we spent the money the wrong way, well that was up to the people themselves. We wanted to take care of it ourselves…You could hardly see a piece of money'. (Islander cited in Sharp, 1993, p. 188)

> They say we can't get freedom till we better educated. But that same talk since before the war. When my father was councillor they ask more education. How long we been ask that thing and never got it yet? Torres Strait people never will get education while they under the Act. While we under the Act we'll always be down. (Islander cited in Beckett, 1987, p.105)

> …I was one of the pioneer teachers to Brisbane. Then we looked back to the life here fenced in. There it was so open in the community. We were free! (Islander cited in Sharp, 1993, p. 84)

There is also evidence that Islanders pursued education, not to be 'white', but to 'know' white thinking or systems of thought and their workings within social, economic and political institutions that overlaid Islander lives. In practice, Islanders were engaged in a synthesis of knowledge from both old and new systems of thought that would allow us to be continuous with our own historical trajectory and still meet our needs and serve our interests within the processes of endless change. This pursuit was antithetical to paternal administration under the Queensland government. Where they saw we must be kept separate from the world that now encircled us, we attempted to find our place in it in our own terms. As one Murray Islander puts it, 'we got the knowledge from the outside world and put it together with our own knowledge' (cited in Sharp, 1993, p. 84).

> At that time [1950s] I knew nothing of English language. Then eventually I started to take an interest because Bob Miles [teacher] was interested in learning *Meriam*. He would teach me English and I would teach him *Meriam Mir*. From then on I started to look at the whole lifestyle in the Torres Strait from a different point of view. One thought was that we have a coin and it has two sides and whilst we're looking at the side the DAIA [Department of Aboriginal and Islander Advancement] dishes out to the Islanders we see there must be another side. It led me to think that I would have succeeded if there was an alternative education in the Strait. (Islander cited in Sharp, 1993, p. 39)

Islanders on the path to political autonomy

By the 1980s the effect of changing discourses in Aboriginal and Islander policy was opening up spaces for Islanders to reassert themselves. Restoration of personal autonomy and the entry of the Commonwealth eventually led to change and opportunities to cut better deals as the Queensland government tried to maintain its position and the Commonwealth tried to build its own spheres of influence. The policy discourse of self-management put forward by the Commonwealth was based on the rights and entitlements of 'special status' citizenship. This engendered a 'new' welfare politics for Islanders' which required 'consent to and participation in, the process' (Beckett, 1987, p. 175).

Islanders now came to the table as negotiators. However, for every determination of the conditions of our participation as culturally distinct but self-determining people, the primary mode of engagement was — and still is — with and through the State. Under this policy, the paradox continues: political autonomy is fostered at the same time that dependence on the State increases (Beckett, 1987).

When this change in the process began in the late 1970s and early 1980s, Islanders were initially advantaged by their familiarity with representations and dealings with the Queensland government through the Island Council system. With the entry of the Commonwealth the political arena became more complex but, as Beckett acknowledged in 1987,

> Somehow these men, only one of whom has had secondary education, have gained a working knowledge of the legal and financial issues arising in negotiations, and learned to use white advisors without being controlled by them. They have mastered the tropes appropriate to these arenas and developed a feel for the alliances and schisms within the political-bureaucratic nexus. (Beckett, 1987, p. 199)

Commonwealth and State governments now share responsibilities in the Torres Strait and the Island Coordinating Council system (ICC) continues to provide the representative structure for Islanders on the outer Islands. The Torres Strait Regional Authority (TSRA), the Torres Strait area regional council of the now dismantled national Aboriginal and Torres Strait Islander Commission (ATSIC) has survived, once again through separate legislation for Torres Strait Islanders, with the arguments being put by Islanders ourselves. TSRA provides a broader representative structure to include all Islanders, including those on Thursday Island and the tip of Cape York.

But what does representation through such structures involve? And what is it that Islanders now confront in our struggle to be politically autonomous? In effect the TSRA operates on a regional basis to make the most of scales of economies and fair distribution of available resources and funding. But the issue is much more complex, because the funding avenues involve three layers of government (federal, state and local) and seventeen discrete local Island councils. In the twenty-first century, the Torres Strait is still remote and distant from the policy- and decision-making centres of the state capital, Brisbane and the national capital, Canberra. But it is a veritable outpost of federal and state bureaucracies. It still lies across an international seaway and an international border but is subject to a complicated international Treaty. It is situated geographically in a sensitive environmental region at the most northern end of the Great Barrier Reef. It is an area of long-time civic and community under-development in an area of long-time marine resource extraction.

7. Disciplining and regulating the body

This reality means that Islander lives are overlaid, not by the singular Queensland government in the form of the Department of Native Affairs or its various nominations. Instead, Islanders go about their daily lives, in times of global terrorism and the tightening of border controls, under the watchful scrutiny of the agents of Foreign Affairs, Immigration, Quarantine, Fisheries, Customs, Federal Police, Queensland Police, Water Police, Defence and Air Surveillance, among others. These are not just jurisdictional referents but involve the physical presence of all these interests in the region. And this is before we get to service provision in the basic areas of health, education, employment, training, housing, welfare, communications, utilities, transport, and justice, all of which are represented by departments and various associated agencies at various tiers of government. As well there are numbers of local community-based organisations.

Some of these government interests (e.g. quarantine and fisheries concerns) are weighted toward regulatory regimes and some (e.g. health and education) are weighted toward service provision. But all impact in some way. Regulatory regimes associated with the border and with marine resource and environmental issues require the co-operation of Islanders. And while Islanders are generally co-operative there are absurdities and ironies that do not escape us in what is a culture of regulation and policing. Islanders may have won free passage across their seas in 1936 but our activities are regulated to an extraordinary degree. Boat licensing, fishing licensing, the ongoing regulation of 'subsistence' and traditional marine activity, safety regulations, quarantine regulations, the limits of protected zones associated with the Border Treaty, and seasonal and catch limits to name some. All these are actively policed and any breaches of regulations carry penalties. Most of these regulations are for good reason — and well understood — some being for our protection, some for resource protection, some for territorial reasons. But although these regulations may be accepted by Islanders for their 'good', the inequities, for example, between the regulation of Islanders and outside commercial fishermen (in effect as well as in intent) lay the grounds for continued grievance and serve to reinforce the ongoing quest for autonomy in the Strait. As in times past, and as in Aboriginal coastal communities, there is evidence in the recent Torres Strait experience that suggests that protection of traditional rights and pursuit of local interests has led to over-regulation of Islanders rather than the external players. What constitutes a legitimate 'subsistence' catch of a particular marine species can be enshrined in regulation down to a particular number and also regulate who may be in the boat and who may not. Trawlers that annually remove around $20 million of prawns, lobsters and mackerel (the profits of which leave the Strait) and damage the sea floor in the process are exercising legitimate commercial rights and do not have to account to either Islanders or the region but rather to licensing boards far away in southern cities. Application of penalties in this web of legislation adds to the growing 'criminalisation' of Islanders who, for customary subsistence or commercial reasons, breach any regulations. This bears resemblance with colonial times where Islanders were harshly regulated by government to 'protect' them from the external interests that intruded into their lives and region.

The struggle to 'self-determine' in the Torres Strait is couched in the language of political autonomy and continues to be concerned with the regulation of external interests in local resources. Islanders are well aware that dependency on the welfare state is a double-edged sword. There is a sense of entitlement due to the legacies of colonialism — but there is also recognition that political autonomy is linked to increasing economic self-reliance. In particular, the issues around the control of marine resources and marine activity are closely associated with regional economic development in Islander thinking. These are becoming increasingly contentious and provide impetus to the pursuit of sea rights as an extension of Native Title (Nakata, 2003).

Ninety-three years after Torres Strait Islanders came under the all-encompassing terms of the *Aborigines Protection and Prevention of the Sale of Opium Act 1987 (1901)*, the final *Report of the House of Representatives Standing Committee on Aboriginal and Torres Strait Islander Affairs (1997) Inquiry into Greater Autonomy for Torres Strait Islanders* was delivered to Parliament. It finalised twenty-five recommendations in support of regional autonomy in the Torres Strait region, and improved processes within the now dismantled ATSIC for Islanders on the mainland. From their consultations, the Committee was convinced that 'Torres Strait Islanders could take responsibility for their own affairs' (1997, p. 43). This conclusion was premised on four grounds. The first was expressed as 'returning a right'.

> These people had total control over their lives, their culture and the local economy, before that autonomy was taken away after European contact and formal annexation to Queensland in 1879. By giving Torres Strait Islanders a greater degree of autonomy, the Commonwealth and Queensland governments will be returning a right that was taken from them. (1997, p. 41)

The second premise was the important role of Torres Strait culture. The Committee accepted arguments about the link between formal decision-making processes and respect for local customs, and recognised 'that by having greater autonomy, Torres Strait Islanders will be able to integrate program design and delivery with their cultural values' (1997, p. 41).

The third premise centred on the link between effective change and greater Torres Strait Islander responsibility for their own affairs. In upholding submissions from Islanders, the Committee cited the Royal Commission into Aboriginal Deaths in Custody arguing that 'substantial change for Aboriginal people in Australia will not occur unless governments and non-Indigenous people accept the necessity for allowing Aboriginals to identify, effect and direct the changes which are required' (1997, p. 42). The Committee accepted that 'if Torres Strait Islanders are given a greater degree of responsibility for making the decisions that affect them, they will then seek their own solutions to problems and establish their own economic initiatives' (1997, p. 43).

The final premise centred on service-delivery issues. It was accepted that greater regional involvement in decision-making processes was also likely to lead to better program coordination and more effective use of resources and funding. But the Committee felt this premise also had the potential to blur distinctions between greater autonomy and greater self-management. It cautioned that self-management (via input and administration of government policy and programs) was complementary to political autonomy but a poor substitute for it. It therefore encouraged specific agreement-making between Islanders and agencies that involved Islanders in 'an integral role in high level policy development' (1997, p. 77).

In this last premise we finally see some recognition of Islanders' desire for control over policy and decision-making in relation to the region in which they live. Islanders were not able to reach consensus on the proposed model for a Regional Assembly and in 2007 are still working on their own model for a Regional Assembly.

Much has changed for the Torres Strait Islander — and much stays the same. In this complex context of administering over the daily lives and futures of people, it cannot be denied that education to understand the language, discourses, bureaucracies and regulatory mechanisms of the external world that is always impinging, always shaping and always serving its own interests is critical to the futures of Torres Strait Islanders. Our bodies may be free but still we remain subject to inscriptions and circumscriptions. We need to always gauge our current position in the changing order of things.

PART TWO

8

Disciplining the Islander in formal education

Tenebris Ad Lucem — From Darkness to Light.
    (School motto on Thursday Island until 1985)

Up until the 1950s it was not uncommon to express the position that Australia's Indigenous people reached a point of intellectual development around adolescence where they could progress no more. The early records from the archives of the New South Wales Department of Education (in 1948 and later in 1955), for instance, cite 'research' to support a position that there was 'common agreement that the intelligence of Aboriginal people is below that of the white population' (cited in Fletcher, 1989, p. 274). This served well to reinforce a community-wide standpoint that Australian Indigenous learners could not rise above 'Fourth Class' standard (Third Class standard in Queensland).

In the Torres Strait, this standard was referred to by Islanders as 'the mark' and the curriculum was systemised during the 1920s.

> ...to impart a knowledge of English, to develop intelligence, to make better what is good in customs and practices, to eliminate what is objectionable, to give a broader outlook and generally to fit these people to live their Island life in a more civilised setting. (Queensland Department of Public Instruction cited in Williamson, 1994, p. 100)

However, by the early 1960s, there were the beginnings of a marked shift in this position. The New South Wales Department of Education's position once again reflects this:

> Research has indicated that the pupils are of average intelligence, and that social deprivation and depressed environment are the reasons for initial retardation than low intelligence; Aboriginal children are

> now seen as disadvantaged members of the general community rather than a substandard racial group. (NSW Department of Education cited in Fletcher, 1989, p. 274)

This shift emerged alongside the wider post-Second World War human rights discourse that underpinned global decolonisation, rather than as any outcome of educational research. Fletcher, in an extensive study of the New South Wales education archival records, could not find any direct educational reference points for the department's shift, indeed reporting that 'there had been no research on the intelligence of Aboriginal children which could have produced such a marked change' (1989, pp. 274–75). However, he did find an early reference by the Teachers Federation to a 'UNESCO [United Nations Educational, Scientific and Cultural Organization] statement that there was no proof that racial groups differed in intelligence or temperament' (p. 275); and noted that the position taken 'had been influenced more by doctrinaire ideas on civil rights and equal rights for all…and it was becoming fashionable to accept that a 'lower' environment rather than a lower racial intelligence could fully explain the school performance' (p. 275).

There was, however, much theorising going on at this time in other parts of the world. Ryan (1971), writing on the African-American context, outlines the shift in thinking by American psychologists towards environmental factors to explain intellectual development. The following extracts provide examples of the deployment of 'unquestioned knowledge' that positions the practices of the middle class as normative to the 'deficit' practices of 'lower classes'. Clear parallels to the inscription of 'savages' in a secondary relation to the 'normative' civilised Europeans are evident in this deployment of 'knowledge' of lower class 'others'.

> …lower-lower class parental patterns, compared to middle class ones, tend to be antithetical to a child's positive mental health… With generally less ego strength (lower self-esteem), the very poor individual is apt to have greater need than his middle class counterpart for security-giving psychological defenses…The subcultural patterns of this group… suggest that their life style…might be termed (within the middle class frame of reference), as immature in a number of respects, such as their greater tendency toward impulsivity, lack of goal commitment, magical thinking, physical learning and behavioral styles, low frustration tolerance, concrete attitudes, and so on. (Chilman cited in Ryan, 1971, pp. 147–48)

8. Disciplining the Islander in formal education

The low SES (socio-economic status) has (1) a weak superego (2) a weak ego, with lack of control or frustration tolerance, (3) a negative, distrustful, suspicious character with poor interpersonal relationships, (4) strong feelings of inferiority, low-self esteem, fear of ridicule and (5) a tendency to act out problems, with violent expression of hostility and extrapunitive tendencies. (Langner & Michaels cited in Ryan, 1971, p. 145)

...to deal professionally with poor people...one must take account of their significant characteristics, particularly as these seem strange or hard to contend with...the deprived are oriented toward the present and, to a lesser extent, the immediate past...the lower class person is handicapped in his efforts to understand change, and he may fear new adjustments...the disadvantaged person is likely to meet difficulties by adjusting to them rather than by attempting to overcome them. (Freedman & Kaplan cited in Ryan, 1971, p. 145)

...if lower class culture is to be changed and lower class people are eventually to be enabled to take advantage of 'opportunities' to participate in conventional society and to earn their own way in it, this change can only come about through a change in the social and ecological situation to which lower class people must adapt. (Rainwater cited in Ryan, 1971, pp. 134–35)

However, Ryan contested psychology's inscriptions of the socially and educationally disadvantaged as one more disposed to absolving the role of Western institutional and disciplinary practices. In his view, the shift in effect 'blames the victim', apologises for and exonerates the role of the state as well as authorises and reinforces 'educated' middle-class values as the unproblematic normative standard.

Ryan was not alone. Freire's text, *Pedagogy of the Oppressed* (1972), drawing on the Brazilian context, saw a very direct relationship between the state and the people, as oppressor and the oppressed. He claimed that the shift in the psychological position was more to do with 'changing the consciousness of oppressed, not the situation that oppresses them' (Simone de Beauvoir cited in Freire, 1972, p. 47). In England, Cultural Studies — through Hoggart's text, *The Uses of Literacy* (1957), Williams' *Culture and Society* (1958) and *The Long Revolution* (1961), and Thompson's seminal work on *The Making of the English Working Class* (1978) — came to focus even more closely on relations of power and how they come to shape cultural practices. Together with Stuart Hall, these theorists re-visioned the environmental influences as a historical phenomenon of changing elements in 'new times'.

In Australia, from the 1960s there was an increasing focus on academic research in Australian Indigenous issues beyond the traditional fields of inquiry in anthropology, archaeology and linguistics. Research related to Australian Indigenous people further accelerated under the Whitlam government in the 1970s and drew academic research and governments into a closer collaboration in instituting reform in Australian Indigenous affairs. Not just the amount of knowledge produced about Australian Indigenous societies or issues increased. New ways of understanding what it meant to be 'Indigenous' in modernising times harnessed more and more of the social sciences as a means to build explanatory models and suggest remedies for eliminating a range of inequities.

So the social inequity that was the prior accepted basis of the education system of Australia's Indigenous people — indeed of the whole of what we now generally refer to as the service provision context — now assumed a central focus in research. Research was well positioned within the discursive shifts underway in the international discourses associated with human rights, equal rights and civil rights, in the developing social sciences, and in Federal government policy reform. This discursively framed a way of understanding 'Indigenous problems' as synonymous with 'disadvantage', 'lack', 'cultural deprivation' and 'cultural difference'. Except for concepts of cultural deprivation, which was quickly reworked as cultural difference, these themes came to dominate policy and practice — to inform both explanation and remedy for past educational failure and the general Islander 'predicament'.

The discursive and material circumscription of the preceding century, when missionaries, scientists and government had used racially-based arguments to rationalise their decisions to separate and protect Islanders from the external influences encroaching on their living environments passed into 'history'. To redress the legacy, by 1971 the shift underway in the disciplines of education, psychology and sociology disposed thinking towards a new scrutiny of social and cultural practice, to develop 'new' ways of knowing Islanders in order to understand what impeded educational progress. To understand generally why Australia's Indigenous people were failing to 'derive benefit from their schooling', investigations came to be directed at '...forces outside the formal education system which seriously affect[ed] the progress of Aborigines within that system...[including] the home, the community, the peer group and the personality and cognitive characteristics of the Aboriginal pupil himself'. (Watts, 1971, p. i).

The policy shifts that occurred post-war from assimilation to integration and then to self-determination, ensured this research did not lead to 'changing' us as Australia's Indigenous peoples. Rather, more knowledge of social and cultural practices was needed in the 1970s to understand what sorts of clashes or barriers impeded progress in formal schooling.

By the 1980s, when education in the Torres Strait eventually became a focus for reform by the Queensland government, the way that Islanders were understood in terms of their social context and as learners influenced the details and extent of curriculum reform. In a very circular way, separate, and now with hindsight, meaningless (rather than substandard or insufficient) schooling was to give way to equal but necessarily different schooling. As a result there was much more research on Torres Strait Islander education (e.g. Kale, 1988; McDonald, 1988; Orr, 1977, 1982; Osborne, 1979, 1982, 1985, 1986, 1988; Osborne & Bamford, 1987; Osborne & Coombs, 1982, 1987, 1988; Osborne & Francis, 1987; Osborne & Henderson, 1985; Osborne & Sellars, 1987; Shnukal, 1984a; 1984b).

Research into education in the Torres Strait became largely a reaction to the view that schooling, as experienced by Islanders prior to commencement of educational reform, was a colonial institution that was mono-cultural, assimilatory and incongruent to Islander culture, ways of knowing and values. Curriculum, likewise mono-cultural, was seen as irrelevant and as inhibiting the conceptual development of Islander children. Pedagogical practices were recognised as culturally inappropriate and incongruent with Islander learning styles and cultural ways. The use of English as the language of instruction was questioned not only as being assimilatory but also as unmindful of the linguistic background of Islander students and of the role that language played in the cognitive and intellectual development of children.

Over the past twenty-five years, research on education in the Torres Strait concentrated in three main areas: history, language and culture. Much of the research can be read as interesting, useful and adding to knowledge about Islanders. But, as in times past, the theoretical premises and assumptions are founded in the disciplines and parallel disciplinary developments. And despite improvements little headway has been made in terms of relative disadvantage as measured in education outcomes.

History

In the accounts of earlier educational history (see Finch, 1975; Langbridge, 1977), Islander experiences were represented through a simple description of formal schooling practices — that is, the forms of education that missionaries and government instituted and the effects of these on the educational outcomes of Islanders. Other accounts can be found in the work done by Orr and Williamson (1973) and Boxall and Duncan (1979).

Orr and Williamson (1973) captured the harsh reality of educating Torres Strait Islander children in broken-down buildings, with an almost unmodified state curriculum, with white teachers who had little understanding of Islander values or languages, and with Islander teachers who had inadequate levels of English and teacher education. In a following paper, Williamson (1974) highlighted the 'incongruence' for the Islander child as a learner in a school system based on 'white middle-class Australia' and its values. He argued that policy and reform makers needed to pursue 'different' educational goals, and that the difficulties experienced by the Islander children in current schooling situations would not be overcome unless there was 'intensive research into the distinctive learning needs and motivations of these children' (1974, p. 60).

Boxall and Duncan's (1979) survey of the school system was more extensive, and included recommendations similar to ones put forward by Finch (1977). These included a case for further research into bilingual education, Islander learning styles and the developmental patterns of Islander children to enable the development of programs that would reflect the children's local experience while at the same time opening up the world beyond the islands. They also encouraged community involvement and direction in programs to encourage and promote cultural identity. Both these surveys also flagged an urgent need to upgrade the training of Islander teachers. In the main these were early descriptions of a 'broken-down' school system and more attuned to progress resources and resourcing issues for the schools.

More recently, educational historians like Williamson (1997) grappled with how to represent the complexity and the dynamics that shaped Islander historical experience between 'the colonizer and the colonized' (p. 407), and signalled a much needed shift in research of Torres Strait Islander education experiences. Here was an opportunity to consider the Islander standpoint and provide some insights into how Islanders viewed the role of education or the experience of schooling in relation to their position within the changing order of things. To do so might reveal, disrupt or disturb the ways that Islanders were generally inscribed as subjects of others' understanding. If this could emerge, then the contradictions and ambiguities that emerge in the contemporary concerns that Islanders have about their educational position may come to be seen within its own historical formation, within their historical experience of it. Further, the ambiguities, contradictions and risks of Western education become a continuous theme in what Islanders need to manage and shape and so inform what Islanders prioritise as goals of education in changing times. These contradictions and risks can never be completely resolved; they require ongoing consideration as the ever-changing context of life in the Torres Strait shifts and alters according to external agendas and interests.

Williamson's history of colonial Torres Strait schooling provides a useful site for investigating contemporary disciplinary practice in relation to understanding Islanders at the interface of changing times. What Islanders like myself get excited by when Williamson and other writers of our history and educational priorities talk of moving beyond the limitations of their conventions and their past writings, is that they will come closer to understanding that Islander calls for education, for 'proper' schooling, for 'university education' were not simply misguided aspirations to become 'white'. An Islander such as me would hope to find evidence of Islanders reading their own diminished position, seeing their secondary relation and understanding the need to 'know' the ways of this intruding world that refused us a position on a level with others. For example, Islanders who worked on government boats had no means to check government assessments and balance sheets.

> We had no education to check the scales, we knew no arithmetic, subtraction, addition. If we brought up 5 or 7 tons [of pearl shells] and the price was say £155 per ton, we might get, ah £5 or £6?...just pocket money. (Ganter, 1994, p. 72)

Our calls were never simply about schooling in English or just about becoming literate in that language for its own sake. Rather, they were about working out what the language of 'white' people and their institutions do that keeps us at a disadvantage, that keeps us as the lesser 'knowers' in situations.

> We been work for JW Bleakley. He come out [to] all the islands, he said, 'Oh, I'm your big mamus, here are two sticks of tobacco, here are two blankets'...so we bend the knee and bow down to him...I get one stick tobacco; that's my pay for Chief Councillor. Well we used to go down to the office and you know those little Pass Books? They stop me if I want to draw money today...'You have to wait for next week'. (Islander cited in Sharp, 1993, p. 127)

>...they kept the books, you had no proof. (Islander cited in Ganter, 1994, p. 87)

> But still the government weighed the shell. It looks like they cheated. They didn't let you know how much it weighed. (Islander cited in Ganter, 1994, p. 90)

> You see my mind opened to the world the first time I heard about university when a signalman during the War said he's going back to uni. It's a new language the blokes spoke during the War. They'd often come to me and talk about things...So I thought to myself...I'll be able to learn more by serving next door to a white bloke and be able to ask him things. Because I want to know like a white man...Then I wanted to join the fortress signals, to learn about the radio and talk to someone to improve my English. I think it's just that I always wanted to find out more about things and inquire about them. At the end of the War I wanted to become a leader of Torres Strait. (Islander cited in Sharp, 1993, p. 167)

As we moved through the latter half of the twentieth century, the ongoing calls for schooling in English continued to be about an understanding of what it is in the language of the emerging community around us that continues to provide conditions to all of our possibilities. What people do not seem to understand is that these calls emerged out of particular moments in the Islanders' historical trajectory when certain things impacted on our lives that made it imperative that we take action.

The Islander calls for 'proper' schooling in English emerge at times when we are most concerned about our futures. But as well it is crucially about defending ourselves against the constant intrusions into our lives, and about maintaining our stature in the face of others. We are not content with being subjected as 'Other' to everybody else. We reference ourselves to an entire universe not just to Western imperialist projects. At an international language and education conference in Greece in 2001, I put it to Donaldo Macedo, a colleague of Paulo Freire, that just because we have not yet exacted a science on how to teach English to Indigenous people without threatening the place of Indigenous languages and cultures it should not equate to a free and open attack on calls for English as being 'ideologically unsound'. We simply refuse to be treated as 'overgrown children', and as if the 'adult' always knows better. As Audre Lorde (1984) suggested, 'it is not [our] difference that immobilises us, it is silence [emphasis added]. And there are many silences to be broken' (p. 44). This, for me, added to the need to critically review liberal sentiments and projects that underpinned the past thirty years of educational reform. We could do well with reassessing how these have come to hold the higher position in determining 'what is good for us' and, in turn, how they have come to silence our views on the way we might prioritise reform in our communities. Even when 'outside experts' acknowledge that perhaps Islanders have a reading of how it is they have come to be positioned by the outside world over the past century and have developed the means to negotiate their way, they feel a need to redirect, to correct and to reposition this reading as incomplete understanding. It may be more useful to Islanders, if listening required suspension of the tendency to call us in to other systems of thought and logic.

This is why I read Williamson's (1997) approach to the documentation of educational histories with much hope. I saw that it may open up spaces for the Islanders' call to be included as a crucial reference point for recounting the history of formal schooling in the Torres Strait, and I looked forward especially to the kinds of methodological innovations he promised beyond 'imperial' (p. 407) reference points. Central to Williamson's approach in his article, 'Decolonizing Historiography of Colonial Education', is the realisation that 'the colonial context of education appears to have been more dynamic than is commonly acknowledged and more powerful in shaping schooling's practices and outcomes than conventional accounts would have us believe' (p. 408), and thus his thesis that 'educational policies...might not have been as coercive and exclusionist as at first appeared' (pp. 413–14).

From his review of early accounts of both Aboriginal and Torres Strait Islander schooling under colonial rule, Williamson (1997) found that writers were mostly caught up with 'imperial concerns' (p. 407) and 'ignored important elements in the interrelationship between colonizer and colonized' (p. 407). As he went on to suggest, 'what has emerged, until recently, has been an "official view of history"' (p. 407). By contrast, and from his review of later accounts, he noted important progress being made by the shift away from 'imperial' or 'official' viewpoints. Since the 1970s, as he pointed out, both Indigenous and non-Indigenous historians were beginning to show Australian Indigenous people as having a history 'in terms of family and community concerns...attachment to their land, and the roles of family, kin, and community in validating, and passing on their histories' (Working Party cited in Williamson, 1997, p. 408). As well, they were being shown as having a history of confronting, resisting and adapting creatively to colonial encounters, and indeed 'less as the "fatal impact" found in European post-colonial critiques and more as "subtle and complex levels of mutual exploitation and accommodation"' (Howe cited in Williamson, 1997, p. 409).

Williamson goes on to position himself with Carter to argue that in the attempt to move out of histories being written from the 'vantage point of the west' (1997, p. 407) the 'revisionists' were still caught up in writing histories using colonial referents and criteria. I think the methodological point is a very good one in that the recent shift in recounting Australian Indigenous experiences by the revisionists produced 'a narrative of non-contact rather than contact because the material from the Aboriginal side of the frontier is interpreted by the same criteria used to establish and interpret that from the white side, whose reference is the external world' (Williamson, 1997, p. 409).

To move beyond extant positions and their modes of representation, Williamson aligned himself with Mullins (1995) to chart the complexities in encounters between Islanders and the colonialists, as well as with Carter (1992) to seek 'referents internal to each side and to the contact situation itself' (Williamson, 1997, p. 409) and thus a framework for interpreting and representing, in research terms, 'what is going on'. Following Carter's line, he saw colonial encounters as having 'spatial and temporal characteristics charged with symbolic meaning as newcomers and original inhabitants, total strangers, attempt to dissolve the physical and psychological distance between one another, and open lines of communication in the search for coexistence' (1997, p. 409). I am confident that these will be crucial elements in any future methodological position taken to representing Indigenous histories as we move further into the twenty-first century. I am also in agreement that such a position has the potential to bring out important 'dynamics of the educational contexts'. It will be enlightening for us all, especially in the field of Torres Strait Islander education, if intervention in formal schooling processes, for instance, becomes based on such dynamics and not solely on histories told through some Western canon.

Getting to the 'dynamics', however, is more easily said than done for this type of methodological innovation has even evaded founding intellectuals. This has resulted in disciplines narrowing to only accepting elements that are continuous with their own — a take-up that reflects more a taking of sides rather than a push forward to rediscover elements of complex intersections that people negotiate in the everyday. To explore elements of continuities and discontinuities with Western systems of thought, people who see a need for improved theoretical configurations need to understand first that the Islander people are not just the all-encompassed colonised people in the far north of Australia. We can never simply be a people just of the past or singularly the 'victim' of external influences; we are a people with an active past of adapting our traditions to better place ourselves and our heritage in changing times.

Williamson, in trying to get to a better understanding of colonial encounters, buys into grounded theory and symbolic interactionist sociology (Mead, 1964). This particular interpretative framework seeks to get to the bottom of 'what is going on' (Denzin, 1992; Woods, 1986) at various points of intersecting historical trajectories by prioritising local viewpoints to explain, if you like, 'what is happening here' (McDermott, 1982). It tries to stand apart from anthropological approaches to 'native cultures' as exotic traditions of a people, to avoid the notion that there are cultural 'truths' out there waiting to be recorded.

The alternate framework tries to concentrate on engagements between smaller groups of people (or sub-cultures), with a particular view to re-presenting the interactive processes from the viewpoint of those who engage in them. This framework tries to provide for a position that gives primacy to how people make sense of the world they live in — as they do — as well as a focus on smaller groups of people whose symbolic sense-making processes are often obscured by, or not visible to, the dominant group. Osborne and Dawes (1992), for example, studied classroom encounters between an English as a Second Language (ESL) teacher and her Torres Strait Islander students (from videotape recordings and from subsequent interviews with students and the teacher) by 'immersing' themselves into the discourse of classroom processes to get a better understanding of the 'ways the teachers and the class (or parts of it at various times) worked with each other to sustain an activity' (p. 3). It was an important attempt by them to move away from canonical readings of the state versus its subjects, to step away from always seeing Islanders as objects of educational practice, and to shift more toward understanding how such encounters are conditioned by all who participate in them. Williamson makes the simple point that if we look at Islander education from the 'local level' we see that the colonisers may not have been as much in control as they thought they were. The corollary of this is to shift the Islander from the position of being always already 'victims' and this alone is a significant methodological step.

However, I am uneasy about the ways that Williamson has undertaken the task to bring into focus 'the dynamics of the educational context', 'processes of interaction' and 'the active engagement of Islanders in negotiating culture contact' (1997, p. 407). What is offered as his interpretative framework is a position that is said to be 'eclectic', even 'loose' (p. 412). As he says, this framework is based on a theory that emerged '[a]s data were gathered and analysed...[and later] adjusted to the judgement and creativity of the researcher' (p. 412). He goes on to say that this framework is about producing a history 'grounded in written reports and the voices and observations of protagonists and eye-witnesses' (p. 413). And I agree — there is value in innovating the age-old practice of only using external referents and by moving towards theories grounded in data but how does a researcher leave history — their cultural and intellectual baggage — at the door before entering the Islander classroom?

This is where it begins to get interesting. In Williamson's attempt to legitimate a theoretical position for recounting historical events, past writings and people's recollections, we read a whole lot about the new conventional orthodoxy in his approach to theory and little about the primary referents of his interpretative framework. Without this, we are left wondering what his theoretical position on data is — his elected methodological position. Does he see, for example, data gathered from Islanders and other people or from the archives as emerging out of a particular history? What is that history? Is it one where everything is continuous to Western systems of thought or one that is continuous with Islander systems of thought? Or is it a history of the contesting positions where one loses and others win? Or is it one of strategically moving between them, borrowing from and adapting to ensure the continuance of one alongside the other? In short, what provided the context for the data to have meaning? I am not reassured by the statement, '[a]s data were gathered and analysed, theory emerged as concepts or relationships acting as "centres for the crystallization of later ideas"' (Phillips cited in Williamson, 1997, p. 412). How, for instance, will he see recollections by individual Islanders? Do we focus on data from the archive and the individual as belonging to a history that tells of an uninterrupted chain of events, or do we try to focus on the systems of thought in the messages that they convey (i.e., the context in which things are said and that which provides its meanings)? And do we seek, in either of these positions, continuities or links with other factors/events/readings to re-present to readers what was stated or written, or do we seek discontinuities, ruptures, thresholds and constraints to allow readers to see what conditions the possibilities in what is stated or written.

I do not want to imply here that 'grounded' theory is questionable but do note the lack of clarity in the approach to it — a question of a situation that poses as a problem for all researchers but not often resolved by them. Williamson himself suggests at the beginning of his discussion that, 'the researcher needs to make explicit the theoretical views guiding the study, decide the data that are most appropriate to gather, and the ways these data may best be analyzed' (1997, p. 412).

Nor do I want to impose questions upon Williamson from so-called 'post-structuralist' or 'post-colonial' positions. Rather, mine is a valid methodological question about the new referents and criteria in his interpretative framework for re-presenting data, for instance, from the Islanders; or is it really the case that they can be found in the data? If so, how will one identify such elements after electing to abandon their intellectual baggage at the gate before entering the field of inquiry — is it really possible for one to step outside of history?

We are left then to scrutinise his approach from his use of data gathered in the field. What follows in his key themes is a recount of schooling events in the Torres Strait that to me, as an Islander, seems to stand in defence of the state (despite its legislative power to officiate over its many institutions, employees and constituents). Williamson, for instance, argues that although there are those who perceive that early colonial governmental regimes were about 'dampen[ing] down Islanders' aspirations for equality of status' (1997, p. 414), they 'might not have been as coercive and exclusionist as at first appeared' (pp. 413–14).

However, he acknowledges that 'the government spent less on Islanders' education than on education for whites' (p. 13) but, as he tries to convey, the state was, at least, 'forced to do more for Islanders in the Torres Strait than for Aboriginal people on the mainland' (p. 414). I guess then that we, as Islanders, need to be at least half grateful rather than ungrateful. Nevertheless, as he goes on to show, schooling on the islands was delivered under many constraints. For example, schooling was to be delivered in a very remote part of the state, under a policy of Protection and Segregation, by 'teachers of indifferent quality' (p. 413), and with little prospect for schooling leading to employment. Schooling also progressed under pressure from many quarters, including the different priorities of regional administrators, the churches and the Islanders themselves who were demanding a 'better deal' (p. 414). Moreover, at any one time in the islands, as he goes on to explain, there 'were never more than two resident white missionaries during LMS [London Missionary Society] times...while in 1932, at the peak of government schooling, only eight of the 41 teachers in the schools were white' (p. 414). In short, schooling 'was placed largely in the hands of [a few] white teachers of indifferent quality and Islander teachers lacking in higher schooling and teacher training' (p. 413). There were, however, some teachers (Firth and Turner, cited in Williamson, 1997, pp. 416–17) who were able to take Islander students beyond the standard (Third Class) set by the State of Queensland. This, he says, was achieved because of the isolation of Islander communities and, amongst other things, the lack of supervision by the officials. Thus, curriculum activity over the years was adapted to suit the 'locale of reserve life' (p. 420).

The schooling that ensued from such a situation did, as Williamson puts it, 'provide insights into white custom' (p. 418) and did not deter Islander parents or grandparents from teaching 'their own language and culture' (p. 420). And, in these ways, schooling did not lead to a segmentation of the community along the lines of educational achievements because, as he surmises, '[b]eing white was the essential prerequisite' (p. 418). For Williamson, '[t]he deciding issues were the strength of custom, the quality of teachers, their relationships with them [Islanders], and the opportunities schooling offered them' (p. 420). This was, as he argues, 'no mere function of colonialism. Rather, it was 'a dynamic process in which its practices and outcomes were shaped less by policy statements and the institutional infrastructure of mission and government than by what took place at the local level' (cited in Nakata, 1997, p. 429).

My concern is raised when Williamson moves to conclude that the Islanders' call for 'proper schooling [was a] misplaced' hope (cited in Nakata, 1997, p. 429). He acknowledges that school learning 'was not always functional to the political, economic and social contexts of life in the islands' (Williamson, 1997, p. 419) and contends this was mainly due to the aforementioned constraints and pressures, 'segregation, limited employment opportunities, and racism' (Williamson, 1997, p. 420). Besides, he adds, proper schooling on the mainland at the time 'had little to offer working class Australians, let alone Aboriginal people and Islanders' (cited in Nakata, 1997, p. 429). What does not figure as a priority in this equation is a view to the Islander perspective that the 'hope' for formal schooling was, and continues to be, a political call to be rid of an intrusive form of governmentality set on entrenching Islander dependence on welfare.

As far as Williamson is concerned, Islanders' desire for education 'grew out of their perceptions of its power to bring benefits to them in the new order' (Williamson, 1997, p. 414). The 'benefits', according to Williamson, were mostly to do with gaining a 'share in the benefits of other introduced institutions such as the commercial fisheries, wage labour and the church. They wanted a share of the power of Europeans and their material goods' (pp. 414–15). Schooling, in this sense, is seen to be prioritised by Islanders. Indeed Williamson claims, it is 'perceived as a "route to the cargo"...[as having] the potential for gaining "equality of power" with Europeans...[and] tapped the power of Christianity' (cited in Nakata, 1997, p. 429). This is perplexing. Was it not the intention to leave external referents at the door before going into the classroom?

This view, however, does not come altogether as a surprise to me. The call for formal schooling has been treated in such ways over and over again in the literature. Outside experts just do not seem to get it. It is not a simple case of wanting an education in 'white ways' to gain material benefits from 'the new order' — a 'route to the cargo'. Neither can it be simply about gaining power and equality with others. Nor is it to find the right path to Heaven. While the anthropological construct of a ship bringing back Indigenous ancestors (as white people) and a cargo of material goods from another world as a spiritual phenomena viz., 'cargo cult' (Worsley, 1968) may be a manipulation of the experiences of people in Papua New Guinea and Melanesia in general, or of the Tanna people of New Hebrides and their encounters with American GI soldiers in particular, it is certainly not a practice I am familiar with in the Torres Strait. But it is an identifiable process in a long history of peculiar practices: in the ways literature on cannibalism in other parts of the world was assembled to appoint Islanders in history as cannibals; in the ways that scientific disciplines from other parts of the world designated us as savages even before they arrived in the islands; and in the ways a 'commonsense' from other parts of the world prevailed in government regimes to see us only as overgrown children even after decades of living alongside fiercely independent Islander leaders in their communities. These are the kinds of elements of what prominent Aboriginal intellectual Marcia Langton (1996) refers to as a deep psychosis in Western systems of thought, which continues to harbour the logic for colonial settlers to legitimise their presence and occupation of lands and seaways that do not belong to them.

Islanders have called for an education not simply so we gain benefits from it. It is so that we can gauge and understand the external influences in our lives, what it is we are up against, and what it means for our survival in colonial environments. I don't think we can simply discount the political vision in this as 'misplaced' hopes. This is indeed a dimension where we, as Islanders, are aligned politically. It is about how to appropriate a better position for ourselves — to cut better deals for ourselves and our traditional heritage in changing times. This is a reference point that must be given primacy in any recount of the Islander schooling. If it was, we would begin to comprehend a very different picture when Islanders say 'schooling had failed them..."No way to go — no way to go...we want education from school, but we got nothing"' (cited in Williamson, 1997, p. 415), or when Williamson reports that though 'their curiosity to know more might have been dulled by their school experiences it was never extinguished' (p. 415). Likewise, it makes a different sense to me when I read in Williamson's data that, 'Islanders appear to have connected schooling in English with their material and political advancement and were not put off by its failure to bring results immediately' (p. 415).

Furthermore, I certainly hear something different when I read his account of Islanders who 'acquired insights into their social and racial inferiority in the Islands and displayed attitudes which some whites thought were above their station...[and about reports in 1905] that school leavers had been rendered '"cheeky, conceited, and indolent"' by their schooling (cited in Williamson, 1997, p. 419). It's frustrating when Islander statements like this are taken simply as displays of negative behaviour: '[w]hether this outcome contributed to subsequent labour unrest among Islanders can only be speculated upon' (p. 419). Why are we so caught up with what others thought, reported or speculated? Is it really that hard to understand what is said by Islanders? If, for a moment, we consider Islander statements as political acts strategic to the ways they negotiate intersecting historical trajectories then we may begin to hear what Islanders are trying to express. Maybe it was because Islanders had learned something in schools and had come to some understanding of their position vis-a-vis 'whites'. And maybe it was because they were able to articulate to those in charge, with confidence and in a language they could understand, what they thought of that. Or maybe it was simply because of a realisation that 'whites' were not as smart as first perceived.

If we do provide primacy in the interpretations of Islanders as 'negotiators', 'actors', or informed players in their own historical trajectories, and try to understand that what is said by them emerges out of a political position, we would get a very different reading when an Islander is reported to have said something. What do we get, for instance, if we consider what Islanders mean when they say that after gaining insights into 'white ways' from their schooling they believed 'there was even greater power in their island custom' (Williamson, 1997, p. 419). If an Islander is reported to have said that he 'plussed' 'three quarters of his island custom with one-quarter of "knowledge from the outside world" in his "new life" under white rule' (Sharp cited in Williamson, 1997, p. 419), it is not a novel phenomenon to be posed in a paradoxical situation, nor can it be regarded simply as an implication 'that underscored schooling's diverse and complex character in the islands' (p. 419). It could be read simply as this Islander's realisation of the shortfalls of 'white' knowledge, his reinstatement of Islander knowledge as credible and valid, his recognition of the political advantages to knowing about the outside world, and importantly, his reiteration of the political project to maintain Islander positions, despite those revolutionaries who perceive all conditions to be hegemonic 'under white rule' (p. 420).

We get the important message from Williamson's recount that the history of schooling has been a dynamic interplay of many elements, and more complex than previously acknowledged. The primary perspective used by Williamson about the history of schooling in the islands requires that we take particular consideration of the constraints in the local contexts in order to see a history of colonial governments and their policy as involved, but not altogether responsible for generations of extremely poor educational outcomes. I also see the need for the inclusion of government teachers, Islander teachers, Islander people and the broader aspects of community relations (e.g. segregation, racism, under-resourcing) as part of the explanation as to what delimited the schooling processes, and thus by association, see them also responsible in part for the poor educational outcomes. But when there are no priorities given to the Islanders' perspective in the 'negotiated situations' (p. 421), when Islander contributions do not find a place in this new approach to the documentation of histories that speaks in relation to the political position which Islanders find themselves in, and when I see statements by Islanders used to bolster what appears to be Williamson's defence of the early colonial projects, I see no advance from earlier writings of Aboriginal and Torres Strait Islander histories in Australia.

Yes, it does need to be written that we are all part of the formalities of schooling. But those involved must be considered as having an active past of moving in and out of socially contested terrains, consciously making and remaking themselves as a unique group of Australian Indigenous people — a political disposition that provides the foundations to what Islanders say and an epistemological locatedness that informs what is possible by them. Otherwise, data can be misconstrued and recounts can end up being read as an apology for the state. When Islander positions are simply incorporated as part of the array of factors involved in schooling, and implicated in its processes, it signals to me that primacy has been given in the interpretative framework to represent neither the historical nor the epistemological locatedness of the Islanders in the so-called 'negotiations'. And to borrow from Williamson's own text, to not go beyond this point demonstrates that this approach to Islander histories 'does less than it intends and achieves more of what the context in which it is set allows' (1997, p. 421).

Language

Much of the general literature on Torres Strait Islander education in Australia begins from an assumption that oral traditions and the first language of the student are fundamental elements that can have a profound effect on educational achievement. Advocates of bilingual education, for example, argue for the beginning years of formal schooling to be undertaken in the student's first language. For an effective transition into the literate traditions of English-based classrooms, they argue, a student from an oral culture needs to be literate in their own language first. English as a Second Language (ESL) advocates argue for, in situations where English is the primary medium for teaching and learning, recognition of the student's first language and treatment of English as their second language. Traditionalists, on the other hand, argue for teaching and learning to be entirely in the student's first language and for English to be learned as a foreign language.

All assume a beginning position with students who come from an oral tradition. Interestingly, the 'oral tradition' factor sits in their equation almost without question. Little is made of the fact that locating students within an 'oral tradition' narrows down their presence in history to 'something' that is 'not' part of the literate traditions, and as separate and apart from the complex world of negotiating colliding historical trajectories over the past two hundred years. It is so simple a proposition that it is stunning. I turn here to a linguistic model devised for learning mathematics to chart this thinking further.

As part of an attempt to explain mathematics education as it relates to people from an oral tradition, Watson's (1988) continua consider an analysis via a theoretical framework built on socio-demographic and linguistic differences between orate and literate traditions. But how easy is it to identify where Islanders are on an oral/literate continuum (cf. Goody, 1978)?

Helen Watson's approach not only helps to exemplify the key components of the language-specific approaches to improving educational outcomes of Aboriginal people but also accepts that 'there exists the same type of continuum linking use of Torres Strait Islander languages and English' (1988, p. 257). If anything, it is a very good example of the assumptions made in language areas of formal education as they attempt a level of complexity to represent Islander lifeworlds in new times in Australia. My concern here is not with the application of this model to maths education or Aboriginal people. Rather, it is to draw to the light underlying positions about the languages used by Torres Strait Islanders and gauge how well the theoretical model devised by Watson deals with 'oral traditions'. This is a fundamental issue that sits at the heart of proponents advocating priorities for education to be in the first language.

To investigate the appropriateness of the application of such continua to Torres Strait Islanders, I attempt here to chart Watson's theoretical construction of the model through its various stages. To gain an insight into the suggested relatedness to Torres Strait Islander linguistics, Anna Shnukal's extensive research work in the Torres Strait on the Torres Strait Creole in *Broken: An introduction to the creole language of Torres Strait* (1988), will be employed to plot Islanders along the continua using Watson's criteria. From the outset, it is interesting to note that Torres Strait communities are located at one end of Watson's continua as a separate group but fail to appear as a group anywhere else. This reflects the tendency to treat Aboriginal people and Islanders as one and the same, and to assume that traditional Islander communities are subjected to the same influences as traditional Aboriginal communities. In many research studies, policies and legislations in Australia Islanders are, to borrow a phrase from feminist theory, 'commatised' (O'Brien, 1984).

Watson (1988) primarily 'examines mathematics education as it relates to the Aboriginal-Australian community' (p. 255). In this analysis, she takes the view that mathematics is a 'linguistic enterprise' (p. 259). To distance herself from past assimilationist policies on schooling, Watson aligns herself with an educational curriculum and pedagogy that addresses the bicultural experience of Australia's Indigenous people. With this perspective, she claims, '(b)icultural education will reproduce the economy and culture of Aboriginal Australia through dynamic interaction with European Australia' (1988, p. 255).

To describe how far removed the student is from the maths register of the English language, Watson constructs a linear model to map subgroups according to their linguistic characteristics. This model employs two continua. The first continuum on the horizontal plane relates to the 'ordinary everyday' language spoken amongst a group. The second continuum on the vertical plane concerns the degree to which oral or literate communication predominates in community groups.

The first continuum involves differences in semantic structures of the ordinary everyday language spoken in Indigenous communities, with the English and traditional languages at opposite ends of the continuum. Watson argues that the systematic ordering of reality which occurs with traditional languages has profound differences in semantic or meaning structures to those of the English language and its dialects, hence their location along the continuum at opposite ends. Different language groups categorise their world distinctly. On this basis, Watson is able to locate the different language dialect use along the continuum. Consequently, traditional communities are located at one end of the continuum with a trend towards communities dispersed in metropolitan and urban areas at the other. There they live as members of the European-derived Australian community and speak dialects of English.

The second continuum attempts to locate the extent to which oral and literate modes of communication predominate in each community. Watson maps groups from traditional communities where print does not figure in their modes of communication on one end of the continuum, moving towards metro-urban Aboriginals whose modes of communication are heavily involved with the use of the printed material.

Here Heath's (1983) major ethnography of literacy among Southern US African-Americans is significant, particularly in its systematic demonstration that stereotypes of 'oral culture' among 'non-mainstream' groups can be erroneous and ethnocentric.

For instance, according to Finch (1975), formal education was first established in the Torres Strait by LMS missionaries in 1891. A teacher training institute was also established soon after by the missionaries on Murray Island and later a theological college at St Paul's Mission on Moa Island. Indeed, the Torres Strait region can claim over a century of exposure to missionaries of most all denominations, Government protectors and administrators, a cash economy, and the presence of literature as part of the daily life. With the arrival of new communication technology to the region, and at the time Watson was developing this continua, there was a regular television program to the islands, a local radio program and telephone connection to all the islands. All entailed, directly and indirectly, the use of various texts or at the least exposure to them. The availability of video on all islands also provided similar access to (video displayed) print and 'the world of the literate'. Regular transport within the region also improved the distribution of newsagent texts. But not all Islanders chose to partake in the literate traditions. At the same time a seventy-year-old member of the regional education committee is able to read and write fluently in English, a fifteen-year-old leaves school in the 1990s with only the basic competencies in English literacy. These observations and influences hint at the wide variance possible in the effects and presence of literate texts to the region.

With this in mind, consider that Watson's continuum primarily acknowledges that the further removed geographically a group is from Western society then the less the degree to which they become involved with print, and consequently the less such textual 'ways with words' influence their speech registers. Hence her continuum appears to deal with the interaction of the written forms only in general terms of 'contact' and does not in any way address the qualitative aspects of interaction with the text.

Even adding into Watson's continuum the variety of language use in each of her settings serves only to illustrate what we already know: that because Torres Strait Islander communities have only been involved with print texts since the latter part of the nineteenth century and because groups vary in their degree of involvement with 'mainstream' society, English speakers, their disciplines and their institutions, they also vary in the degree to which they are able to make sense of the more 'specialised' registers of English.

Watson's continua, while an ambitious preliminary attempt to identify 'differences' among Indigenous groups to the English language, and therefore starting points to engage in formal learning processes, stops short of placing constituent communities appropriately. For example: the limited investigation of the influence of the printed material on speech registers in each community; the lack of consideration given to the influence of the second language; the low priority given to migratory movements between constituent communities; the inconsistencies of groupings from continua to locating communities on the grid (e.g. the merging of rural non-traditional, metro-urban and rural-urban communities); and the statement that inclusion of Islander people would group along a similar continua, all point to the need for a better understanding of the sociology of language of both Islander and Aboriginal groups.

Categorising these groups to position discussions on appropriate curriculum and pedagogy would best be treated with caution. Placing groups along an oral/literate continua is to generalise, perhaps inaccurately, about certain groups of people. Amongst educators and curriculum developers, such categorisation can lead to standardisation, which when reflected in pedagogy and curriculum, leaves teachers no closer to addressing the complexities of individual linguistic and social backgrounds.

In reference to Torres Strait Islander students, consideration of only the predominate language used in the community is insufficient. The assumption with language specific approaches — whether they be bilingual, ESL or traditional language focused — is that all students have a common language and, as shown here, it is no longer tenable to assume they have the same linguistic background or resources. The first, second and oftentimes third language spoken, also become significant factors in understanding the characteristics of Islanders, and make any categorisation of Torres Strait Islanders more complex and problematic. It is therefore necessary to pay closer attention to the individual capabilities of each student before assuming linguistic relationships to the English language.

But where to start, and how practical is it for teachers of classrooms with such diversity of linguistic backgrounds? Which language does the teacher start with — the common language or the student's first language? Which first language? Who decides? What linguistic resources do 'white' teachers have to deal with this? This is the cause of so much ambivalence in classrooms today, leaving teachers bewildered with basic pedagogical questions like: how to conference Kriol texts produced by students and in which language; how to connect representational resources in these texts to link students to core curriculum areas; what constitutes a linguistic resource, grammar, knowledge and skills. Herein lies the very reason why student writing experiences in primary schools are limited to recounts from one year level to the next (Nakata, Jensen, Nakata, 1995). It is one thing to recognise important representational resources of the learners but it is a very strategic pedagogical task to capture them as 'hooks' to engage learners in other learning activities — an area where we, as educators, are still to learn a great deal more.

However, it is the effect that worries me greatly. The readiness with which the Islanders' unproblematised 'oral tradition' comes to constitute a fundamental component to a linear model is troublesome. Constituting Islander language communities at one end of the spectrum and English language communities at the other effectively sets up the way to understand educational matters as well as the direction of the reform process. Thinking about educational matters then must begin at one point and progress must be staged: there needs to be mastery of one stage before the other; failure at any stage breaks the chain and therefore the link to the next. This is evident in the argument of language advocates that literacy in one language provides the 'readiness' for literate competencies in another.

The ready acceptance of a linear model also sutures over the fact that English language communities come from and still are part of an oral tradition. The oral and literate world are not separate but entwined, inter-textual and continue to evolve as traditions and artefacts of our engagements with each other; we all continue to live in times where there are oral traditions. Just as Saussure failed to give primacy to the dialectics of the material world in the identification of a language group, bilingual advocates fail to explore in more detail the value of complexities in the lifeworld of Islanders in their everyday communications.

Like Williamson, approaches to the language issues in 'new times' promise much more than it delivered. And to leave basic points unresolved in theoretical frameworks, in turn, can serve directly to frustrate progress of the educational issues in professional practice.

Culture

Just as the early literature inscribed Islanders as 'lost souls', 'savages' and 'child-like', the educational literature of the 1980s and 1990s continued the same mode of abstracting to another disciplinary plane the material realities and conditions of the Islander as exotic experiences, habits, languages, economies and cultures — a preoccupation with universal cultural categories where images of the Islander people remain undifferentiated, and unproblematised as 'Western talk'. As Raymond Williams (1977) and Roland Barthes (1972) noted of bourgeois practice, transformations of realities into images of the world are not only an intellectual production but also an ideological one.

The following reading of 'culture' is to explicate the politics of 'taken-for-granted' positions, to again disrupt the 'givens' and to highlight what has become habitual in practice and 'natural' in its historical transformation. The cultural Islander represented in the *National Aboriginal and Torres Strait Islander Education Policy* (Department of Employment, Education and Training, 1989) is a particularly good example for this. It exemplifies well the third area of concentration by non-Islanders with cultural difference and contemporary discourse in the formal education process.

In the National Policy Statement the Islander appears as one of Australia's Indigenous people with distinctive cultural attributes: 'Aboriginal people and Torres Strait Islanders are the Indigenous peoples of Australia. Their distinctive cultures are a rich and important part of the nation's living heritage' (Department of Employment, Education and Training, 1989, p. 5). Likewise, education is redefined as a cultural event:

> The historically-developed education processes of...[Islander] culture have been eroded in many communities for a variety of reasons. The education arrangements and procedures established from... [Western] traditions have not adequately recognised and accommodated the particular needs and circumstances of...[Islander] people. (Department of Employment, Education and Training, 1989, p. 5)

Societal relations are similarly implicated with 'culture': 'Not only have...[Islander] people been consequently disadvantaged, but Australian society has not come to understand and appreciate the significance of...[Islander] culture' (1989, p. 5).

In the process of developing this national policy statement, those who were consulted also agreed to an education policy to be developed 'in harmony with employment development policies...[to] enable...[Islander] people to pursue their own goals in community development, cultural maintenance, self-management and economic independence' (1989, p. 8). Furthermore, it is claimed that the national policy statement 'represents a co-operative effort to develop more effective processes for the education of...[Islander] people' (p. 5). This becomes hard for anyone to ignore. And when it is said to be 'predicated upon the principles of social justice, equity, economic efficiency and cost-effective service delivery' (p. 6) and with a 'major purpose...to achieve broad equity between...[Islander] people and other Australians in access, participation and outcomes in all forms of education' (p. 9), the national policy appears as a logical, coherent, all-encompassing educational policy.

As a sign from within the domain of anthropology, 'culture', if we consult a basic undergraduate text book by Harris (1985), 'refers to the socially acquired traditions. When anthropologists speak of a human culture, they usually mean the total socially acquired lifestyle of a group of people' (p. 114). These include ways for 'speaking, thinking, feeling, and acting' (p. 114) which also serve as norms or standards to 'society's culture of domestic [and public] life' (p. 114). To refer to the Islander as a cultural subject, the national policy statement of 1989 borrows an anthropological schema of how the Torres Strait Islander is seen as an organised group, regardless of what the Islander perceives of herself/himself. Culture, in these ways, sets up from the outset priorities to represent the collective habits of a people. As the collective experience of a group of people, 'culture' in policy is a referent to inter-group relations with little emphasis on intra-group diversity. In other words, individual members, their age, their gender, their religion, their schooling needs, their interests, their economic needs, their politics, their individual persuasions and their own experiences remain undifferentiated, and suffice under the common group norm as the 'cultural other'.

Next, when the national policy statement argues that 'historically-developed education processes of...[Islander] culture have been eroded' (Department of Employment, Education and Training, 1989, p. 5), the dynamic nature of the cultural phenomenon takes on a new role. As a socially constructed and historically situated entity, culture is in process of change and adaptation. 'Erosion', however, is a metaphor that begins from the perception of culture as a foundational and potentially static entity (Luke, Nakata, Singh and Smith, 1993). This covers over the notion of culture as constantly changing. What then emerges is a viewpoint of 'culture' as museum pieces for the anthropological gaze, as unitary static objects, which renders the Islanders' historical presence in some distant anthropological schema of a different tradition.

The acceptance of a universal term in these ways stands to omit the array of factors that contribute to 'the most educationally disadvantaged group in Australia' (p. 7). For instance, the diagnosis of the Islanders' situation as 'eroding' leads policy one way to prioritise an educational agenda reliant on adding in, restoring and preserving strategies to reinstate the 'nation's living heritage' and relegates to the margins extant teaching and learning practices that have failed students for decades.

Yes, the discourse of a 'culturally different' agenda has enabled researchers to gain considerable insights into the alienation of the Islander in schooling. For instance, research into incongruent strategies in curricula and pedagogical techniques highlighted practices that were not appropriate to Islanders. But without an analysis of differential power affiliated with particular cultural discourses and practices, the recognition of 'difference' can amount to a resignation to 'difference' and to a 'lack' of 'institutional power' and 'capital'. That is, while teachers, curricula and academic institutions across the country have become aware of and implemented projects based on culture, the recognition of cultural differences has mostly resulted in ways for researchers and practitioners to explain the Islander's existence, the Islander's resistance and the Islander's failure. Relevance or sensitivity to cultural differences alone however does not change traditional classroom practices from alienating the Islander in formal learning processes.

It may appear here that future policies require a departure from the more favoured cultural premise to other conceptual themes and representations. Or, it may appear to others that policy only requires additional themes. However, to represent the Islander in other thematic schemas without making problematic 'culture' as in a political position would be to accept underpinning schemas, and to accept apparatuses that will again serve to embed fundamental apolitical positions between the state and the Islanders. Allow me to turn to this now.

Culture, in a political position, and as it sits in the national policy statement, has been a term used to posit within defined boundaries allowable, apolitical identities and traditions. For example, while interpretations of the Islander as the nation's living heritage are acceptable in policy, political interpretations of the Indigenous peoples with prior rights to this continent are posited outside acceptable definitions. That is, Indigenous people can have a presence in a history that belongs to some distant tradition 'culture' but not in a history of invasion and stealth of their land and resources. Culture, then, can be seen as the premise for a system of inclusionary and exclusionary practices where ideas are either won or lost. The supremacy of one over the other prevails as authority over the other, as either honoured or silenced, as positive or negative.

As an inclusionary/exclusionary apparatus, the cultural subject in policy offers in a public domain a premise where the Islander can be read about as culturally exotic, understood as traditionally oriented, or predicted as aesthetically rich; and, in turn, it offers the content to hold Islanders to account for their traditions without ever visiting the islands. Hence, the anthropological exotica of native culture (e.g. Said's Orientalist) is composed as a new pantheon of quasi-metaphysical conditions and standards to live up to (Williams, 1977). If I fail to conduct myself according to the exotic standards I could be seen as 'un-Islander like', or to be neglecting traditional values, or worse still as 'buying into Western values'. In short, the imposition of disciplinary and disciplining standards calls in the Islander to measure herself/himself against the new public knowledge and to juxtapose what she/he does daily as marginal and private.

Culture in policy as defined within acceptable categories is no threat to the state because it sets up a public knowledge where individuals can self-regulate their own behaviours (e.g. internalising culture as the rudimentary premise for viewing and solving problems). Control and discipline are assured through self-regulation and yet operate outside the state. The effect of culture as a disciplining concept, then, not only works as a self-regulating device for the Islander but also serves as the mechanism that works for those in charge — except power is not exercised over another. Once regulated and positioned in the cultural discourse, the culturalised Islander exercises power over herself/himself.

As a disciplinary concept, culture has become the mode to identify with a position to assert rights, a guide to develop a future; and yet to conform with the cultural identity as an apolitical, ahistorical, docile subject of the past, the Islanders give up their standpoint on the material realities confronting their own situation. This is because culture constitutes simultaneously the premise where the Islanders can be disciplined, divided and marginalised.

Nevertheless, culture does set out the positive thesis, the ideal and the target of government initiatives. All are able to view the governments as doing the best they can. And as a document with humanitarian appeal, culture in policy stands as an authorised domain either for anyone to romanticise the Islander or recall the Islander to account for herself/himself. For example, ongoing government projects and ongoing low-performances in schooling have led the general public to form an opinion of the education of Islander people as 'not trying hard enough' or that the government is dealing with an 'intractable problem'. Yet the national policy, as a public (i.e. democratically processed with Indigenous education consultants) document, which sets — and has set for the past eighteen years — the educational agenda for the schools (i.e. schools that continue to fail Islander students), receives little attention.

Culture in policy as authorised knowledge, as public knowledge, as manufactured knowledge is a treatise on the Islander that provides the means for education experts to measure, gauge, evaluate and forecast future priorities in schooling, curricula, pedagogics, research, funding and other educational programs for the Islander. As a precursor to the classroom, the Islander student can be made accountable through the cultural apolitical themes: where cultural values are honoured and where political statements are shunned; where conformist behaviours are rewarded and deviants are punished; where positive aspects of the cultural interpretations (e.g. art, song and dance) are applauded, Land Rights 'attitudes' are ridiculed and claims to Sea Rights are held to be an 'unreasonable' demand.

The culturalist agenda has become practice among education experts who have taken up positive aspects of the myths of their discipline and, in turn, constituted new knowledge without any knowledge of the Islander people. It has set up as a positive (liberal) goal that preserves primary disciplinary and disciplining apparatuses already in place between the state and the people and, in these ways, reifies a long practice that continues to silence the standpoints of the Islanders.

As 'culture' continues to be deployed today without a critique of underlying theoretical schemas, the various forms of representation of the Islander will effectively continue as a fundamental part of the problem as readily as it has been shown to be a fundamental part of the solution. As Foucault (1977) found with prison reforms, the innovation and not the displacement of the great models of punitive imprisonment meant that, 'before providing a solution, [the models]…themselves posed problems: the problem of their existence and the problem of their diffusion' (p. 120).

9
Disciplining Indigenous Knowledge

>...another information set from which data can be extracted to plug into scientific frameworks. (Nakashima & de Guchteneire, 1999, p. 2)

In colonial times, and residually in so-called postcolonial times, Indigenous peoples' knowledge was relegated to the realm of the 'primitive'. Aspects of this knowledge were incorporated into the discipline of early anthropology so that others could understand us. But the knowledge systems that underpinned everyday life in Indigenous people's contexts were generally considered as obstacles to progress along the path to modern civilisation. In many places, our knowledge was largely ignored or suppressed; and as a result of Indigenous peoples' dispersal and dislocation from land and way of life, much of it was lost.

Until the 1980s Indigenous Knowledge surfaced in very few academic disciplines, for example, 'anthropology, development sociology and geography' (Warren, von Liebenstein & Slikkerveer, 1993, p. 1). However, Indigenous Knowledge now surfaces in academic and scientific circles, in the fields of ecology, soil science, veterinary medicine, forestry, human health, aquatic resource management, botany, zoology, agronomy, agricultural economics, rural sociology, mathematics, management science, agricultural education and extension, fisheries, range management, information science, wildlife management, and water resource management (Warren, von Liebenstein & Slikkerveer, 1993, p. 1).

Understandably, Indigenous peoples welcome the elevation of status that comes with increased recognition of their knowledge systems after centuries of dismissal and disintegration (Eyzaguirre, 2001). As well, the emergence of re-valued and revised 'Indigenous Knowledge' for inclusion into program and course content in formal education programs also excites those who see it as a source of 'unmediated' knowledge, untainted by the 'white man' and containing the possibility to reclaim, regenerate and reinstate Indigenous practices and ways of understanding the world (e.g. Battiste & Youngblood Henderson, 2000).

But what happens, or what do we need to consider, when Indigenous Knowledge is brought into relation with the disciplines in the academy? In their differences, Indigenous Knowledge systems and Western scientific ones are considered so disparate as to be 'incommensurable' (Verran, 2005) or 'irreconcilable' (Russell, 2005) on cosmological, epistemological and ontological grounds. In our arguments to include such knowledge in disciplinary content in Indigenous higher education, how these differences frame possible understanding and misunderstanding at the surface levels of aspects of Indigenous Knowledge requires some attention. As well, the discursive framing of arguments that now elevate the value of Indigenous Knowledge are worthy of examination.

The renewed interest in our knowledge systems and practices is widespread and global. It has emerged in times of 'new configurations in global relations…[where] the centrality of knowledge…[is] the emerging currency in that relationship' (Hoppers, 2000, p. 283). The global discourse on Indigenous Knowledge is overwhelmingly driven by research into sustainable development practices in developing countries (supported mainly by United Nations [UN] programs and Non-government Organisations [NGOs]) and the scientific community's concern about loss of biodiversity of species and ecosystems and the future implications of that for the whole planet (Myer, 1998). The disciplines noted here reflect these two areas of humanitarian and scientific concern. In the human sciences the elevation of Indigenous Knowledge has been driven more by the academic interrogation of dominant discourses and the recognition and valuing of social and cultural diversity (Agrawal, 1995b).

Within the humanitarian and scientific areas, a number of other interested parties emerge (see special issue of the Indigenous Knowledge and Development Monitor, 1993). These include scientists who recognise that Indigenous Knowledge needs to be recorded or validated if any of it is to be incorporated into the scientific corpus and utilised. Also interested are the agencies operating in developing countries that realise the importance of 'local' knowledge in solving problems at the local level. These two lead to the interest of researchers and those professionals involved in documentation and recording systems. Conservationists have developed a special interest in the environment and species degradation and the disappearing knowledge base of societies under pressure from development and industrialisation. There is increasing overlap between conservation and scientific interests as bio-prospecting and gene-harvesting assume greater priority. In response to much of this interest, political advocates interested in the tensions between North and South have emerged (e.g. Saw, 1992). This advocacy is carried out by various people and means, including activism from Indigenous peoples themselves and different bodies and mechanisms within the UN. Overarching all these interests is the capitalist interest. To capitalist interests, Indigenous Knowledge is merely another resource for potential profit.

Out of these sectorial interests, we see the conceptualisation of Indigenous Knowledge becoming detached from holistic notions of 'culture' in the human sciences, and to be more reflective of the humanitarian, practical, environmental and scientific interests that are promoting its use and documentation in developing countries. It has become an umbrella term, not limited to Indigenous peoples but inclusive of those in the developing countries who struggle to survive and who still rely on traditional forms of knowledge whether they be Indigenous within developed and developing nation-states, formerly colonised, or distant or recent migrant groups in developing countries. One estimation of this group of people is some 80 per cent of the world's population who rely on Indigenous Knowledge for either medicine or food (Rural Advancement Foundation International (RAFI) cited in the United Nations Development Programme's (UNDP) Civil Society Organisations and Participation Programme (CSOPP), 1995). At the same time, Indigenous Knowledge has become more fragmented and specialised as scientists and humanitarians pick at the bits and pieces that fit with their interests and disciplines.

Excepting the role of political advocates but not their presence, all these interests illustrate how totally a Western interest this interest in Indigenous knowledge is. The documentation of such knowledge by scientists, the storage of information in databases in academic institutions, whether they be gene banks or electronic networks, all looks remarkably similar to former colonial enterprises which co-opted land, resources and labour in the interest of their own prosperity through trade and value-adding. According to documentations at the UNDP, Indigenous Knowledge fuels multi-billion dollar genetics supply industries, ranging from food and pharmaceuticals in developed countries to chemical product, energy and other manufactures (UNDP's CSOPP, 1995, p. 9).

Yet developing countries and NGOs struggle to find ways to ensure the disadvantaged of the world have access to sustainable supplies of clean water and basic food staples, and international bodies struggle to enact and implement mechanisms for ensuring Indigenous peoples' knowledge is protected and recompensed (e.g. UNDP, UN Food & Agriculture Organisation, UN Convention on Biological Diversity etc.).

One thing is certain in all of this. Indigenous knowledge is increasingly discussed by all as a commodity, something of value, something that can be value-added, something that can be exchanged, traded, appropriated, preserved, something that can be excavated and mined. Or, as Douglas Nakashima and Paul de Guchteneire (1999) put it, 'another information set from which data can be extracted to plug into scientific frameworks' (p. 2).

Indigenous Knowledge is therefore different things in different places to different people. There is contention about some of its characteristics. However, a quick and crude distillation of some of its elements from various sources gives a reasonable picture of how it is conceptualised broadly in this global discourse. As a system of knowledge it is understood in terms of its distance from 'scientific knowledge'. What is many, many systems is currently and variously recognised from Western perspectives as 'local knowledge' — knowledge that is 'unique to a given culture or society' (Warren, 1991, 1993), and as being 'oral, rural, holistic, powerless, and culturally-embedded' (Indigenous Knowledge & Development Monitor, 1993; von Liebenstein, 2000). This is the result of 'dynamic innovation' although informal and unsystematised (UNDP's CSOPP, 1995) and it is 'continually influenced by internal creativity and experimentation as well as by contact with external systems' (Flavier, de Jesus & Navarro, 1995). An African perspective reminds us that, 'an understanding is required of Indigenous knowledge and its role in community life from an integrated perspective that includes both spiritual and material aspects of a society as well as the complex relations between them' (Morolo, 2002, p. 1). A number of terms also are used interchangeably: local knowledge, traditional knowledge (TK), Indigenous knowledge (IK), traditional environmental or ecological knowledge (TEK), or Indigenous technical knowledge (ITK).

An important aspect of Indigenous Knowledge that is overlooked in some definitions is that Indigenous peoples hold collective rights and interests in their knowledge (Casey, 2001; Davis, 1997, 1998). This, along with its oral nature, the diversity of Indigenous Knowledge systems, and the fact that management of this knowledge involves rules regarding secrecy and sacredness (Davis, 1997, 1998) means that the issues surrounding ownership and therefore protection (see Hunter, 2002; Janke, 1997, 1998) are quite different from those inscribed in Western institutions. Western concepts of intellectual property have for some time been recognised as inadequate (Casey, 2001; Janke, 1997, 1998). This is a most complex area for many reasons (see also work by Ellen & Harris, 1996; Ellen, Parkes & Bicker, 2000). Much work is being done in the UN (e.g. United Nations Conference on Trade and Development [UNCTAD], 2002) and by Indigenous groups to develop adequate principles and a different system for Indigenous intellectual and cultural property protection.

Accepting these conceptions of Indigenous Knowledge immediately points to some of the contradictions in current activity — scientific, developmental and in information management. One contradiction is that the strategy of archiving and disseminating Indigenous Knowledge runs contradictory to the very conceptual basis of what is seen to be 'indigenous' in Indigenous Knowledge (Agrawal, 1995a, 1995b). Strategies of conservation involve the collection, documentation, storage and dissemination of Indigenous Knowledge (Koenig, 2001). When it employs methods and instruments of Western science, which involve fragmentation across categories of information, isolation and *ex situ* storage in regional, national and international archives and networks then it begins to lay itself open to the same criticisms as 'Western science', which has largely failed in development contexts. It becomes not embedded in local meanings and contexts but separated from its original context — an entity to be studied, worked on, developed, integrated, transferred and ultimately changed to fit another. Pablo B Eyzaguirre, a senior scientist at the International Plant Genetic Resources Institute in Rome, expresses similar concerns:

> [t]aking 'validated' nuggets of Indigenous knowledge out of its cultural context may satisfy an outside researcher's need, or even solve a technical problem in development, but it may undermine the knowledge system itself. (2001, p. 1)

Of course these are the very reasons for which Indigenous Knowledge is of interest. I am not going to argue the extreme position that Indigenous Knowledge should be left alone and forever isolated. And I am not going to argue that it should not be documented. Recovery and preservation of lost and endangered knowledge is extremely urgent and important for Indigenous communities (see Langton & Ma Rhea, 2005). I venture to say, however, that knowledge recovery led by Indigenous communities would not look the same as that led by scientists, developmental technologists and conservationists — even when participatory. For without a doubt, the collection and documentation of Indigenous Knowledge by the development and scientific communities is a very partial enterprise, selecting and privileging some Indigenous Knowledge while discarding and excluding others. Of course, if what Indigenous communities choose to document is of no apparent value to others, then the cost of documentation may be an obstacle for those communities.

These concerns aside for the moment, there is in the development literature an acceptance of the value of integrating two systems of knowledge — traditional and scientific — in order to produce new knowledge and practices that provide solutions for sustainable development and developing countries and communities. Some authors (e.g. von Liebenstein, 2000), aware of the dominance and perceived superiority of scientific knowledge, take care to stress the complementarity of the two knowledge systems. In much of the literature, there is an emphasis on incorporation of Indigenous Knowledge into strategies for application (e.g. UNDP's CSOP, 1995), or for scientific validation (The World Bank, n. d.), or further research (Morolo, 2002), or for developing foundations for sustainable development (von Liebenstein, 2000). Some have been prepared to argue for the need for models of community information management when integrating knowledge information systems (von Liebenstein, 2000).

However, this literature on the integration of knowledge systems rarely interrogates in any critical way the distinctions drawn between Indigenous Knowledge and scientific systems of knowledge. This is to be expected. Developmentalists are primarily concerned with what works in practice, and the discussion of binary systems of thought is the realm of the theoretical. But I would argue that addressing the theoretical underpinnings of practice is critical to any substantive understanding of knowledge systems. Arun Agrawal (1995b) makes the point that in the elevation of and talk about Indigenous Knowledge, people 'commit them[selves] to a dichotomy between Indigenous and Western knowledge' (p. 2) when theoretically the attempt to separate them cannot be sustained.

First he argues that because there are similarities across the categories and substantial differences within each of them that a simple separation on the basis of characteristics as announced in the literature on Indigenous Knowledge fails in substance. Second, he suggests that the duality between them assumes fixity of both knowledge systems in time and space that is inherently false. The conceptualisation of Indigenous Knowledge currently promotes the idea of more fixity for that system than for Western knowledge, which is seen to move ever onward in time and space. Whatever, Agrawal argues, that the development of knowledge systems everywhere 'suggests contact, diversity, exchange, communication, learning and transformation among different systems of knowledge and beliefs' (p. 3). Third, he interrogates the suggestion that Indigenous Knowledge is socially and culturally embedded but Western scientific knowledge is not. He cites contemporary philosophers of science who reveal the 'social moorings' of science, who foreground a view of science as culture and practice, and who see science as 'relative to culture', or 'relative to interests', to illustrate just how much Western knowledge is as 'anchored in specific milieu as any other systems of knowledge' (p. 3). Arguing the limitations of the duality, he argues that 'to successfully build new epistemic foundations, accounts of innovation and experimentation must bridge the Indigenous/Western divide' (p. 3) rather than be founded on the simple separation of the two systems as expressed in the literature. Perhaps the key issue to note is that the global push to describe and document Indigenous Knowledge is gaining momentum without little commensurate interest in the epistemological study of Indigenous Knowledge systems.

However, the literature on Indigenous Knowledge is growing internationally and is a worthy area for analysis and assessment. It crisscrosses from critique to caution, to advocacy, to theory, to innovation and to examples in practice (see Agrawal, 1995a, 1995b, 1996; Battiste & Youngblood Henderson, 2000; Christie, 2005; Ellen & Harris, 1996; Gegeo & Watson-Gegeo, 2001; Langton & Ma Rhea, 2005; Russell, 2005; LT Smith, 1999; Verran, 2005). It is important to read it critically enough to situate the arguments of various positions taken in this literature. The work in Australian Indigenous contexts by Helen Verran (2005) and Michael Christie (2005), in particular, provide cautions about the difficulties associated with documentation and translating and working Indigenous and Western knowledge systems alongside each other.

Differences at epistemological and ontological levels mean that, in the academy, it is not possible to bring in Indigenous Knowledge and plonk it in the curriculum unproblematically as if it is another data set for Western knowledge to discipline and test. Indigenous Knowledge systems and Western knowledge systems work off different theories of knowledge that frame,

> who can be a knower, what can be known, what constitutes knowledge, sources of evidence for constructing knowledge, what constitutes

truth, how truth is to be verified, how evidence becomes truth, how valid inferences are to be drawn, the role of belief in evidence, and related issues. (Gegeo & Watson-Gegeo, 2001, p. 57)

One knowledge system cannot legitimately verify the 'claims to truth' of the other via its own standards and justifications (Verran, 2005). So incommensurable are the ways these systems 'do' knowledge, that even with understanding of epistemological and ontological differences and endless descriptions of them in various sites of knowledge production, we cannot just 'do' Indigenous Knowledge in the curriculum. In universities, we subscribe to the institutional arrangements and practices of the Western and scientific knowledge traditions. Learning and 'doing' knowledge in this context is mediated by the disciplinary organisation of knowledge and its discursive and textual practices. In this context, we deal with representations of Indigenous Knowledge already circumscribed by the Western disciplines and the discursive positioning of various disciplinary practices, including scientific paradigms, historical understandings, particular sets of interests, various theoretical positions, technologies of textual production, and so on. These representations may carefully and usefully describe the application of different approaches of each knowledge system to a common point of focus to generate understanding. But the way we come to know and understand, discuss, critique and analyse in university programs is not the way Indigenous people come to know in local contexts.

However, in the academy and on the ground, the talk of Indigenous Knowledge systems, rather than of cultures, does bring Indigenous Knowledge, its systems, its expressions and traditions of practice into a different relation with Western science than was possible through the discipline of anthropology. As early chapters in this book have described, early anthropological studies of Indigenous societies and cultures were used to provide the evidence for disciplinary theories of human evolution and development (Peterson, 1990). Knowledge production in this area served to rationalise an array of practices and activities of liberal capitalism as it expanded across the globe. But, despite a shifting basis of inquiry over the last century, all knowledge production about Indigenous people still works within a wider set of social relations that rationalise, justify and work to operationalise a complicated apparatus of bureaucratic, managerial and disciplinary actions that continue to confine the lives of Indigenous people.

We can argue that interest in Indigenous Knowledge systems begins in a different place, but we have to concede that Indigenous Knowledge is similarly positioned within discursive fields as any other knowledge production 'about us'. Still, this does not deny the argument that the current interest in Indigenous Knowledge is emerging at a different historical moment where Indigenous peoples are much better positioned within the legal-political order where issues of rights, sovereignty, self-determination and historical redress provide a better base for the assertion of Indigenous interests.

So, even though it is still predominately non-Indigenous or Western parameters that give shape to the Indigenous Knowledge discourse, it does ask questions that relate to its usefulness and value in a variety of contexts, including Indigenous contexts. This brings a focus in some — but by no means all — contexts to more collaborative and locally-generated practice on the ground (Gumbula, 2005; Christie, 2005), more opportunities to preserve and maintain Indigenous Knowledge within communities (Langton & Ma Rhea, 2005) both through documentation processes and through reinvigorated interest in its future utility (Anderson, 2005, Hunter, 2005), and especially for strengthening Indigenous social, economic and political institutions (Ma Rhea, 2004). It also brings a focus to sharing and transferring aspects of Indigenous Knowledge across contexts for much wider human benefit. In best practice circumstances, the transferring and/or integration of Indigenous Knowledge across knowledge domains provides due recognition and legal protection to those aspects and innovations of knowledge that are Indigenous in origin. In worst practice, of course, global interest in Indigenous Knowledge threatens its integrity and exploits it on an even greater scale.

In the academy, and in Australia — whether Indigenous or non-Indigenous, lecturer or student — most of us develop our general and/or detailed understandings of Indigenous Knowledge, traditions and practices via the interpretations and representations of it in the English language by Western knowledge specialists or scientists. This is not to deny that some Indigenous students and lecturers develop knowledge *in situ* in Indigenous contexts. But it is to suggest that the larger conceptualisation and characteristics that describe and situate Indigenous Knowledge vis-a-vis Western knowledge, comes to us through the filter of its discourse. What aspect of Indigenous Knowledge gets representation, and how it is represented in this space reflects a complex set of intersections of interests and contestations: from what aspects of knowledge are recognised or valued, what can be envisioned in terms of representation or utility, what sorts of collaborations are practical or possible, the capacity of current technologies to represent aspects of Indigenous Knowledge without destroying its integrity; to what research projects are funded, to the quality of experts in both knowledge traditions, to the particular interests of scientists or disciplinary sectors, to what is finally included in databases, or published and circulated in the public or scholarly domain. And importantly, the negative of all of those: what is not of interest, or value; what is not able to attract funding; what is not investigated, documented or published; what is misinterpreted during the process of abstracting Indigenous Knowledge; and what remains marginalised at the peripheries and at risk of being written out, not recognised as valid knowledge or forgotten.

In this contested space between the two knowledge systems, things are not clearly black or white, Indigenous or Western. In this space are histories, politics, economics, multiple and interconnected discourses, social practices and knowledge technologies which condition how we all come to look at the world, how we come to know and understand our changing realties in the everyday, and how and what knowledge we operationalise in our daily lives. Much of what we bring to this is tacit and unspoken knowledge, those assumptions by which we make sense and meaning in our everyday world. On the ground, in practical contexts where Indigenous Knowledge experts are in direct contact with scientific experts, this is the space of difficult translation between different ways of understanding reality (Verran, 2005). But, in the intellectual discourse, translation has already occurred. Indigenous Knowledge is re-presented and re-configured as part of the corpus 'about' us and is already discursively bounded, ordered and organised by others and their sets of interests.

In the academy, then, we come to learn 'about' Indigenous Knowledge in similar ways to how we came to learn 'about' Indigenous cultures and issues via the emerging or established disciplines. It is important for those wanting to bring Indigenous Knowledge into teaching and learning contexts to understand what happens when Indigenous Knowledge is conceptualised simplistically and oppositionally from the standpoint of scientific paradigms as everything that is 'not science'. It is also important to understand what happens when Indigenous Knowledge is documented in ways that disembody it from the people who are its agents, when the 'knowers' of that knowledge are separated out from what comes to be 'the known', in ways that dislocate it from its locale, and separate it from the social institutions that uphold and reinforce its efficacy, and cleave it from the practices that constantly renew its meanings in the here and now. And it is also important to consider what disintegrations and transformations occur when it is redistributed across

Western categories of classification, when it is managed in databases via technologies that have been developed in ways that suit the hierarchies, linearity, abstraction and objectification of Western knowledge — all of which are the antithesis of Indigenous Knowledge traditions and technologies.

In incorporating understandings of Indigenous Knowledge into curriculum areas, in asking our students to read accounts of it, or to discuss its potential applications in a range of professional contexts, or use it in applied ways, it must be acknowledged that we are screening it through a filter that positions it to serve our educational objectives, and which draws on our own prior theoretical investments in knowledge and knowledge practice.

PART THREE

10

The Cultural Interface

> Either you think — or else others have to think for you and take power from you, pervert and discipline your natural tastes, civilise and sterilise you.
>
> (Scott Fitzgerald, 1993, p. 269)

In earlier chapters, I raised questions about the documentation of Torres Strait Islanders. The University of Cambridge expedition to the Torres Strait islands just over a century ago gathered extensive field data, which was then used to describe Islanders in terms of their distance from 'civilised' societies. The research team tested and described many of our physical, mental and social characteristics on a comparative basis with people in Western communities. A full reading of their scientific method, and particularly their interpretation of data and conclusions drawn, is an excellent example of just how culturally-embedded their thinking and practices were, and how much they were, to use an expression that Michel Foucault (1970) coined, merely 'in the vicinity of science'.

This does not lead me to wish these texts had never been produced or that they should not stand on library shelves today. Quite the opposite, I would like to see them as basic reading for Torres Strait students. What better way to develop critical reading skills, to gain some understanding of systems of thought and knowledge production and to anchor down a Torres Strait or Indigenous standpoint in students' analyses of systems of thought and knowledge. My interest in them as texts for critical study is not to contest 'what is the truth about Islanders' but to rediscover the methods of knowledge production and how particular knowledges achieve legitimacy and authority at the expense of other knowledge.

Earlier chapters also revealed the historical inscription of Islanders as the exotic 'Other'. The viewing of Islanders as 'artefacts of the past' enabled them to be viewed as the legitimate and natural subjects and objects of study and of social, economic and political reorganisation. For example, the conceptual and theoretical distance produced by the construction of Islanders as children was paralleled by a very real and tangible distance established between Islanders and others as it manifested in differential treatment and all the unequal relations that accrued from that. The effects of the 'paternal–child relationship' in this differential treatment reaffirmed the 'sense' or 'truth' of the assumptions that underpinned it.

Contemporary theories of Islanders as culturally different but equal interpret us more positively through our cultural behaviour and customs, which demonstrate Islander distinctiveness, history and tradition. This framework is about returning to Islanders, in both theoretical and practical terms, our 'equal' humanity and reinstating the value of our 'different' former lives in the past. This approach makes sense and is useful in explaining the Islander position because it seems to capture the best of both worlds. It allows Islanders some link with the past and it insists on equality in the present to eliminate any unequal effects of their distance from others.

In seeking a better basis for explaining the position of Islanders, the point is not to deny that Islanders are equal or different. The evidence of Islanders as culturally different and of equal humanity and capacity is observable in the everyday and once again reaffirms the 'sense' or 'truth' of this basic framework through which we order thinking about Islanders. But that previous construction of Islanders as savage, as child, as being in moral danger could also be evidenced in the everyday as six volumes of the Cambridge Anthropological Expedition and decades of government reports provided. Islanders have not essentially changed from inferior beings to equals, or from savages to culturally different people; the thinking around them has constituted them to cohere with the evolution of changes in a Western order of things.

The point is to consider a configuration that may be more productive for understanding our constitution within the broader society, its knowledge and interests, and the complex sets of social and discursive relations that position us and to consider possibilities for change that may emerge from that understanding. To do this requires the deployment of a different set of assumptions about Islanders in theory and practice. This, as I have already intimated, first requires a rethinking of the space in which Islanders interact with others. Second, it requires a deeper consideration of the ways in which the specificities of Islander experience are constituted in that space.

In the production of theories, understanding and knowledge of Islanders, whether we are Islanders or non-Islanders, we draw on already formed understandings from many points. In complex or contested terrains of overlapping knowledge systems different understandings often conflict, contradict, produce incoherence and make it difficult to 'make sense' of these contradictions. To make sense and bring order to it we organise our thinking according to a position that we believe is useful in explaining or making sense of all the elements. Building a theoretical configuration that will be more useful in explaining the position of Islanders in relation to the interaction between different historical systems of thought and complicated by the plurality of meanings that have been produced in the interactions between these systems for several generations will, of necessity, depend on generating a new set of understandings to inform analysis.

My thesis here is that if the assumptions underpinning a new theoretical framework were to take more account of Islander experience of these complex terrains and the ongoing Islander analysis that has remained subjugated by Western attempts to explain the position of Islanders, then more useful theories of the Islander position can be generated. How Islanders and others come to form the understandings and work from the assumptions that they do is of interest to any analysis of the Islander position entangled in the Western order of things.

The proposition here is not simply another perspective. It is foremost a proposition to expand assumptions underpinning theory based on a reading of how Islanders have been inscribed in Western systems of thought over the past century and more. It is a proposition to draw into theory principles that give primacy to the Islander lifeworlds as a complex terrain of political and social contests. In this terrain we have developed a reading of ourselves at the interface of colliding trajectories: we continue to maintain our values as a people of tradition; we have actively shaped new practices and adapted our own to deal with the encroaching elements; we are fighting against the odds; and we are making and re-making ourselves in the everyday. My proposition also draws into view the fact that we have some agency in history.

Understanding complex trajectories at the Interface

For the purposes of understanding the context of ongoing transformation of Islander lives, understanding Islanders is explicitly about understanding 'us' as we have been and continue to be constituted in our relations with others. Even in the way we now understand ourselves, we define ourselves primarily in our difference to others and the descriptions and characteristics of this difference have been firmly developed within the Western knowledge tradition. While we have maintained continuity with our former knowledge tradition, much of the content of this tradition has been transformed in its interactions with Western knowledge systems and continues to evolve in interactions with Western knowledge and its institutions, technologies and practices. Islanders exist, live and are positioned in a particular relation to other knowledge, interests and people as we pursue the dual goals of equality with other Australians while maintaining and preserving cultural distinctiveness. For Islanders, these dual goals address three critical interests viz., our ongoing continuity with former pre-colonial lives and traditions, our equal status with other Australian citizens rather than continued acceptance of a disadvantaged and marginalised status, and our aim to determine and manage our own futures.

Islanders in the Torres Strait, and many on the Australian mainland, operate on a daily basis in a space that is commonly understood as the intersection between two different cultures — the Islander and the non-Islander, the latter expressed as Australian, Western, mainstream or whatever. This position is often represented theoretically as a simple intersection of two different and often contesting elements that give rise to a 'clash of cultures', a 'cultural mismatch', 'cultural dissonance' or the dominance of one culture over the other, despite the efforts of Islanders to maintain 'our way'. The reality of this intersection, however, is much more than this.

To capture this complexity it is helpful to conceptualise this space, not as an intersection, but as a much broader interface. To connect with common understandings I use the term *Cultural Interface* but this is not restricted to cultural specificities. Neither can the Interface be viewed solely in structuralist terms though it does quite clearly have structural elements and effects, and it is in the structures of institutional practice that change and transformation is sought. It is much more complex than structural conditions suggest or can describe. Nor can its complexity be fully described in terms of the intersection between the theoretical and the 'real', expressed via the contestations and contradictions between textual and inter-textual representations of Islanders and the largely unrecorded, lived Islander experience of the everyday that constitutes Islanders' understanding and consciousness of their position. It is more than these intersections suggest, though this also explains and describes elements and effects of the complexities of the Interface. Nor can the position of Islanders at the Interface today be understood in the present without understanding some of the historical specificities of this Interface, for both historical constructions of Islanders and Islander responses in the historical everyday continue to inform the way we understand the Islander position in current times.

The Cultural Interface is constituted by points of intersecting trajectories. It is a multi-layered and multi-dimensional space of dynamic relations constituted by the intersections of time, place, distance, different systems of thought, competing and contesting discourses within and between different knowledge traditions, and different systems of social, economic and political organisation. It is a space of many shifting and complex intersections between different people with different histories, experiences, languages, agendas, aspirations and responses. As much as it is currently overlaid by various theories, narratives and arguments that work to produce cohesive, consensual and co-operative social practices, it is also a space that abounds with contradictions, ambiguities, conflict and contestation of meanings that emerge from these various shifting intersections. All these elements cohere together at the Interface in the everyday to inform, constrain or enable what can be seen or not seen, what can be brought to the surface or sutured over, what can be said or not said, heard or not heard, understood or misunderstood, what knowledge can be accepted, rejected, legitimised or marginalised, or what actions can be taken or not taken on both individual and collective levels.

The intersections between all these sets of relations shape the personal and interpersonal, the textual and inter-textual, the discursive, the inter- and intra-discursive, the theoretical and the structural and institutional frameworks through which people are understood, explained and regulated, and through which they understand, contest, resist, explain, self-regulate and uphold themselves. The elements, interests and relations between them in this space provide the conditions that shape thinking, understanding, knowledge, identities, history and change in a constant state of process. Most importantly, they shape how we can speak of ourselves and of each other, how we understand one another and the ongoing relations between us, and how we describe and represent our 'lived realities'. The elements at the Interface provide the conditions that allow or disallow the types of conversations and dialogue that can occur, and therefore are both derivative and constitutive of the relations that Islanders have with others in the everyday, in relation to institutional practice and in theoretical terms. For once others speak of and explain Islanders they are involved in the ongoing practice of shaping understanding about who and what Islanders are and how we can be understood. In that process they shape conversation and dialogue with an allegiance to their own ways of understanding and making sense of the complex, which in turn shapes any transformation of practice. Islanders have their language and conversation shaped and constituted by the conditions of the Cultural Interface, positioned as they are by these myriad intersections, even though their understandings of themselves and their position within these sets of relations may be quite different from those of others and at times from one another.

If we conceptualise the lived space of Islanders in these terms, then explanations of the Islander position through (op)positions such as 'black–white', 'them–us', 'traditional–Western' and 'Islander–mainstream' do not go nearly far enough in providing a useful framework for explaining the complexity of the Islander position. Yes, the Islander position may be conditioned in such intersections but the Interface can never be reducible to any one relation such as 'traditional–Western'. If we begin to consider what constitutes our understanding of 'traditional' and what constitutes our understanding of 'Western', then the boundaries between these notions become much less clear and the oppositional nature of the relation becomes much less useful as a way of explicating the Islander position within them. In the lived realities of Islander lives, conflicts and contestations of meaning often cut across Islander/Western domains of knowledge and understanding. The choices and options that emerge in these spaces do not emerge neatly from one domain or the other or in support of one or the other but from this complex space where many sets of understandings are now inextricably interrelated with each other.

The Cultural Interface cannot be viewed then in deterministic ways. It is a space of possibilities as well as constraints, which can have negative or positive consequences for different people at different times. That historically the negative consequences manifested to suppress Islander freedom and re-organise many aspects of our lives does not mean that all Islanders were uniformly oppressed throughout the entire period, or that there were no positives for us in that reorganisation, or that there were no spaces in which we could act, or assert, or be ourselves. Nor can it be determined from these historical circumstances that Islanders will always be negatively positioned at the Interface. Indeed, history tells us, that ongoing intersections at the Interface, which have deployed different theories about relations of Islanders to 'others', have re-positioned Islanders in ways that mean, for example, that a regional governmental model in the Torres Strait islands is now an accepted proposition for Islanders — a model of autonomy that reconfigures the relation between Islanders and local, state and federal authorities.

In all these different intersections, however they come together, there are spaces where people operate on a daily basis making choices according to the particular constraints and possibilities of the moment. People act in these spaces, drawing on their own understandings of what is emerging all around them, drawing on collective understanding, drawing on historical ways of understanding. All these sets of understandings may themselves draw from many different and/or contested points of understanding, including those that derive from traditional knowledge, from Western knowledge, from previous experience of the intersections between them and so on. In this process people are constantly producing new ways of understanding and at the same time filtering out elements of all those ways of understanding that prevent them from making sense at a particular point in time and trying in the process to preserve a particular sense of self or, in the case of collective efforts, a particular sense of community, always itself a subject of ongoing discussion and ongoing change.

It is useful in understanding the positioning of Islanders at this Interface to explore some of the a priori elements and relations that condition possibilities for Islander experience. This conceptualisation of the Cultural Interface suggests that Islander experience may be critical in understanding the constitutional elements of the Interface. If a new theoretical perspective is to be generated to harness this Islander experience at the Interface — the space where Islanders make meaning of their lives — to provide a framework through which this experience can speak back to other ways of understanding, then some of the constituting elements need to be explored in greater depth. Any new theoretical approach must be open to the idea that Islander experience is constituted in complex sets of social and discursive relations.

Islander positions in theories

We do not have, I would argue, a good understanding of the ongoing effects of subscribing to the theoretical construction of Islanders as being from and in the human past, as we now do of our construction as 'other' (Attwood, 1996). Nor do we tend to view the colonial period as a historical attempt in practice to bring Islanders from this past into the present. But this is how Islanders were positioned. Theoretically, Islanders were positioned as people from the past who were being catapulted into the present by the presence of intruders into their previously timeless and unchanging lives — not by intruders into their present lives but intruders into their lives from the past. Understanding Islanders came to be about understanding this distance between the past (represented by Islander thinking, understanding and organisation of their world, which were all present and could be observed in the here and now) and the present (represented by European understanding, thinking and ways of organising their world which were also in the here and now and could be observed by Islanders). Understanding Islanders came to be not so much about Islanders as about understanding the distance between them and others — and managing the difference and disjuncture between the two.

This point about being theorised as people from the past, and the nexus between past and present and notions of the past in the present, may seem rather nonsensical — logic and historical observation tells us that Islanders were present in the here and now and that they were dealt with there in real terms, not in a theoretical space or timeless void. But it is exactly this intersection between the theoretical (that has constructed these notions of past and present) and the real, which has positioned Islanders in this way through particular practices (including particular ways of thinking), which tends to be overlooked.

Once understood as people from the past who needed the benefits of differentiated social policies to guide them into the present, Islanders in the everyday, as actors in the present, begin to be theoretically submerged and marginalised. They begin to disappear as people at the centre of their own lives as they are co-opted into another history, another narrative that is not really about them but about their relation to it. When Islanders, in this analysis of their present circumstances, are positioned as secondary, then no primacy can be given to the things that Islanders do, their daily experiences of a life lived in changing circumstances and how they might see their position within these dynamics. The story of that other side does not get told as they see it unfold, as they experience it, or as they make sense of it. Rather, it is written over and retold in a way that gives primacy to the logic of the new order to which Islanders have been inscribed and prescribed in a particular relation. The analysis of that other story — the Islander explanations for Islander responses — is not heard or understood.

In describing Islander culture as an artefact of the past, Islander knowledge — thinking, understanding and organisation of their world — is itself viewed as something of the past. But in fact it has always been something of the present, evolving and responding to all that is new and changing in Islander contexts. Islander consciousness and systems for thinking about, reflecting on and analysing their place in unfolding events — Islander 'history' — while subjugated in Western accounts, are nevertheless continuing. By this 'Island' history, I do not just mean 'historical events'. I include as well the whole trajectory of the past that Islanders carry with them into the future: ways of being, thinking, understanding, systems of knowledge and epistemology, the historical effects from former experiences that may have conditioned in part how they responded in the ways that they did. This is more than the deployment of current constructs of traditional culture can capture. Culture as it is used as an explanatory framework of what Islanders once were (the subjects of their own course of history) weakens — indeed hijacks — this notion of Islanders' own construction of historical understanding into something apolitical — descriptive, explanatory and yes important and useful, but lacking the politics of analysis and action and lacking too a reason and logic of its own that is as legitimate as others. This is because others must 'read' and interpret Islanders' responses through their own notions of what Islanders were and are and what the meanings of their experiences were and are. They cannot get to the Islanders' experience of this history because they did not experience it in that way and because other forms of understanding the historical context of Islanders structure their thinking.

In contemporary times, Islanders are read through the prism of culture, itself a construction of others that, as applied to the current context, misses the Islander experience of their engagement with past 'before time', colonial and more recent events. The more recent accounts that make use of extensive contact and interviews with Islanders (e.g. Beckett, 1987; Sharp, 1993; Osborne, 1997) are notably quite different accounts of Islanders than previous ones, precisely because they have included parts of that 'untold' side of the historical context. Islanders may not be able to 'tell' this untold side of their history themselves in a way that would satisfy the discipline of history, but nevertheless they have brought down through experience, memory, consciousness, passed-on knowledge, stories, dance and contemporary cultural practices something that is of that history and that will still speak of it in ways that others may not have fully understood via external observation and analysis of it. What Islanders 'bring down' through the generations informs their standpoint in the present. Whether it satisfies the standards of historical 'truth' imposed by Western historians is not the point; how it helps explain the Islanders' view of the present position and what they view as the imperatives and priorities of the future is of interest.

Any new framework needs to consider the way — or whether — it calls in Islanders as people from the past as well as the residual racism and ongoing colonial project within this. While we may wish to retain a distinct collective identity, and while much of this might be linked to historical and cultural traditions in its specificities, this does not mean that Islanders are oriented to the past. To the contrary, we are outward-looking and future-oriented. Cultural preservation and maintenance, the hallmarks of nearly thirty years of Indigenous policy, are noble goals that in effect rewrite Islander determinations to be in control of their historical trajectory into a more politically benign plan of inclusion and tolerance of aspects of a past culture that can atone for the injustice of colonial intervention. It is an extension of largesse that does not address the continued exclusion of Islanders' analyses of their experience of history or their desire to be in effective control of their futures. It is embraced by Islanders because it is an important part of Islander life. But it is also embraced because it is the basis for political assertion on the part of Islanders — it sets the parameters within which we are permitted to assert ourselves without penalty and we make good use of it. But it falls short of dealing with the complex realities of Islander lives at the Interface. In developing a better theoretical basis for the inclusion and expression of Islander standpoints that are constituted in the complex space of the Interface, the residue of 'the past in the present' needs to be reconsidered. One way is through notions of continuity and discontinuity.

Understanding continuity and discontinuity as a framework for the political space

Notions of continuity and discontinuity (Foucault, 1989) provide a better way for considering Islander relationships with different systems of knowledge and different historical trajectories, and for thinking about paths between the past and present. We can consider the colonial period as an historical period that placed Islander societies under tremendous pressure through its various and often successful attempts to 'discontinue' many of our practices. Religious practice was completely transformed; economic and social organisation was greatly reformed. As earlier chapters have illustrated, the greatest triumph of rendering Islanders discontinuous with their own histories was through the inscription of Islanders into other systems of knowledge — the Western order of things. This textual inscription of Islanders was achieved through the very act of denying Islanders as actors in their own present.

But Islanders were actors in their own present. As more recent textual inscriptions confirm, at the Interface there is a multitude of evidence of Islanders maintaining, in the midst of change and in the midst of our diminished position, in the midst of discontinuities with former lives, continuity with former selves, with our own histories and narratives of who and what we were. In what we did and what we still do, individuals and the collective find continuity; we continue our own narratives, even as they change with individual and collective circumstances. There is not a singular narrative or the same narrative, rather a collection of narratives to parallel the complex history and position of Islanders. In sum, these form a collective Islander narrative. The vibrancy of contemporary Islander customary practices is testimony to the practice of continuing on our own path while reconstructing, renewing and regenerating familiar forms with alien content whether these alien forms were coercively imposed or taken up voluntarily.

The history of Islanders' experiences and social practices at this Interface then is not a history of Islanders that is of no import in the analysis of either the historical or current Islander position. This history of Islander agency during the colonial period should not be forgotten. Nor should it be cast as merely a period of diminishment, powerlessness and loss. Although it was those things, it was also a history of strength, of changing and re-making ourselves, of remaining ourselves — a history of dignity, intelligence, forbearance, anger, resentment and frustration; of some selling out perhaps, getting it wrong no doubt, of pragmatism certainly and so on. It is a history of how we acted in the present in that historical period. We lived in the present and responded to its changing circumstances as human beings everywhere do. While the historical experience of Islanders at this Interface constitutes an important part of Islander history, it can only now emerge as a recovered history. It cannot be a definitive history because the everyday cannot be fully recovered. The accounts that are being written of it are always partial although they help build a more complex picture of Islanders during this period.

Historically, Islanders — always with a view of themselves in the present — became occupied with negotiating the terms and conditions of their position in the changing circumstances. They yielded, compromised, embraced and rejected. At particular points of crisis — the 1936 Maritime Strike, the 'border no change' campaign and the Mabo litigation, for example — they drew a line in the sand and stood ground. These defining moments are the most visible part of Islander agency. Less visible and available for inclusion into analysis are the daily ongoing experiences of individual Islanders, families and communities as they responded to the new, incorporated and accommodated, changed some ways and not others, developed analyses of their situation, and negotiated and responded as people in the present. As their circumstances were transformed so they transformed themselves and added to, adjusted and complicated their meaning-making systems to reflect the changed 'reality' of their daily lives. In this process, they were able to remain Islanders even if Islanders today bear little resemblance to Islanders past. They may not have been well positioned in this process but they were active.

But even as people make difficult, pragmatic or constrained choices they are often well aware of what has to be given up or let go in making a particular decision or buying into a particular logic of argu-ment and so on. As people give up their position, their preferences, their practices, they do not necessarily 'forget'. They make judgments and move forward, finding ways to maintain themselves and/or their community in the changed circumstances. They manage loss. They reconstruct their stories. This is the stuff of the everyday where individuals, families, groups and communities transmit important values by reconstructing them if necessary into different forms and practices. In this way, Islanders 'domesticated' outside practices to fit with Islander ways of understanding — the stuff of cultural appropriation. The Christian religion replaced many of the functions of former beliefs but while those former practices have disappeared they were not forgotten entirely. The residue carries on in different ways alongside commitment to Christianity, in the ongoing practice of 'superstitious' belief and the practice of 'magic', and in Islanders' religious analysis (see Sharp, 1993). The threads of continuity weave on through time into the modern fabric of Islander life. These are not uniform in uptake; they are transformed in process in most cases, but they are still there for the uptake, for ongoing transformation and evolution. Old practices associated with the transmission of knowledge continue: some Islanders are still 'chosen' to be bearers of traditional knowledge; traditional knowledge is still 'passed down' in the form of gift. That every Islander does not carry this knowledge does not mean that the presence of this continuing knowledge does not inform the current conditions of Islander life in imperceptible ways. Islander practices of maintaining continuity enable the ongoing transformations of Islander identity that reflect the complex and multi-dimensional — that is, distinctiveness as Islanders but broader shared identities in other shifting intersections — as citizens, workers, consumers, youth, students, women and so on.

The ways that Islanders have transformed themselves as they were being transformed by others is the ongoing development of their place in their own history. If concerns about cultural preservation can be seen in terms of continuity and discontinuity we can be less obsessed with maintaining the past by constantly demanding the evidence of it in our present and become more concerned with the process of maintaining continuity with the past as we look to the future — of retaining a distinct but necessarily shifting identity in line with changing times and imperatives. We may look after the past and preserve traditional knowledge in different or as yet unimagined ways and we can continue as we have. This is fundamentally about the process of making meaning as we go about our daily lives. In this we are well practised if not well positioned. Implicated in this once again is the everyday experience of Islanders. As well, systems of knowledge, our access to them, and the positioning (subjectivities) produced by our relation to them are implicated in understanding and improving our position in this process.

Locating Islander agency

The everyday — where active, knowing Islanders were (and still are) negotiating changes manifested in their everyday lives — must be theorised into any analysis of the Interface, otherwise the position of Islanders at the Interface cannot be understood via their experience of it. Rather, understanding of the Islander position gets drawn back to sit within the prescriptions of the theoretical frameworks because these provide an order and logic that makes sense. Moreover, these analyses make sense because in the narratives they produce there are partial truths that cannot be denied. For example, Islanders were and are different and distinct; they have been subjected to oppressive state control, have endured the loss of former cultural practices and so on.

It is in the everyday that the enactment of the theoretical constructions position Islanders and constrain or enable them in real terms. Understanding this is a critical notion if we as Islanders are ever to untangle ourselves from colonial histories and understand our present position more fully — and if others are to understand our present responses more fully.

In the everyday, as we saw in previous chapters, there is evidence of Islanders who were not the prescribed Islander, who did not conform to this prescribed view, who did not agree with the engendered relationship, who were not averse to changing circumstances, who were transforming and remaking themselves in their present circumstances and daily activities even as the constraints and conditions of those circumstances meant a constant refusal of the Islander position as capable of being part of the present on the same terms as others. There is also evidence of Islander refusal via disobedience, indifference, and minimal co-operation with the emerging order as they tried to negotiate the new on their own terms. In all accounts, from whatever position they were written, we are able to see that Islanders were living in the present; they were actors in their own lives, they were not a passive group of people previously frozen in a time warp and now patiently thawing out under coconut trees waiting to be given new directions to the future. Missionary accounts, government records and reports, maritime companies' records, visitors' accounts, and historical assessments from past and more recent times all provide glimpses of active, assertive, thinking Islanders responding and negotiating their way as daily circumstances and imperatives required, as they had always done with each other, with their closer neighbours and with visitors from earlier periods. Islander memory and consciousness passed down also provides glimpses of Islanders who did not internalise the prescribed position.

To the Queensland government, the intelligent Islander was seen to be the one who could be trusted to be reasonable, who could see the logic of his administrators: the Islander who knew what was in his/her best interests. Of course, the co-operative Islander was an intelligent Islander positioning him/herself in the best way possible within the constraints of the circumstances. The unco-operative Islander was also an intelligent Islander refusing to be positioned in the prescribed way. These two Islanders could often be the same Islander responding to different circumstances or different Islanders responding to the same circumstances. Thus in the everyday, despite the theoretical prescriptions that positioned Islanders and which had real material elements and effects in the everyday, there was nothing prescribed in the ways that Islanders responded.

It is important not to romanticise Islander agency in this process. Islanders were — and in most situations still are — positioned in restrictive terms at the Interface. What Islanders may understand or the ways in which they make sense of things at the Interface is itself both constitutive and derivative of their position at the Interface. The Interface is in this sense the space of ongoing historical continuities and discontinuities as people discard and take up different ways of understanding, being and acting in a complex and changing environment.

Incorporating everyday experience into theory

Throughout this book, a proposition has been building that ways of understanding Islanders have been limited in usefulness because they interpret Islander 'realities' from another standpoint. I have also progressively suggested that centralising Islanders as the agents of ongoing continuity in their everyday lives via the inclusion of their interpretation of their everyday experiences within the ongoing and changing order may go much further in providing more useful representations of Islander 'realities' and more useful knowledge about the position of Islanders. Such 'Islander' accounts and understandings would better enable those involved in transforming Islander lives (in the ongoing reform process to redress historical disadvantage) to develop, implement and evaluate policies and programs that reflect, act in, serve and uphold the interests of Islanders as determined by Islanders.

But what would constitute such an 'Islander' standpoint — and how this might be brought to bear on policy and practice via any inclusion or interpretation of Islander experience — requires much more than simple inclusions of Islander 'accounts' of experience. It also requires much more than the inclusion of Islander 'perspectives' on issues as garnered through the now well-established 'advise and consult' practices of the reform process and much more than the presence of Islanders in the bureaucracies that determine and/or implement policy and practice.

The interpretation of experience is always mediated by theoretical underpinnings of analyses as the differences between earlier and later historical analysis demonstrate. Giving primacy in analysis to Islander experience in the everyday is not to be conceived in simple terms as something naïve and akin to individual perception. Islander experience of the everyday is already located and conditioned within a complex set of relations and any analysis of descriptions of that experience needs to reveal the politics of those relations by including the conflicts, the contradictions, the incoherence of contesting positions as people make sense of their experience. The idea here is not to think of this experience simply in terms of the production of individual accounts of it. Although individuals do give different and varied accounts of their lived realities, and although these accounts produce valuable insights, individual accounts of that are personal narratives. Instead, the idea is to provide some analysis of why and how these complex sets of relations construct or give rise to different 'realities' for the collective of Torres Strait Islanders as compared with other Australians as well as the diversity within the collective.

Furthermore, the idea is to provide some inclusion of the validity of this experience of Islander lives positioned within complex sets of relations, as worthy of inclusion into theories of who and what Islanders are and more importantly how they are positioned

Without it, Islander understanding of this position will be confined to the narrative as it largely is now — the authoritative, personal voice that is then re-inscribed into the theoretical without disrupting or complicating that other major narrative — whatever it may be at the time. Islanders will be left to 'tell their stories' or to 'advise' so that others can understand them, but the complicated world of analysing and interpreting change as it manifests in Islanders' lived realities will be left for others to oversee as in the past. Personal narrative can explain the everyday experience from the Islander side but it does not equate to incorporating this explanation of one's position in the more complicated web of the Interface where many narratives, histories and elements come together in ways that cannot always be articulated coherently into a different theoretical explanation of the Islander position. It does, however, provide the evidence of it. And it does introduce Islander accounts to be included in the content of analysis. This content needs to be interrogated to generate more useful explanations of the position of Islanders. So what are the parameters to consider at the Cultural Interface for an Islander standpoint?

Towards an Islander standpoint

The Cultural Interface has been named as the space where Islanders live and act on a daily basis and is in this sense both the personal space and the civic space — the place where we make sense of our individual and collective experience. It is a lived location. However, lest we be tempted to begin thinking of the Interface as a physical space, it is important to reiterate that the Cultural Interface is the overlay of myriad intersections of sets of relations and in this sense it is also a theoretical space. Islander experience is constituted in a complex nexus between 'lived experience' and discursive constructions that play out in many shifting intersections that are never reducible to any one intersection (for example, the relation between the traditional and mainstream). Islander experience is itself mediated by the ways in which it is constituted and in the ways it is explained. Our experience sits within complex sets of relations and is therefore open to interpretation. There can be no 'authentic' account of Islander experience that can represent any single 'truth' of our reality. In this sense, any new theoretical framework that attempts to include Islander standpoints must see the Interface as primarily a site of struggle over the meaning of our experience.

Islander perspectives emerge in the differences between interpretation of Islander experience between Islanders and those others who understand Islanders' experience from another vantage point. Without contradictions and conflicts between others' constructions of Islanders and/or institutional readings of us and our own experience of them, there would be no need to consider Islander perspectives — it is in this contested space that a distinct Islander perspective is produced.

It is important to recognise that this struggle over meaning also includes struggles over meaning between Islanders themselves. Islanders are positioned differently in relation to the Interface by such things as differences in gender, heritage, levels of education, access to different knowledge, geographical location, historical experience, religious affiliation, age, social roles, other beliefs and so on. No Islander 'experiences' the Interface in exactly the same way as another because how we make sense of our experiences is mediated constantly by a whole array of factors, including both externally imposed and subjectively produced mediations. It is important not to make the mistake of thinking that differences between Islanders' individual or group perspectives are directly an outcome of some Islanders having had more 'authentic' experiences of being an Islander than others or that the more 'authentic' accounts of Islander experiences are those that derive from Islanders who live a more 'authentically' traditional life.

It is important too to recognise that Islanders have been and still are positioned at the Interface in ways that produce different realities. An Islander elder who has lived a largely subsistence life in a remote community and has been educated to Year 3 level is no more 'authentic' an Islander than a younger Islander raised on Thursday Island who has a tertiary qualification and works for the government. They are both Islanders whose experiences may lead them to interpret the meaning of their lived realities in different ways but these interpretations are equally as legitimate as each other. In reaching general conclusions about the meaning of their experiences as Islanders they may in fact arrive at similar analyses of their position though the content of them may be quite different. They may also have different analyses of their position which also allow for the production of more useful explanations of the Islander position because they bring to light the different effects of the many elements which condition the experiences of Torres Strait Islanders.

Because Islanders are already constituted in their relation to others and in their differential relations to each other, experience is open to a range of often contradictory interpretations. We can argue that the sensibilities of the Islander collective derive from consensus surrounding the meaning of their experiences and the goals for their future. This is true, but consensus manifests most strongly at points of crisis which produce a unity of purpose in the face of external threats. In the day to day of less pressured circumstances — when Islanders reflect or discuss within the collective the details of designs for the future, and the ways to change practices in their own interests — consensus is more elusive. To read any lack of a singular or fixed Islander perspective as the evidence of either deep divisions or that some Islanders have lost their way in relation to Islander priorities, threatening the collective notions of what it means to be an Islander, is once again to miss the point. The collective can maintain consensus on future goals while being quite fragmented about the various paths to achieve them. Contestation over the meaning of experience and inclusion of this in analysis of our position surely facilitates an enriched discussion of the issues and helps to clarify the critical elements that have to be brought to consensus in the interests of Islander collective cohesiveness.

Building an Islander standpoint into a theoretical framework requires then more than the inclusion of Islander perspectives and narratives. It requires the recognition of the existence of the contested nature of these, the many vantage points through which they can be analysed and the theorising of these constitutive aspects of Islander experience as integral to understanding the complexity of the Islander position. That is, the Islander standpoint can never be reduced to the inclusion of Islander content, or the expression of Islander opinion through data, survey, consultation or advisory processes. These may provide the content but any Islander standpoint needs to emerge in the process of analysis. This involves not understanding the Islander position via experience of it as some certainty, as something to be fixed in its meaning, as essentially cultural, as something that is waiting to be uncovered and that just needs to be 'told'. Including experience in this way is problematic if we accept it as a 'true' or 'authentic' account of what it means to be an Islander. It is much more about understanding and explicating the complex positioning that is constitutive of Islander experience at the Interface as the playing out of the constant struggle for meaning, the contestation over meaning; it is about the various readings that can be applied to give this experience meaning in a way that makes sense to those involved in understanding Islanders. Islander standpoints are conditioned in these complex sets of relations that exist at the Interface and understanding the Islander standpoint involves understanding that complexity and making it a primary interest of any theory that informs analysis.

11

An Indigenous Standpoint theory

> We are in a closed box and wait for the lid to be taken off.
> (Torres Strait Islander to the Deputy Chief Protector in Report 22 February 1936, p. 3, cited in Sharp, 1993, p. 197)

The discussion in the previous chapter begs the question of how to undertake analysis that accounts for Islander experiences at the Cultural Interface. At this point I take the opportunity to expand discussion to address an Indigenous standpoint theory generally. How are Indigenous students, academics and researchers in the disciplines to navigate the complexities of Indigenous experience within such contested spaces? The term standpoint is often substituted for perspective or viewpoint, but these do not adequately represent the use of the term in theory, which is quite complex and contested as a theoretical approach.

Feminist standpoint theory emerged in the 1970s and 1980s in an attempt to deal with the problem of articulating women's experience of their world as organised through practices of knowledge production, and which theorised women's positions as rational, logical outcomes of the natural order of things, when in fact they were socially constructed positions that were outcomes of particular forms of social organisation that supported the position and authority of men over women (Smith, 1987). As a method of inquiry, standpoint theory was utilised by a diversity of marginalised groups whose accounts of experience were excluded or subjugated within intellectual knowledge production. However, analysis from the standpoint of people's everyday experience is not the aggregation of stories from lived experience. It is not the endless production of subjective narrative to disrupt objectified accounts. According to Polhaus, it works off the premise that

> [f]irst the social position of the knower is epistemically significant; where the knower is socially positioned will both make possible and delimit knowledge. Second, more objective knowledge is not a product of mere observation or a disinterested perspective on the world, but is achieved by struggling to understand one's experience through a critical stance on the social order within which knowledge is produced. (Pohlhaus, 2002, p. 285)

Standpoint accounts, then, depend on reflexivity and the distinction between experience and standpoint (Pohlhaus, 2002). Bringing the situation of ourselves as 'knowers' into the frame does not make ourselves the focus of study but will 'involve investigating the social relations within which we as "knowers" know' (p. 287). This will also involve knowing where to look, and which social relations might be informing our knowledge. Importantly, and to borrow again from Polhaus, 'being… [an Indigenous knower] does not yield a ready-made critical stance on the world, but rather the situation of…[Indigenous knowers] provides the questions from which one must start in order to produce more objective knowledge' (Pohlhaus, 2002, p. 287). Standpoint, then, does not refer 'to a particular social position, but rather is an engagement with the kinds of questions found there' (Pohlhaus, 2002, p. 287), and this engagement moves us along 'to forge', following Harding (1991), a critical Indigenous standpoint.

An Indigenous standpoint, therefore, has to be produced. It is not a simple reflection of experience and it does not pre-exist in the everyday waiting to be brought to light. It is not any sort of hidden wisdom that Indigenous people possess. It is a distinct form of analysis, and is itself both a discursive construction and an intellectual device to persuade others and elevate what might not have been a focus of attention by others. It is not deterministic of any truth but it lays open a basis from which to launch a range of possible arguments for a range of possible purposes. These arguments still need to be rational and reasoned; they need to answer to the logic and assumptions on which they are built. Arguments from this position cannot assert a claim to truth that is beyond the scrutiny of others on the basis that, as a member of the Indigenous community, what I say counts.

This, then, is not an Indigenous way of 'doing knowledge'. Nor would standpoint theory allow that it is enough for Indigenous students (or academics) to authorise themselves solely on the basis of their experience. Rather, it would encourage the drawing in of that experience to bear on a critical analysis of accepted positions and arguments. In this way, an Indigenous standpoint theory argues for what Harding calls 'strong objectivity' (Pohlhaus, 2002, p. 285) by bringing in accounts of relations that 'knowers' located in more privileged social positions are not attentive to. It is a particular form of investigation. It is the explication and analysis of how the social organisation and practices of knowledge through its various apparatuses and technologies of the textual production organise and express themselves in that everyday, as seen from within that experience. People's lived experience at the cultural interface is the point of entry for investigation, not the case under investigation. It is to find a way to explore the actualities of the everyday and discover how to express them conceptually from within that experience, rather than depend on or deploy predetermined concepts and categories for explaining experience. For Indigenous students this requires the development of complex analytical and writing skills.

Standpoint theory did not develop as a singular theory but has congealed around different interpretations of other theories associated with Marxist approaches, post-structuralism, and postmodernism. It has come under a lot of criticism and has fallen somewhat out of favour (see Moore & Muller, 1999; Walby, 2000). Criticisms have been levelled at its weaknesses: the defeatism of what some call the tendency to 'epistemic relativism'; the endless fragmentation across categories of difference; an unfortunate emphasis on 'who can know' rather than 'what can be known'; the preoccupation with politics of identity and location that reify boundaries between groups who also have common concerns; and the containment of politics and action to recognition and location rather than redistribution and transformation. These weaknesses need to be engaged with by Indigenous academics so that accounts can be produced that articulate forms of Indigenous agency created in local sites through the social organisation of knowledge and its technologies, and which give content to how people engage and participate in and through them.

For Indigenous students, academics and researchers, standpoint theory in my mind is a method of inquiry, a process for making more intelligible 'the corpus of objectified knowledge about us' as it emerges and organises understanding of our lived realities. I see this as theorising knowledge from a particular and interested position — not to produce the 'truth' of the Indigenous position but to better reveal the workings of knowledge and how understanding of Indigenous people is caught up and implicated in its work.

This to me is a useful starting point for a first principle of an Indigenous standpoint theory viz., that Indigenous people are entangled in a very contested knowledge space at the Cultural Interface. It would therefore begin from the premise that my social position is discursively constituted within and constitutive of complex sets of social relations as expressed through the social organisation of my everyday. As an interested 'knower', I am asking to understand how I come to understand — to know within the complexities at the interface where our experience is constituted in and constitutive of the corpus.

A second useful principle for an Indigenous standpoint theory would recognise Indigenous agency as framed within the limits and possibilities of what I can know from this constituted position — to recognise that at the interface we are constantly being asked to be both continuous with one position at the same time as being discontinuous with another (Foucault, 1972). This is experienced as a push–pull between Indigenous and not Indigenous positions; that is, the familiar confusion with constantly being asked at any one moment to both agree and disagree with any proposition on the basis of a constrained choice between a whitefella or blackfella perspective. For me, this provides a means to see my position in a particular relation with others, to maintain myself with knowledge of how I am being positioned, and to defend a position if I have to.

A third and connected principle that may usefully be incorporated is the idea that the constant 'tensions' that this tug-of-war creates are physically experienced, and both inform as well as limit what can be said and what is to be left unsaid in the everyday. To factor this tension in helps us to get beyond notions of structuralist power and the resultant causal analyses. This will allow us a more sophisticated view to the tensions created between Indigenous and non-Indigenous dualities, not as the literal translation of what is said or written in propositions, but the physical experience and memory of such encounters in the everyday, and to include them as part of the constellation of *a priori* elements that inform and limit not just the range but the diversity of responses from us.

These three principles allow that although I have knowledge of my experience at the interface and can forge a critical standpoint, I am not out singularly to overturn the so-called dominant position through simplistic arguments of omission, exclusion or misrepresentation but rather out there to make better arguments in relation to my position within knowledge, and in relation to other communities of 'knowers'.

We see and act on things in these ways all the time. Think of something like Indigenous humour — it emerges from this locale where we form a community around some shared inter-subjective understanding of our experience, where we can understand the jokes. Witness Mary G's poor guests on SBS TV; they are the outsiders in this world of experience and they must fathom our accounts of it and feel what it is like *not* to be a 'knower' of this world. Humour and satire are particular forms of social analysis and comment. Comedians like Mary G are right in there 'doing' social analyses that illuminate our way of looking at our experience, which drag into the analysis our experience of dealing across a space where our shared subjectivities have been constituted.

Indigenous humour is a way of making sense from within this experience. It recognises the tensions and complexities of everyday life and reflects this back into this space and the fact that we all 'get the joke' provides evidence of our knowledge of how complexities in this space emerge in our everyday experience. The joke doesn't resolve anything but it does articulate something known but unsaid. We laugh because it expresses something we recognise, something we already know. In that we often send up ourselves, humour reveals our incomplete understandings of how the world beyond us works and the mystery of its ways. It also captures an important dimension of our experience in this locale. And Indigenous humour reveals the ignorance of outsiders of how we operate in and understand our world — and many a merry laugh we have all had at whitefellas' expense in this regard. In humour, there is scrutiny of ourselves as actors in our world and acknowledgment of that world beyond that is omnipresent and often not coherently logical from our point of view.

This is why we need a theory that as its first principle can generate accounts of communities of Indigenous people in contested knowledge spaces, that as its second principle affords agency to people, and that as its third principle acknowledges the everyday tensions, complexities and ambiguities as the very conditions that produce the possibilities in the spaces between Indigenous and non-Indigenous positions. In these ways we can deploy an Indigenous standpoint to help unravel and untangle ourselves from the conditions that delimit who, what or how we can or can't be, to help see ourselves with some charge of the everyday, and to help understand our varied responses to the colonial world.

Concluding remarks

The focus of this book has been on Torres Strait Islanders but much of what I have put forward has relevance to other Indigenous peoples and contexts. There are clear implications for the way we consider Indigenous learners in the disciplines of higher education. In this concluding section I now want to return to specific academic issues associated with the inclusion of 'Indigenous' content into the disciplines and the position of Indigenous students and academics within these relations. How are we to assist students to engage with the disciplines in ways that provide them the space to contest and shape the way forward without incurring the personal cost often associated with alienation and anger? How are we to assist students to engage in ways that do not simply accept the position afforded to them by the imaginations of others? How are we to assist students so that their educational experience is of intellectual engagement with the content and methods of the disciplines in the light of their own experiences of being Indigenous, rather than of retreat into intellectual separation and isolation?

In the faculties and disciplines attention to Indigenous issues and content has been a focus of reform and development with varied results over the last two to three decades. Until the late 1960s 'Indigenous' content was taught through the disciplines of archaeology, anthropology and linguistics (Peterson, 1990). Reform in Indigenous affairs, particularly from the time of the Whitlam government (1972) brought forth a burgeoning of research in areas associated with the improvement of the social conditions of Australia's Indigenous people, particularly in education and health. But there was also increased research interest in the ways colonial practice has impacted on us and on revised ways of understanding Indigenous histories, cultures and philosophies. This research now provides much of the content for, and informs, the way we understand Indigenous people and issues within the disciplines.

However, in many of the reviews and research projects associated with factors affecting the success of Indigenous university students, issues around the content and teaching of Indigenous subject matter have been consistently mentioned (see for example, Sonn, Bishop & Humphries, 1996; Penfold, 1996; Walker, 2000; Malcolm & Rochecouste, 2002; Usher, Lyndsay, Miller & Miller, 2005). Concerns about not enough Indigenous content and the tendency to 'add it on' as one of many 'multicultural' perspectives, about the disrespectful treatment of some Indigenous content, about the non-consideration of Indigenous knowledge systems and 'ways of knowing', and about the lack of accommodation of 'cultural learning styles' are consistently mentioned as reasons for student withdrawals or alienation.

In an ongoing response to the paucity and invisibility of Indigenous content and issues, some universities have put great effort into incorporating 'Indigenous perspectives across the curriculum'. Some Australian universities have established schools of Indigenous studies to concentrate the effort, rather than disperse it; some retain and develop Indigenous content within the relevant disciplines; and many have established specialised courses and degree programs for Indigenous students in particular professions such as health, community education, business management and so on.

The movement towards making curricula more inclusive, whichever way it has been approached, relies largely on non-Indigenous research into Indigenous issues and has encouraged the extraction of elements of Indigenous ways of understanding the world — mathematical knowledge, astronomy, stories, mythology, art, environmental knowledge, religion — and insertion of these elements to fit with particular curriculum areas. The purpose of such inclusions is to develop students' understanding of Indigenous Australia and current predicaments and much of this content contributes to that goal.

But there are other considerations which need some reflection before we discuss any teaching and learning issues associated with Indigenous Knowledge at the higher education level. These revolve around the location of Indigenous learners at the Cultural Interface.

For many Indigenous students and lecturers, regardless of our distance from what we understand as 'the traditional context', the Indigenous epistemological basis of knowledge construction and the ways of 'doing' knowledge are not completely unfamiliar. These are embedded, not in detailed knowledge of the land and place for all of us perhaps, nor perhaps in Indigenous environmental or ecological knowledge, but in ways of storytelling and of memory-making; in music, art and performance; in cultural and social practices; in ways of of relating to kin and socialising children; in ways of thinking and of transmitting knowledge, even in creolised languages; and in that all-encompassing popular, though loosely used term, 'worldview', and so on. My own daughters who have spent most of their lives outside of the Torres Strait nevertheless have a view of themselves and their position in the world generated within the historicities and contemporary practices in this space.

But Indigenous students and academics are all also grounded in Western disciplines, through historical experience, through Christianisation, through the English language, through interventions of and interactions with colonial and contemporary institutions, through formal education, through subscription to the law, through subscription to the world of work, to democratic values, through everyday living, through use of technology, through popular culture, and so on. This is also familiar and recognisable, and we may accept it, refuse it, assimilate it, domesticate it, use it or subvert it, but nevertheless we are constantly engaged with it, as we move forward in a constant process of endless and often unconscious negotiations between these frames — or reference points — for viewing, understanding and knowing the world.

Negotiating between these is a transforming process of endless instances of learning and forgetting, of melding and keeping separate, of discarding and taking up, of continuity and discontinuity. We participate in these ways of viewing, being and acting in the world, often in quite contradictory, ambiguous or ambivalent ways. We subscribe with varying degrees of commitment, both in time and space, to various positions depending on the moment, depending on what experiences, capacities, resources and discourses we have to draw on, according to what is at stake for us, or our family, or our community, and so on, and according to past experiences, current realities, aspirations and imagined futures.

In this locale at the Cultural Interface Indigenous students who study the disciplines are discursively constituted as subjects vis-a-vis that 'matrix of abstracted discourses that constructs a consciousness of ourselves which is outside of the local, outside of how life is experienced' (following D. Smith 1987, 1990, 1999). And it is via understanding what constitutes and is constitutive of Indigenous experience in this locale that university academics need to re-theorise Indigenous students as prospective learners.

Whatever the particularities of their prior experiences, learners come into university programs already variously constituted and positioned discursively to take up the knowledge which has inscribed their position. The socio-historical discourses which have constituted their position are, in this learning context, organised and given their order through the disciplines and the corpus, through a Western order of things. Some of the theoretical framings within this order have come to form a commonsense and consensus position about the Indigenous community. Contestation of knowledge is easier for students at content and ideological levels within these accepted positions. Contestation is also easier if sites of interrogation are considered in terms of simple intersections.

But, Indigenous students often feel the contradictions and tensions within having to align to one or the other, especially when they see weaknesses in examples and arguments on both sides of the divide. However, it is more difficult to problematise the major theoretical concepts and pursue inter-subjective mapping of our many relationships at the Cultural Interface because these demand explication of broader sets of discursive relations beyond the literal interpretation of the text or the theoretical framings within a particular approach to a topic.

For example, when we deploy the concept of sovereignty or that of self-determination, how are those situated within wider sets of discursive relations of colonial discourse, legal discourse, rights discourse and so on? How has it provided a priori conditions to our thinking? How does it frame thinking in a range of implicated areas of practice? How does our subscription to it allow or not allow certain sorts of discussion about it? And when is it possible that we can talk of something else to achieve our goals? For instance, when legal-political concepts work through and are constituted in complex relations with anthropological discourse and on into health or education, and are then further complicated by the apparatuses of policy and managerial and bureaucratic discourse, how are these all to be brought to the surface? How are students to suspend accepted thinking in one area without suspending allegiance to Indigenous interests? Can they take up other positions without being tagged either essentialist or assimilationist? If so, what are they? Not opening up theoretical propositions for more complicated discussion means that the dynamics of the Cultural Interface are sutured over in favour of the Western order of things and its constitution of what an Indigenous 'opposition' should be.

Indigenous students, especially younger students, also often do not have a fully articulated experiential basis for contesting knowledge about things Indigenous in the disciplines. In that much cultural practice is implicitly understood, it is often difficult for Indigenous students to contest the interpretations of the corpus on the basis of what they know of their own culture. For example, the inner workings of customary adoption are not always revealed to young Torres Strait Islanders. They may know enough to be uneasy with a textual interpretation under discussion in a Law tutorial, but not certain enough of their own knowledge to make some sort of counter-claim. This uneasiness has to be suspended to make sense of legal discourse. The choice becomes one between silence or laying themselves open to challenge from the more authoritative elements of the corpus or the more confident speakers in their tutorial group. How are Indigenous learners to be supported to explore their experiential knowledge beyond the classroom and to bring it in to inform how particular Indigenous positions are contested via engagement with the corpus? The learner, in reaching a position under these conditions must suspend one or the other. It is often the case that Indigenous learners are unsettled and confined by both the accepted or orthodox Western and Indigenous interpretations of their experience, as I was in my undergraduate studies. But they cannot easily forge a deeper understanding without being called into alignment with one position or the other. Under these conditions, the Indigenous student does not have opportunities for developing ways of reading, ways of critically engaging with accepted Indigenous discourse, as this itself is constituted within wider sets of social relations, without betraying accepted positions within the Indigenous body politic. Thus it is difficult to work through the inherent tensions of the everyday world. Currently, professional preparation is inadequate in terms of equipping graduates to work the relevant elements of two knowledge systems together in the interests of better practice.

There is no doubt that my experiences growing up in a remote Island community towards the end of the era of paternal exclusion coupled with my educational history and university experience have shaped my thinking in relation to the project of Indigenous education. The desire to understand my position in relation to the wider world that encircled and diminished us historically has stimulated an ongoing interest in our current discursive positioning within knowledge and institutional practice. Understandings of the Indigenous lived locale as a place of deep and layered complexity, contradiction, and ambiguity have led me to be suspicious of simple explanations and remedies to improve the Indigenous position. My dissatisfaction with the discourse of culturalism stemmed largely from being certain about who I was (an Islander) and uncertain about why we were treated the way we were. Something about the re-writing of earlier racial discourses into a cultural discourse grated deep within my mind and soul. Why would I accept such a shift that said in effect 'Oops, sorry, we were wrong but we've rethought this and, here, we think this is a better explanation of you and your predicament'.

This discontent led me to reject the orthodox view and to turn to explore the practices of those in the disciplines. In my undergraduate years, there was the possibility that my oppositional stance could have developed into a radically 'dumb' one and at many times sheer anger at our historical circumstances threatened my sanity and my study. In the ensuing years, I have observed the difficulties other Indigenous students, including postgraduate students, have in dissenting from established and accepted Indigenous positions at the same time as being dissatisfied with the content and practices within disciplines. To inves_ tigate or criticise ways of thinking and theorising that are accepted in the Indigenous community and in Indigenous academic practice is a risky and painful business and invokes alienation from both sides of the Indigenous and non-Indigenous divide. To contest the accepted practices within the Indigenous education context is difficult if it conflicts with the politics of the orthodox Indigenous positions. And yet, as our problems persist, it will be the academic inquiry of those Indigenous people now entering higher education that will have to shape and improve educational practices.

As we move on towards the end of the third decade of Indigenous higher education, it seems timely to make a few observations in relation to the teaching and learning issues for Indigenous students. First, we need to recognise that our students live and will work in a very difficult and complex space. We do not serve them well if we conflate our understanding of the 'here and now' with an imagined distant past that can be brought forward to reconfigure a future embedded in our traditions and bounded off and separated from the global.

Second, the tendency of some arguments within Indigenous academia to fixate on cleaving the Indigenous from the 'white' in order to elevate the Indigenous also does not serve our students well. The discursive entanglement of Indigenous knowledge and experiential understanding within the disciplines should provide the grounds for deeper engagement with the disciplines and not the grounds for departure and separation or superficial contesting of 'truth' claims. We cannot easily separate them once they are inscribed in intellectual and disciplinary discourses. And on whose authority do we deploy our own understanding of Indigenous traditional knowledge — the authorities within textual or database productions? Yes, we may use our experience, gained within our own historical experience of our passed down traditions to unsettle and speak back into these discourses but that is different from claiming and using

Indigenous knowledge from various groups to underwrite any truth claims vis-a-vis Western knowledge. Nor do we serve our students if we allow or encourage them to reject Western knowledge sources and their practices on the grounds of them not being Indigenous. The task is to engage them to work against them or with them in productive and useful ways. To reject Western knowledge on ideological grounds needs to be thoroughly examined by those who advocate it.

Third, we need to keep in focus that future graduates into professions must be able to work in complex and changing knowledge terrains — knowledge production stands still for nobody. Many Indigenous students are already familiar with the complexities of the Cultural Interface and the contradictions and ambiguities of a life lived there surround them daily. To ask them to submerge this complexity in favour of simpler explanations of our predicament is to question their capacity for thinking and reconstructing meaning in this complex space once again.

Fourth, we need curriculum designs to build on these capacities and experiences of Indigenous students and to create opportunities for learners to achieve a balance of knowledge, skills and processes for exploring disciplinary boundaries. The solutions to problems in the Indigenous context do not lie only in finding the right content for students to digest but will also depend on the sort of engagements they have with it.

Fifth, and very importantly, educators, especially Indigenous educators, need themselves to develop their scholarship in contested knowledge spaces of the cultural interface and develop some facility with how to engage and move students through the learning process.

However, at the same time, Indigenous students need much stronger support than they currently have to engage more rigorously. The challenges they face need much more attention in curriculum and assessment design. Many Indigenous students in higher education are intellectually lonely. They must layer in the meanings from another unrepresented world and process these alongside disciplinary concepts and meanings. In some cases, they do not even articulate this aspect of their learning to anyone, for they can find no spaces in which to do so, not in the content of their courses, not in tutorials and not in assessment.

Within university courses, especially those concerned with the preparation of students for the professions, the practice of 'adding in' Indigenous content developed within the Western disciplines is the norm and likely to remain the only real avenue for inclusion. The more recent attempts to include relevant aspects of Indigenous knowledge systems to develop deeper appreciation of these knowledge traditions are largely engaged in the same process of incorporation or inclusion.

Even those who have opportunities to go into the field to learn directly from Indigenous people are learning more about the limits of their own knowledge practices than they are about the complexities and meanings of Indigenous knowledge traditions, which in my view makes this perhaps the most valuable exercise of all.

The important thing, in my view, is not to be deluded about what we can achieve in higher education in relation to controlling Indigenous content or in shaping knowledge and practice to be uniquely and identifiably 'Indigenous'. It is not that productive to separate it out and lay claim to a separate domain of knowledge with any authority.

The knowledge within the disciplines that circumscribes the ways Indigenous people are understood is now accessible to Indigenous people. We need to scrutinise it for how it discursively and textually produces a position for us (and others) to read ourselves in this world. We need to recognise at the same time that our historical and ongoing experience also informs the way that we read the world and the knowledge positions which inscribe us into that world and this gives us an alternate reading of our position.

It is important then that those concerned with the teaching of Indigenous content or issues in the disciplines orient students to approach this knowledge, not as the facts of Indigenous realities but as the context that provides the conditions for intellectual reflection and engagement with contemporary Indigenous issues.

These concerns for Indigenous students undertaking higher education mirror the concerns I have always held for my children as they grew up. In a world premised on difference, I felt — as my father, grandfather and great-grandfather did — that what they all needed most was an understanding of the political nature of their position, and that required both the language and the knowledge of how that positioning is effected in the everyday world. They also needed a way of maintaining themselves in the face of it, as well as working against that knowledge system that continues to hold them to the position that it has produced for them. They know who they are and where they are from but they need to be clear about the wider world which shapes the ways they can enact their lives.

References

Agrawal, A 1995a. Dismantling the divide between Indigenous and Western knowledge. *Development and Change*, 26 (3), 413–439.

—— 1995b. Indigenous and scientific knowledge: some critical comments. *Indigenous Knowledge and Development Monitor*, 3, 314. Retrieved 25 July 2002, from http://www.nuffic.nl/ciran/ikdm/4-2/articles/agrawal.htm

—— 1996. A sequel to the debate (2). *Indigenous Knowledge and Development Monitor*, 4 (2), 3–4. Retrieved 25 July 2002 from http://www.uffic.nl/ciran/ikdm/4-2/articles/agrawal.htm

Anderson, J 2005. Indigenous knowledge, intellectual property, libraries and archives: Crises of access, control and future utility. In M Nakata & M Langton (eds), *Australian Indigenous knowledge and libraries*. Kingston, ACT: Australian Academic & Research Libraries, Australian Library and Information Association.

Attwood, B 1996. The past as future: Aborigines, Australia and the (dis)course of history. In *Australian Humanities Review* at http://www.lib.latrobe.edu.au/AHR/archive/Issue-April-1996/Attwood.html

Barrett, C 1946. Torres Strait Islanders. *Walkabout*, 30 (1), 6–11.

Barthes, R 1972. *Mythologies*. London: Paladin.

Battiste, M & Youngblood Henderson, J 2000. *Protecting Indigenous knowledge and heritage: A global challenge*. Saskatoon, Saskatchewan: Purich.

Beckett, J 1987. *Torres Strait Islanders: Custom and colonialism*. New York: Cambridge University Press.

Bishop, R 1995. Freeing ourselves from neo-colonial domination in research: An Indigenous approach to creating knowledge. Keynote address at the New Zealand Association for Research in Education Conference, Massey University, Palmerston North.

Bleakley, W 1961. *The Aboriginal people of Australia: Their history, their habits, their assimilation*. Brisbane: Jacaranda Press.

Boxall, R & Duncan, W 1979. *Education in Torres Strait (the mid-1970s)*. Brisbane: Curriculum Branch, Department of Education, Queensland.

Carter, P 1992. *Living in a New Country: History, travelling and language.* London: Faber & Faber.

Casey, D 2001. Indigenous ownership of digital material: Is organised crime getting out of hand? Paper presented at the ALIA 2000: Capitalising on knowledge conference, Canberra Australia, October 2000. Retrieved 29 January 2002, from http://www.alia.org.au/incite/2001/06/museum.html

Christie, M 2005. Aboriginal knowledge traditions in digital environments. Online paper at Charles Darwin University, Darwin Australia. Retrieved 15 May 2006 from http://www.cdu.edu.au/cedntres/ik/pdf/CHRISTIE_AJIEpaper.pdf

Davis, M 1997. Indigenous peoples and intellectual property rights, Research paper no. 20, 1996–97, Information and Research Services, Department of the Parliamentary Library, Canberra. Retrieved 7 August 2002, from http://www.aph.gov.au/library/pubs/rp/1996-97/97rp20.htm

——1998. Biological diversity and Indigenous knowledge, Research paper no. 17, 1997–98, Information and Research Services, Department of the Parliamentary Library, Canberra. Retrieved 5 August 2002, from http://www.aph.gov.au/library/pubs/rp/1997-98/98rp17.htm

Denzin, N 1992. *Symbolic interactionism and cultural studies: The politics of interpretation.* Oxford: Blackwell.

Department of Employment, Education and Training 1989. *National Aboriginal and Torres Strait Islander education policy: Joint policy statement.* Canberra: AGPS.

Douglas, J 1899–1900. The islands and inhabitants of Torres Strait. *Queensland Geographical Society,* 15, 25–40.

Ellen, R & Harris, H 1996. Concepts of Indigenous environmental knowledge in scientific and development studies literature: a critical assessment. Online paper presented at the East–West Environmental Linkages Network Workshop 3, Canterbury UK, 8–10 May 1996. Retrieved 27 July 2002, from http://www.ukc.ac.uk/rainforest/SML_files/Occpap/indigknow.occpap_TOC.html

Ellen, R, Parkes, P & Bicker, A 2000. *Indigenous environmental knowledge and its transformations: Critical anthropological perspectives.* Amsterdam: Harwood Academic Publishers.

Eyzaguirre, P 2001. Global recognition of Indigenous knowledge: is this the latest phase of globalisation? *Indigenous Knowledge and Development Monitor,* 8 (1), 1–2. Retrieved 25 July 2002 from http://www.nuffic.nl/ciran/ikdm/9-2/column.html

Finch, N 1975. Torres Strait Island education: Past, present and a proposal for the future re-organisation of the primary school system. Unpublished master's thesis, Faculty of Education, University of Queensland, St Lucia, Brisbane.

——1977. *The Torres Strait Islands: Portrait of a unique group of Australians.* Brisbane: Jacaranda Press.

References

Flavier, J, de Jesus, A & Navarro, C 1995. The regional program for the promotion of Indigenous knowledge in Asia. In D Warren, L Slikkerveer & D Brokensha (eds.), *The cultural dimension of development: Indigenous knowledge systems*. London: Intermediate Technology Publications.

Fletcher, J 1989. *Clean, clad and courteous: A history of Aboriginal education in New South Wales*. Marrickville: Southwood Press.

Foucault, M 1970. *The order of things: An archaeology of the human sciences*. London: Tavistock.

—1972. *The archaeology of knowledge*. London: Routledge.

—1977. *Discipline and punish: The birth of the prison*. London: Penguin.

—1980. (edited by C Gordon and translated by C Gordon, L Marshall, J Mepham & K Soper). *Power/knowledge: Selected works and interviews 1972–1977*. Worcester: The Harvester Press.

—1989. *Madness and civilisation: A history of insanity in the age of reason*. London: Tavistock/Routledge.

Freire, P 1972. *Pedagogy of the Oppressed*. Harmondsworth: Penguin.

Ganter, R 1994. *The Pearl-shellers of Torres Strait: Resource use, development and decline 1860s–1960s*. Melbourne: Melbourne University Press.

Gegeo, D & Watson-Gegeo, K 2001. 'How we know': Kwara'ae rural villagers doing Indigenous epistemology, *The Contemporary Pacific*, 13 (1), 55–88.

Goody, J 1978. *The domestication of the savage mind*. Cambridge: Cambridge University Press.

Gumbula, J 2005. Exploring the Gupapuyna legacy: strategies for developing the Galiwin'ku Indigenous knowledge centre. In M Nakata & M Langton (eds.) *Australian Indigenous knowledge and libraries*. Canberra: Australian Academic & Research Libraries.

Haddon, AC 1890. The ethnography of the western tribe of Torres Strait. *Journal of the Anthropological Institute*, 19, 297–440.

—(ed.) 1901. *Reports of the Cambridge Anthropological Expedition to Torres Straits, Vol II: Physiology and psychology*. Cambridge: Cambridge University Press.

—1904. *Reports of the Cambridge Anthropological Expedition to Torres Straits, Vol V: Sociology, magic and religion of the Western Islanders*. Cambridge: Cambridge University Press.

—1907. *Reports of the Cambridge Anthropological Expedition to Torres Straits, Vol III: Linguistics*. Cambridge: Cambridge University Press.

—1908. *Reports of the Cambridge Anthropological Expedition to Torres Straits, Vol VI: Sociology, magic and religion of the Eastern Islanders*. Cambridge: Cambridge University Press.

—1912. *Reports of the Cambridge Anthropological Expedition to Torres Straits, Vol IV: Arts and crafts*. Cambridge: Cambridge University Press.

—1935. *Reports of the Cambridge Anthropological Expedition to Torres Straits, Vol I: General ethnography*. Cambridge: Cambridge University Press.

Haddon, AC & Seligmann, CG 1904. The training of a magician in Mabuiag. In AC Haddon (ed.), *Reports of the Cambridge Anthropological Expedition* to Torres Straits, Vol V: Sociology, magic and religion of the Western Islanders. Cambridge: Cambridge University Press.

Haddon AC & Wilkin, A 1904. Hero cults: The cult of Kwoiam. In AC Haddon (ed.), *Reports of the Cambridge Anthropological Expedition to Torres Straits, Vol V: Sociology, magic and religion of the Western Islanders*. Cambridge: Cambridge University Press.

Harding, S 1991. *Whose science? Whose knowledge?* New York: Cornell University Press.

Harris, M 1985. *Culture, people, nature: An introduction to general anthropology* (4th edn). New York: Harper & Row.

Hart, K 1998. The place of the 1898 Cambridge Anthropological Expedition to the Torres Straits. Paper presented at the opening session of the Anthropology and Psychology: The legacy of the Torres Strait expedition, 1898–1998 Conference, St John's College, Cambridge, 10–12 August 1998.

Heath, S 1983. *Ways with words: Language, life, and work in communities and classrooms*. Cambridge: Cambridge University Press.

Henriques, J, Holloway, W, Urwin, C, Venn, C & Walkerdine, V 1984. *Changing the subject: Psychology, social regulation and subjectivity*. London: Methuen.

Hoggart, R 1957. *The uses of literacy: Aspects of working-class life, with special reference to publications and entertainments*. London: Chatto & Windus.

Hoppers, C 2000. The centre-periphery in knowledge production in the 21st century. *Compare*, 30 (3), 283–291.

House of Representatives Standing Committee on Aboriginal and Torres Strait Islander Affairs 1997. *Torres Strait Islanders: A new deal*. Canberra: The Parliament of the Commonwealth of Australia.

Hunter, J 2002. Rights markup extensions for the protection of Indigenous knowledge. Paper presented at the 11th International WWW Conference, Honolulu Hawaii, 7–11 May 2002. Retrieved 5 August 2002 from http://www2002.org/CDROM/alternate/748/

——2005. The role of information technologies in Indigenous knowledge management. In M Nakata & M Langton (eds), *Australian Indigenous knowledge and libraries*. Kingston, ACT: Australian Academic & Research Libraries, Australian Library and Information Association.

Indigenous Knowledge and Development Monitor, 1993. Special Edition on the International Symposium on 'Indigenous Knowledge and Sustainable Development', held in September 1992 at the International Institute for Rural Reconstruction (IIRR) in Silang, Cavite, The Philippines, 1 (2). Retrieved 25 July 2000 from http://www.nuffic.nl/ciran/ikdm/1-2/contents.html

Janke, T 1997. *Our culture, our future: Proposals for the recognition and protection of Indigenous cultural and intellectual property*. Canberra: Australian Institute of Aboriginal and Torres Strait Islander Studies.

——1998. Our culture, our future: report on Australian Indigenous cultural and intellectual property right. Retrieved 27 July 2002 from http://www.icip.lawnet.com.au/

References

Jukes, J 1847. *Narrative of the surveying voyage of HMS* Fly, *commanded by Captain FP Blackwood, RN (during the years 1842–1846)*. London: Boone.

Kale, J 1988. Establishing positive learning environments for Aboriginal and Torres Strait Islander children in the earliest years of schooling. *The Aboriginal Child at School*, 16, 45–5.

Koenig, M 2001. Knowledge management, user education and librarianship. Paper presented at the 67th IFLA council and general conference, Boston USA, 16-25 August 2001. Retrieved 10 July 2002, from http://www.ifla.org/iv/ifla67/papers/085-99e.pdf

Langbridge, J 1977. From enculturation to evangelization: An account of missionary education in the islands of Torres Strait to 1915. Unpublished BA Hons thesis, Department of Education, James Cook University, Townsville.

Langton, M 1996. How Aboriginal religion has become an administrable subject. An extract from the opening keynote address of the 6th International Congress on Women, Adelaide, April 1996. Online paper at http://www.lib.latrobe.edu.au/AHR/archive/Issue-July-1996/langton.html

Langton, M & Ma Rhea, Z 2005. Traditional Indigenous biodiversity-related knowledge. In M Nakata & M Langton (eds) *Australian Indigenous knowledge and libraries*. Kingston, ACT: Australian Academic & Research Libraries, Australian Library and Information Association.

Lawrie, M 1984. A forgotten Torres Strait school. *Torres Strait Islander*, 6–8.

Lorde, A 1984. Sister outsider. Freedom CA: The Crossing Press.

Luke, A, Nakata, M, Garbutcheon-Singh, M, & Smith, R 1993. Policy and politics of representation: Torres Strait Islanders and Aboriginal people at the margins. In B Lingard, J Knight & P Porter (eds.), *Schooling reform in hard times*. London: The Falmer Press.

MacFarlane, S 1888. *Among the cannibals of New Guinea*. Philadelphia: Presbyterian Board of Publication and Sabbath School Work.

MacGillivray, J 1852. *Narrative of the voyage of HMS* Rattlesnake, *commanded by the late Captain Owen Stanley RN, FRS ETC. during the years 1846–1850*. London: T and W Boone.

Malcolm, IG & Rochecouste, J 2002. Barriers to Indigenous student success in higher education. Paper presented at HERDSA Annual Conference 7–10 July 2000, Perth, Western Australia. Retrieved 8 February 2006 from http://www.ecu.edu.au/conferences/herdsa/main/papers/nonref/pdf/IanMalcolm.pdf

Matejka, L 1973. Appendix 1: On the first Russian prolegomena to semiotics. In V Volosinov (translated by L Matejka & I Titunik, 1973), *Marxism and the philosophy of language*. Cambridge: Harvard University Press.

Ma Rhea, Z 2004. The preservation and maintenance of the knowledge of Indigenous peoples and local communities: the role of education. Paper presented at the Australian Association of Researchers in Education (AARE) Conference, Melbourne. Retrieved 22 February 2005 from http://www.aare.edu.au/04pap/mar04956.pdf

McConaghy, C 2000. Rethinking Indigenous education: Culturalism, colonialism & the politics of knowing. Flaxton: PostPressed.

McDermott, R 1982. Rigor and respect as standards in ethnographic description. *Harvard Education Review*, 48 (1), 321–8.

McDonald, H 1988. Succeeding against the odds: Torres Strait Islanders at university. *Queensland Researcher*, 4, 21–43.

McDougall, W 1903. Cutaneous sensations, muscular sense, variations of bloodpressure. In AC Haddon (ed.), *Reports of the Cambridge Anthropological Expedition to Torres Straits, Vol II Part II*. Cambridge: Cambridge University Press.

McInnes, A 1983. *The wreck of the* Charles Eaton. Windsor: Diamond Press.

Mead, GH 1964. *On social psychology*. Chicago: University of Chicago Press.

Mollison, P 1949. The administration of the Torres Strait Islands, Parts 1 & 2. *South Pacific*, 3, 197–200; 3, 217–20.

Moore, R & Muller, J 1999. The discourse of 'voice' and the problem of knowledge and identity in the sociology of education. *British Journal of Sociology of Education*, 20 (2), 189–206.

Morolo, T 2002. Indigenous knowledge system, National Research Foundation website. Retrieved 10 July 2002, from http://www.nrf.ac.za/focusareas/iks/

Mullins, S 1995. *Torres Strait: A history of colonial occupation and culture contact 1864–1897*. Rockhampton: CQU Publishing Unit.

Myer, L 1998. Biodiversity conservation and Indigenous knowledge: Rethinking the role of anthropology. *Indigenous Knowledge and Development Monitor*, 6 (1), 1–6. Retrieved 25 July 2002, from http://www.nuffic.nl/ciran/ikdm/6-1/myer.html

Myers, CS 1903. Hearing, smell, taste, reaction-times. In AC Haddon (ed.), *Reports of the Cambridge Anthropological Expedition to Torres Straits: Vol. II Part II* Cambridge: Cambridge University Press.

Nakashima, D & de Guchteneire, P 1999. Science and other systems of knowledge: A new impetus for Indigenous knowledge from the World Conference on Science. *Indigenous Knowledge and Development Monitor*, 7 (3), 1–3. Retrieved 10 July 2002, from http://www.nuffic.nl/ciran/ikdm/7-3/nakashima.html

Nakata, M 1991. Placing Torres Strait Islanders on a sociolinguistic and literate continuum: A critical commentary. *The Aboriginal Child at School*, 19, 39–53.

—— 1993. Culture in education: For us or for them? In N Loos & T Osanai (eds.), *Indigenous minorities and education: Australian and Japanese perspectives of their Indigenous peoples, the Ainu, Aborigines and Torres Strait Islanders*. Tokyo: San-You-Sha.

—— 1997a. Who's reading 'misplaced hopes'? *International Journal of Qualitative Studies in Education* 10 (4), 425–431.

—— 1997b. The Cultural Interface: An exploration of the intersection of Western knowledge systems and Torres Strait Islander positions and experiences. Unpublished doctoral thesis. James Cook University, Townsville.

References

—— 2002. Indigenous Knowledge and the Cultural Interface: Underlying issues at the intersection of knowledge and information systems. *IFLA Journal*, 28 (5/6), 281–91 (abridged version). Also in AH Hudson, J Matthews & A Woods (eds.) *Disrupting preconceptions: Postcolonialism and education*. Flaxton: Post Pressed.

——2003. Treaty and the self-determination agendas of Torres Strait Islanders: A common struggle. In H McGlade (ed.), *Treaty: Let's get it right*. Canberra: Aboriginal Studies Press.

—— (forthcoming). The Cultural Interface. *Special Issue of Journal of Indigenous Education*.

Nakata, M, Jensen, J & Nakata, V 1995. *Literacy issues in communities and schools on three Torres Strait islands: Report submitted to the management team of the Torres Strait cluster of schools participating in the Queensland Education Department's 'Striving for Success: The School Enhancement Project'*. Townsville: James Cook University of North Queensland Printery.

O'Brien, M 1984. The commatisation of women: Patriarchal fetishism in the sociology of education. *Interchange*. 15 (2), 43–60.

Orr, G 1977. Education, language and ideology: A Torres Strait case study. Unpublished Master's thesis, University of Queensland, Brisbane.

Orr, G 1982. Language instruction in Torres Strait Islander schools: Some preliminary considerations for school-based curriculum development. *The Aboriginal Child at School*, 10, 48–57.

Orr, M 1979. Language instruction in Torres Strait Island primary schools: A case study in the initiation and promulgation of cultural democracy. Unpublished PhD thesis, Florida State University, Florida.

Orr, K & Williamson, A 1973. *Education in the Torres Strait: Perspectives for development*. Canberra: The Research School of Pacific Studies, Australian National University.

Osborne, B 1979. A justification of the new strategies to prepare teachers of Aboriginal and Torres Strait Islander pupils in Queensland. Unpublished Master's thesis, James Cook University, Townsville.

—— 1982. Field dependence/independence of Torres Strait Islander and Aboriginal pupils. *Journal of Intercultural Studies*, 3, 5–18.

—— 1985. Reflections on education in the Torres Strait: Zuni insights. *The Aboriginal Child at School*, 13, 3–11.

—— 1986. *Torres Strait Islander styles of communication and learning (Torres Strait Working Papers 1)*. Townsville: James Cook University of North Queensland.

—— 1988. Teachers' initial perceptions of teaching at Thursday Island State High School. *Queensland Researcher*, 4, 45–65.

Osborne, B & Bamford, B 1987. *Torres Strait Islanders teaching Torres Strait Islander II (Torres Strait Working Papers 4)*. Townsville: James Cook University of North Queensland.

Osborne, B & Coombs, G 1982. Teaching Aboriginal and Torres Strait Islander pupils who are field-dependent. In P Beinssen & J Parker (eds.) *Focus on *practice (Volume 1)*. Aitkenvale (North Queensland): Queensland Special Education Association.

—— 1987. *Setting up an intercultural encounter: An ethnographic study of 'settling down' a Thursday Island High School class (Torres Strait Working Papers 6)*. Townsville: James Cook University of North Queensland.

—— 1988. Research into Torres Strait Islander Education. *Queensland Researcher*, 4, 75–84.

Osborne, B & Francis, D 1987. *Torres Strait Islanders teaching Torres Strait Islander III (Torres Strait Working Papers 5)*. Townsville: James Cook University of North Queensland.

Osborne, B & Henderson, L 1985. Black and White perspectives of teaching practice 1: Supervising teachers' perspectives. *South Pacific Journal of Teacher Education*, 13, 30–43.

Osborne, B & Sellars, N 1987. *Torres Strait Islanders teaching Torres Strait Islander I (Torres Strait Working Papers 3)*. Townsville: James Cook University of North Queensland.

Osborne, E 1997. *Torres Strait Islander women in the Pacific War*. Canberra: Aboriginal Studies Press.

Osborne, B & Dawes, G 1992. Preparation, negotiation and teacher vulnerability in a Thursday Island classroom. Paper presented at ATEA conference July 1992, James Cook University of North Queensland, Townsville.

Penfold, C 1996. Indigenous issues in the mainstream curriculum: Help or hindrance for Indigenous law students? Paper delivered at the 1996 Australasian Law Teachers Association Conference.

Peterson, N 1990. Studying man and man's nature: The history of the institutionalisation of Aboriginal anthropology. The Wentworth Lectures 1990. Retrieved 20 November 2003, from http://www.aiatsis.gov.au/lbry/dig_prgm/wentworth/m0006639_a.rtf

——1996. Mills family report. Unpublished manuscript.

Pohlhaus, G 2002. Knowing communities: An investigation of Harding's standpoint epistemology. *Social Epistemology*, 16 (3), 283–93.

Prideaux, P 1988. *Somerset, Cape York Peninsula, 1864–1877: From spear to pearl-shell*. Brisbane: Boolarong Publications.

Raven-Hart, R 1949. *The happy isles*. Melbourne: Georgian House.

Ray, SH 1907. Linguistics. In AC Haddon (ed.) *Reports of the Cambridge Anthropological Expedition to Torres Straits: Vol III* Cambridge: Cambridge University Press.

Rivers, WHR 1901. Physiology and psychology. In AC Haddon (ed.) *Reports of the Cambridge Anthropological Expedition to Torres Straits: Vol II*. Cambridge: Cambridge University Press.

——1904. Genealogy, kinship, totemism, personal names. In AC Haddon (ed.) *Reports of the Cambridge Anthropological Expedition to Torres Straits: Vol V*. Cambridge: Cambridge University Press.

——1908. Social organisation. In AC Haddon (ed.) *Reports of the Cambridge Anthropological Expedition to Torres Straits: Vol VI*. Cambridge: Cambridge University Press.

References

Roldan, A 1993. Looking at anthropology from a biological point of view: AC Haddon's metaphors on anthropology. *History of Human Sciences* 5 (4), 21–32.

Russell, L 2005. Indigenous knowledge and the archives: Accessing hidden history and understandings. In M Nakata & M Langton (eds), *Australian Indigenous knowledge and libraries*. Kingston, ACT: Australian Academic & Research Libraries, Australian Library and Information Association.

Ryan, W 1971. *Blaming the victim*. New York: Vintage Books.

Saussure, F 1959. *Course in general linguistics*. New York: The Philosophical Library.

——1972. *Course in linguistics* (edited by C Bally, & A Sechehaye, with the collaboration of A Riedlinger; translated and annotated by R Harris). London: Duckworth.

Saw, G 1992. Indigenous knowledge: The librarian's role in reversing the north-south flow of information resources. In *Libraries: the heart of the matter, proceedings of the Australian Library and Information Association 2nd biennial conference, 27 September–2 October 1992*. Port Melbourne: D. W. Thorpe.

Scott Fitzgerald, F 1993. *Tender is the night*. London: Orion Publisher.

Seligmann, CG 1904. Birth and childhood customs, women's puberty customs. In AC Haddon (ed.) *Reports of the Cambridge Anthropological Expedition to Torres Straits: Vol.V.* Cambridge: Cambridge University Press.

Sharp, N 1993. *Stars of Tagai: The Torres Strait Islanders*. Canberra: Aboriginal Studies Press.

Shnukal, A 1984a. Torres Strait Islander students in Queensland mainland schools — Part 1: Language Background. *The Aboriginal Child at School*, 12, 13–21.

—— 1984b. Torres Strait Islander students in Queensland mainland schools — Part 2: Language Background. *The Aboriginal Child at School*, 12, 27–33

—— 1988. *Broken: An introduction to the Creole language of Torres Strait*. Canberra: Department of Linguistics, Australian National University.

Singe, J 1989. *The Torres Strait: People and history*. Brisbane: University of Queensland Press.

Smith, D 1987. *The everyday world as problematic: A feminist sociology*. Boston: Northeastern University Press.

—— 1990. *The conceptual practices of power: A feminist sociology of knowledge*. Boston: Northeastern University Press.

—— 1999. *Writing the social: Critique, theory & investigations*. Toronto: University of Toronto Press.

Smith, LT 1999. *Decolonizing methodologies: Research and Indigenous peoples*. Dunedin: University of Otago Press.

Sonn, C, Bishop, B & Humphries, R 1996. Risk and protective factors that influence the participation of indigenous students in mainstream courses: Preliminary findings [1]. Different approaches: Theory and practice in higher education. Proceedings HERDSA Conference 1996. Perth, Western

Australia, 8–12 July. Retrieved 8 February 2006, from http://www.herdsa.org.au/confs/1996/sonn.html

Thompson, E 1978. *Making of the English working class*. Harmondsworth: Penguin.

Torres Strait Islander Regional Education Committee 1985. Policy statement on education in Torres Strait. Unpublished monograph.

Trinh T Minh-ha 1989. *Woman, native, other*. Bloomington: Indiana University Press.

United Nations Development Programme's (UNDP) Civil Society Organisations and Participation Programme (CSOPP) 1995. Conserving Indigenous knowledge — integrating new systems of integration. Retrieved 10 July 2002, from http://www.undp.org/csopp/CSO/New Files/dociknowledge.html

United Nations Conference on Trade and Development (UNCTAD) 2002. The state of the debate on traditional knowledge. Paper presented at the International seminar on systems for the protection and commercialisation of traditional knowledge, in particular traditional medicines, New Delhi, 3–5 April 2002. Retrieved 25 July 2002, from http://www.unctad.org/trade_env/test1/meetings/delhi/statedebateTK.doc

Usher, K, Lindsay, D, Miller, M & Miller A 2005. Challenges faced by Indigenous nursing students and strategies that aided their progress in the course: A descriptive study. *Contemporary Nurse*, 19 (1–2), 17–31.

Verran, H 2005. Knowledge traditions of Aboriginal Australians: Questions and answers arising in a databasing project. Draft published by Making Collective Memory with Computers. School of Australian Indigenous Knowledge Systems, Charles Darwin University, Darwin, Northern Territory. Retrieved 15 May 2006 from http://www.cdu.ed.au/centres/ik/pdf/knowledgeanddatabasing.pdf

Volosinov, VN (translated by L Matejka & I Titunik, 1973). *Marxism and the philosophy of language*. Cambridge: Harvard University Press.

Von Liebenstein, G 2000. Interfacing global and Indigenous knowledge: Towards an Indigenous knowledge information system. Paper presented at the 6th UNESCO-APEID international conference on education, Bangkok Thailand, 12–15 December 2000, Bangkok Thailand. Retrieved 26 July 2002, from http://www.developmentgateway.org/ node/130646/browser/?keyword_list=233182&country_list=0

Walby, S 2000. Beyond the politics of location: The power of argument in a global era. *Feminist Theory*, 1 (2) 189–206.

Walker, R 2000. *Indigenous performance in Western Australian universities: Reframing retention and success*. Canberra: Department of Education, Training and Youth Affairs.

Warren, M 1991. Using Indigenous knowledge in agricultural development. The World Bank discussion paper no. 127. Washington, D.C.: The World Bank.

References

——1993. Using Indigenous knowledge for agriculture and rural development: Current issues. *Indigenous Knowledge and Development Monitor*, 1 (1), 1–6. Retrieved 25 July 2002, from http://www.nuffic.nl/ciran/ikdm/1-1/warren.html

Warren, M, von Liebenstein, G & Slikkerveer, L 1993. Networking for Indigenous knowledge. *Indigenous Knowledge and Development Monitor*, 1 (1), 1–4. Retrieved 25 July 2002, from http://www.nuffic.nl/ciran/ikdm/1-1/warren_l_s.html

Watson, H 1988. Language and mathematics education for Aboriginal-Australian children. *Language and Education*. 2 (4), 255–273.

Watts, B (ed.) 1971. *The national workshop on Aboriginal education: Priorities for action and research*. Brisbane: University of Queensland.

Weedon, C 1999. *Feminism, theory & the politics of difference*. Malden, Mass.: Blackwell Publishers.

Wemyss, T 1837. *Narrative of the melancholy shipwreck of the Charles Eaton, and the inhuman massacre of the passengers and crew; with an account of the rescue of two boys from the hands of the savages in an island in Torres Straits*. Stockton: W Robinson.

White, G 1917. *Round about the Torres Straits*. London: Central Board of Missions.

Whittle, P 1997. WHR Rivers: A founding father worth remembering. Paper given to the Zangwill Club of the Department of Experimental Psychology, Cambridge University, 6 December 1997.

Wilkin, A 1904. Tales of the war-path: The feud between Mabuiag and Moa. In AC Haddon (ed.), *Reports of the Cambridge Anthropological Expedition to Torres Straits, Vol V: Sociology, magic and religion of the Western Islanders*. Cambridge: Cambridge University Press.

Williams, R 1958. *Culture and society*. Harmondsworth: Penguin, in association with Chatto & Windus.

——1961. *The long revolution*. London: Chatto & Windus.

——1973. *The country and the city*. St Albans: Paladin.

——1977. *Marxism and literature*. Oxford: Oxford University Press.

Williamson, A 1974. Torres Strait pupils. *New Guinea and Australia, the Pacific and SE Asia*, 8 (4), 50–61.

——1994. *Schooling the Torres Strait Islanders 1873 to 1941: Context, custom and colonialism*. Adelaide: Aboriginal Research Institute Publications.

——1997. Decolonizing historiography of colonial education: Processes of interaction in the schooling of Torres Strait Islanders. *International Journal of Qualitative Studies in Education* 10 (4), 407–23.

Woods, P 1986. *Inside schools: Ethnography in educational research*. London: Routledge & Kegan Paul.

World Bank Group, The (n.d.). What is Indigenous knowledge. Retrieved 10 July 2002, from http://www.worldbank.org/afr/ik/basic.htm

Worsley, P 1968. *The trumpet shall sound: A study of 'Cargo' cults in Melanesia*. New York: Schoken.

Index

Aboriginal and Torres Strait Islander Commission, 148, 150
Aboriginal Industries Board, 135
Aboriginal people, differentiation of Torres Strait Islanders from, 133–4, 173, 177
Aborigines Protection and Prevention of the Sale of Opium Act 1897–1901, 133–4
academy, *see* higher education; research
acidity (taste), 90
Ad, 118
administration of Islander affairs, 129–51
adultery, 122–3
aesthetics, 55–67
agency, 205, 207–8, 216
Agrawal, A, 187–8
Agud (Augud), 112–13, 118–19
algometers, 95, 99
Among the Cannibals of New Guinea, 15–17, 19–25
ancestor worship, 117–18
animal totems/clan groups, 112–14
anthropology, 26–7, 101–28, 189
  biological sciences and, 44
  national education policy statement (1989) schema borrowed from, 178
assimilation policies, 139–40

astigmatism, 50
ATSIC, 148, 150
auditory tests, 76–84, 91
Augud, 112–13, 118–19
Australian mainland, *see* mainland
authority structures, 105–12
  see also Queensland government; religion

bartering, 121–2
Bartlett, Frederick Charles, 109
bêche-de-mer fishing, *see* marine industry
Beckett, J, 143
beliefs, *see* religion
bicultural education, 173
bile, association of words for colours with, 59
bilingual education, 160, 172, 175–6
binocular vision, 68
biology, 44
  see also physiology and physiological investigations
births, *see* childbirth and pregnancy
bisection of lines tests, 69–70
bitterness (taste), 90
Bjelke Petersen, Sir Joh, 141
black (colour), 61, 64, 65, 66
Bleakley, John William, 134, 140, 161
blindness, colour, 57–8, 75

Index

blood, association of word for 'red' with, 59, 60, 61
blood feuds, 127
blood pressure, 98–100
blue (colour), 57, 59, 60, 61–7
　yellow–blue blindness, 58
boats, 111
　trade of canoes, 121
　see also company boats; marine industry
border issue, Australian–Papua New Guinea, 143
Boxall, R & Duncan, W, 160
boys, 126
　dark, vision in, 50–1
　eyes' physiological condition, 46
　hearing, 79, 80
　pain thresholds, 95–6
　reaction times, 91
　size–weight illusions, 97
　smell, 85–6
　spatial perception, 69–73
　see also initiations
brain functions, 44
brightness, sensibility to, 52–3
Brothers Grimm, 102–3
bulu-bulu, 62–3, 64

Cambridge Anthropological Expedition, 26–128
cannibalism, 16, 18–20, 21, 23, 25, 123
canoes, trade of, 121
Cape York, 17, 32, 118, 148
cargo cults, 169
Carter, P, 164
cash economy, 136–7
cataracts, 45
Catholic Convent School, Thursday Island, 4, 6
cerebral cortex, 44
ceremonies, 106–7, 115–19, 127
　funerals, 125
　see also initiations
Charles Eaton, 18–19, 123
childbirth and pregnancy, 116

infanticide and foeticide, 123, 124–6
maternity allowances, 145
children, 124–6
　colour nomenclature, 58
　eyes' physiological condition, 45
　hearing, 80, 81, 83, 84
　knowledge of kinship systems, 109–10
　smell, 84–5, 87, 88
　visual acuity, 47–8, 49–50
　see also boys; girls
Christianity, 115, 125, 206
　clothes worn to church, 66–7
　see also missionaries
Christie, Michael, 188
citizenship rights, 134, 140, 145–6
clans, 112–14
　see also kinship systems
class, 156–8, 160
clothing, 120–1
　worn to church, 66–7
co-operation and unco-operation (agency), 205, 207–8, 216
co-operative lugger schemes, *see* company boats
colonial institutions and processes, 129–47, 201–7
　in education, 160–72
　Indigenous Knowledge and, 182, 184
　Islander lifeworlds in relation to, 7–8
　see also nineteenth century; Queensland government
colour, 56–67
colour blindness, 57–8, 75
colour preference, 66–7
commerce and trade, 121–2, 134–5
Commonwealth government, 139–41, 145, 147–51, 158, 177–81
communication technology, 174
community development, 140–1, 178
company boats, 134–5, 136, 137, 146, 161

Maritime Strike 1936, 131, 138–9, 143, 145
comparative studies, 30, 32–128
conjunctivas, 45–6
conservation and environment, 149–50, 183–4, 187
continuity and discontinuity, 141–74, 204–7
corneas, 45–6
Council system, 131, 132, 145, 148
counting tests, 48
Creole (Kriol), 6, 176
Cultural Interface, 195–212, 215–16, 219–21
Cultural Studies, 157–8
culture, 9–10, 158–9
   bicultural education, 173
   detachment of conceptualisation of Indigenous Knowledge from, 184, 189
   Indigenous students' knowledge of, 219–22
   in policy, 177–81
   see also Indigenous Knowledge; Islander culture; lifeworlds
curfews, 131, 137
curricula, 6, 155, 159, 160, 168
   higher education, 219, 224;
   incorporation of Indigenous Knowledge, 188–92
cutaneous sensations, 92–6

dark, vision in, 50–1
Darnley Island, 16–17, 20
   Council, 146
Dauar, 127
Dawes, G & Osborne, B, 165
deafness and hearing, 76–84, 91
death, 117–18
   infanticide and foeticide, 123, 124–6
   see also warfare and fighting
deities, *see* religion
Department of Employment, Education and Training, 177–81
development literature, 183–7
dialects, *see* languages and linguistics

discipline and regulation, 129–51, 180–1
discontinuity and continuity, 141–74, 204–7
dissection of lines tests, 69–70
distance hearing, 77–8
distance vision (hypermetropia), 49, 50, 53–4
distances, estimation of, 68–75
diving, affect on hearing of, 77, 81–2
divorce, 124
'domestic morality', 122–3
Douglas, John, 134
Duncan, W & Boxall, R, 160

E method visual acuity tests, 47, 48, 49, 52–3
earnings, 134, 136–7, 161–2
ears and hearing, 76–84, 91
eastern Islands and Islanders, *see* Murray Island
education, 5, 23, 145, 146–7, 155–81
   cultural paradigm (culturalism), 9–10
   evangelical, 20, 23, 174
   magicians, 115–16
   Nakata family, 1–11
employment, 131, 135–7, 168, 178
   see also marine industry
English as a Second Language (ESL), 165, 172, 175–6
English language, 4, 6, 147, 160
   colour nomenclature, 59, 60
   as language of instruction, 159, 161–2, 170, 172–7
   Snellen's letter test-types, 47–8
environment and conservation, 149–50, 183–4, 187
environmental factors as explanation of intellectual development, 156–8
Erub, *see* Darnley Island
ethical codes, 119–27
ethnology, 27, 101–28
etiquette, 110–11, 143–4
Europeans, 143–4, 146

first contact, 15–25; Haddon's reconstruction of Islander society before, 104–7, 121
 reincarnation of Islanders as, 117
 teachers, 167–8
the exotic, 177, 180
eyes and seeing, 43–75, 91
Eyzaguirre, Pablo B, 186

family histories (genealogies), 109, 113, 126
 Nakata family, 2–7, 141
 see also kinship systems
Federal government, 139–41, 145, 147–51, 158, 177–81
feeling and touch, 92–8, 100
females, *see* women
feminist standpoint theory, 213
feuds, 127
fighting, *see* warfare and fighting
finances, 4, 146
 wages and earnings, 134, 136–7, 161–2
Finch, N, 160, 174
finger nail pain thresholds, 95–6
fishing, 111, 149–50
 see also marine industry
Fletcher, J, 156
flower names, 60
foeticide and infanticide, 123, 124–6
folktales and myths, 102–5, 118–19, 121, 124
forehead/forefinger nail pain thresholds, 95–6
Frazer, Sir James, 113
freedom of movement, 6, 131, 137, 149
Freire, P, 157
funeral ceremonies, 125

G, Mary, 216–17
gall bladder, association of words for colours with, 59
Galton whistle, 81
Ganter, R, 134, 135, 143
genealogies, *see* family histories

Germany, 102–3
ghosts, 117–18
girls, 124
 hearing, 79
 infanticide, 123, 125, 126
 spatial perception, 72–3
gods, *see* religion
golegole, 64
government teacher-supervisors, 131, 137, 138
grammar, 32–41
green (colour), 59, 60, 61, 64
 preference for, 66, 67
 red–green blindness, 57
Grimm Brothers, 102–3
grounded theory, 165–7
Guillery's method, 48

Haddon, Alfred Cort, 27–9, 101–8, 112–27
 linguistic work, 60
 smelling tests on, 86
 vision tests on, 50
Hasluck, Paul, 139–40
head hunting, 18, 123, 127
hearing, 76–84, 91
Heath, S, 174
Hering's fall experiment, 68
heroes, 118, 120–1
High Court Mabo decision, 143
high school education, 6, 7, 145
high tones, hearing of, 81–3
higher education, 2–3, 8–11, 218–25
 incorporation of Indigenous Knowledge into, 182–92
 see also research
Hill-Barnard sphygmometer, 99
history, 2–7
 educational discourse, 155–81
 of languages, 32–41, 102–3
 'past' and 'present', 201–7
 see also Islander history
HMS *Rattlesnake,* 17
Holmgren's red-green blindness test, 57

House of Representatives Standing Committee on Aboriginal and Torres Strait Islander Affairs report, 150–1
housing, 46
human rights discourse, 139, 156, 158
humour, 216–17
hunting, 111
hypermetropia, 49, 50, 53–4

icons, 118–19
ideology, 177
illusions, 44, 67–85
  size–weight, 96–8, 100
imi, 111–12
incest, 122
Indigenous humour, 216–17
Indigenous Knowledge (local knowledge), 1–3, 182–92, 219–25
  visual powers and, 53–6
Indigenous standpoint theory, 213–17
indigo (colour), 66
indirect rule, 130–1
industry, *see* marine industry
infanticide, 123, 124–6
initiations, 111, 119, 124
  magicians, 115
  Pulu, 123
integration policies, 140–1
intellectual property and Indigenous Knowledge, 185–6
intelligence and intellectual development, 55, 98–100, 155–7
Island Coordinating Council system, 148
Island Council system, 131, 132, 145, 148
Island Funds, 136
Island Industries Board, 135
'Island Law', 138
'Island police', 131, 138
Islander agency, 205, 207–8, 216
Islander culture, 9–10, 101–28, 142–4, 195–212
  Commonwealth government policy, 150–1, 177–81
  MacFarlane's perception of, 16, 19–20, 21–4
Islander education, *see* education
Islander history, 2–7, 15–25, 129–51
  Cambridge Reports as sources, 28
  education, 6, 145, 155, 159–72, 174; Naghir Island, 5
  Haddon's reconstruction of pre-contact society, 104–7, 121
  theoretical constructions, 201–7
  see also family histories

Jackson, John Hughlings, 44
Jukes, Joseph Beete, 21

kinship systems, 109–12, 113
  parent–child relationship, 123, 124–6
  see also marriage
Kiwai Islanders, 47, 57–8, 63–4, 67
knowledge systems, 1–3, 8–11, 169–71, 182–92, 197–207
  culture in policy and, 180–1
  Indigenous epistemological basis, 219–20
  middle class as normative, 156–8
  see also lifeworlds
kogem, 123
kosekerlam, 123
Kriol (Torres Strait Creole), 6, 176
kuasar-kupa, 123
kulka, 60
kupa-kuasar, 122–3

labour, 131, 135–7, 168, 178
  see also marine industry
land rights, 143, 181
languages and linguistics, 10, 32–41, 160, 172–7
  documented by missionaries, 23
  Grimm's Law, 102–3
  Haddon's rendering and distilling of folktales and myths, 103–4
  Torres Strait Creole (Kriol), 6, 176

see also English language; nomenclature; oral traditions; Ray, Sidney H
lease arrangements, Nakata family's islands, 3, 4, 6, 141
legislation, 77, 130–1, 133–4, 148, 149–50
'Island Law', 138
length, estimation of, 69–75
letter test-types, 47–8
lifeworlds, 7–8, 130, 197–201
  colour nomenclature reflecting, 59–60, 62–3
  hearing and, 77–8
  language communities and, 38–9
  smell and, 89
  in Watson's linear model of language, 172, 173–6
lines, spatial perception tests involving, 69–72
linguistics, *see* languages and linguistics
literacy, 4, 47–8, 174–5, 176
local knowledge, *see* Indigenous Knowledge
London Missionary Society (LMS), 15–17, 19–25, 131, 167
  formal education provided by, 3, 20, 23, 174
  Walker, Rev Fred, 134–5, 146
long-distance hearing, 77–8
long-distance vision (hypermetropia), 49, 50, 53–4
Lovibond's Tintometer, 65–6
Lu babat, 118
luggers, *see* company boats

Mabo judgment, 143
Mabuiag Island/Islanders, 42, 116
  colour nomenclature, 61, 63, 64
  hearing, 79, 80
  kinship system, 111–12
  taste, 90
  visual acuity, 47, 51
Macedo, Donald, 162
MacFarlane, Rev Samuel, 15–17, 19–25

MacGillivray, John, 17–18, 21, 117, 118, 122, 123
magic and *maidelaigs*, 113, 114–17, 125, 206
mainland, 17, 131, 148
  languages, 32; colour nomenclature, 64
  pre-contact trade with, 121
  religion, 118
  schools, 6, 7
males, *see* men
maludgamulnga, 64
mamus system, 131
mari, 117
marine industry, 5, 6, 149–50
  Nakata family fleet, 3, 4
  workforce, 29, 131, 133–4, 136; divers, 77, 81–2
  see also boats; company boats
Maritime Strike 1936, 131, 138–9, 143, 145
'the mark', 155
markai, 117
marriage, 122, 137
  couples' colour preferences, 66
  kinship and, 110, 111–12
  Pulu, 123
  totemic system, 113
  see also childbirth and pregnancy
Marxism and the Philosophy of Language, 39
Mary G, 216–17
massacre of *Charles Eaton* shipwreck survivors, 18–19, 123
Masson's Disc test, 52–3
maternity allowances, 145
mathematics education, Watson's approach to, 172–5
McDougall, Dr William, 27–9, 42, 89–90, 92–100
McInnes, A, 18
meaning (semantics), 38–9, 173–4
measles, 76–7
memory, 58–9, 88–9
men, 103, 116
  colour nomenclature, 58–9
  colour preferences, 66, 67

eyes' physiological condition, 45, 46
hearing, 81
kinship, 110, 111–12
pain thresholds, 95–6
reaction times, 91
size–weight illusions, 97–8
smell, 86–8
spatial perception, 69–74
tactile discrimination, 93–4
taste, 90
see also boys; marriage
mental development and intelligence, 55, 98–100, 155–7
Mer, *see* Murray Island
Mills, Frank, 4–6, 141
Mills, James, 3–4, 5
Miriam people, *see* Murray Island
missionaries, 15–25, 118, 125
    Catholic Convent School, Thursday Island, 4, 6
    influences noted by Haddon, 120–1
    see also London Missionary Society
Moa Island, 174
money, *see* finances
morality, 119–27
mother-of-pearl shell industry, *see* marine industry
movement, freedom of, 6, 131, 137, 149
Müller–Lyer Illusion test, 69, 72–4
Mullins, S, 164
Murray, Mr, 20
Murray Island (Mer) and Miriam people (eastern Islands and Islanders), 17–18, 60, 141, 147
    Council, 145, 146
    see also London Missionary Society
Murray Island (Mer) and Miriam people (eastern Islands and Islanders), Cambridge Anthropological Expedition tests and observations on, 27–8, 42
    colour blindness, 57–8, 75
    counting, 48
    cultural movements assumed from folktales and myths, 104, 105
    eyes' physiological condition, 45
    families and population control, 126
    hearing, 76–84, 91
    language, 32–7, 40; adultery, words for, 123; colour nomenclature, 58–65
    pain thresholds, 95–6
    reaction times, 91–2
    smell, 85–8
    social groupings, 108
    spatial perception, 69–74
    tactile discrimination, 94
    taste, 90
    temperament, 127
    trade, 121–2
    visual acuity, 47, 49, 50, 51, 91
Myers, Dr Charles S, 27–9, 42, 76–92, 100, 114
myopia, 49–50, 51
myths and folktales, 102–5, 118–19, 121, 124

Naghir Island, 3–6
nails, pain thresholds for, 95–6
Nakata family, 1–11, 141
naming systems, *see* nomenclature
National Aboriginal and Torres Strait Islander Education Policy, 177–81
Native Title, 150
    Mabo judgment, 143
neurology, 44
New Guinea, *see* Papua New Guinea
New South Wales Department of Education, 155–6
nightly curfews, 131, 137
1912 Island Fund, 136
nineteenth century, 15–25, 130–1, 133–4
    Cambridge Anthropological Expedition, 26–128
    legislation, 77, 130–1, 133
    see also London Missionary Society
'noble savage', 21–2

nomenclature (vocabulary), 35, 36, 55
   adultery, terms for, 122–3
   colour terms, 56–67
   counting terms, 48
   ghost *(markai)* and spirit *(mari)*, distinction between, 117
   kinship terms, 109–10
   Saussure's contentions, 38
   taste terms, 90
   totems and icons, terms for, 111–12, 118–19
Non-government Organisations (NGOs), 183, 184–5
nostrils, 84
nudity, 120–1
numbers and counting, 48

O'Leary, Cornelius, 138–9
olfactory tests, 84–9
oral traditions, 3, 172–7
   myths and folktales, 102–5, 118–19, 121, 124
   see also Indigenous Knowledge
orange (colour), 60, 61
Orr, K & Williamson, A, 160
Osborne, B and Dawes, G, 165
'Other', 195–6, 200–1
   the exotic, 177, 180
   lower class, 156–8
otorrhoea, 76
ownership of Indigenous Knowledge, 185–6

Pacific Islanders, *see* South Sea (Pacific) Islanders
pain thresholds, 95–6, 100
Papua New Guinea, 88
   border issue, 143
   Cambridge Anthropological Expedition in, 28, 32; tests carried out on Kiwai Islanders, 47, 57–8, 63–4, 67
   London Missionary Society in, 15, 20, 23
   trade with, 121

Papuan Industries Limited (PIL), 135, 146
Papuan Institute, establishment of, 20–1
parent–child relationship, 123, 124–6
parturition, *see* childbirth and pregnancy
'past' and 'present', 201–7
pay and earnings, 134, 136–7, 161–2
pearling industry, *see* marine industry
peripheral retinas, vision of, 65–6
personal names, 109, 110
personal relationships, 122–7
   see also kinship systems; marriage; warfare and fighting
perspective, *see* standpoints
philology, 33–4, 57, 59, 63
physiology and physiological investigations, 42–3, 76–100
   of eye, 44–6, 65–6, 68, 71–2; refraction, 49, 51
pinguicula, 45–6
pink (colour), 61, 66
pitch, differences in, 82–3
political autonomy, 143, 145, 147–51, 200
Politzer's Hormesser, 78, 79
population control (infanticide), 123, 124–6
post-colonial critiques, 164
pre-contact society, Haddon's reconstruction of, 104–7, 121
pregnancy, *see* childbirth and pregnancy
'present' and 'past', 201–7
printed material, 174–5
protection of Indigenous Knowledge, 185–6
Protectors and protectionist policies, 6, 131–46
   missionaries, 20–1, 24–5
psychology and psychological investigations, 26–7, 42–75, 158

environmental factors as
explanation of intellectual
development, 156–8
into languages, 32–41
pterygium, 45–6
Pulu, 123
pupils (eyes), 46
purple (colour), 61, 66
puru, 122

quarrels, settling of, 127
see also warfare and fighting
Queensland government, 6, 29,
130–49, 208
dealings with Nakata family, 3, 4,
5, 141
educational policies, 6, 155, 159,
167–8
legislation, 77, 130–1, 133–4

racism, 3–4, 168, 203
see also Protectors and protectionist
policies
Rattlesnake, 17
Ray, Sidney H, 28–9, 32–41, 64
Islander terms for 'adultery', 122–3
Islander words corresponding with
'bitter', 90
kulka, 60
markai ('ghost') and *mari* ('spirit'),
distinction between, 117
reaction times, 90, 91–2
reading (literacy), 4, 47–8, 174–5,
176
red (colour), 57, 59, 60, 61, 62, 65
preference for, 66, 67
red–green blindness, 57
refraction of eye, 49, 51
Regional Assembly, 151
regional (political) autonomy, 143,
145, 147–51, 200
regulation and discipline, 129–51,
180–1
reincarnation, 117
relations, *see* kinship systems
religion, 112–19, 206

clothes worn to church, 66–7
see also missionaries
research, 195–225
Cambridge Anthropological
Expedition, 26–128
educational, 155–81
incorporation of Indigenous
Knowledge into scientific corpus,
182–92
retinas, vision of peripheral, 65–6
rights, 6, 131–2, 140–1, 145–6,
147–51
Government Resident Douglas'
opinion, 134
over Indigenous Knowledge,
185–6
Rivers, Dr William HR, 27–9,
42–75, 89, 127
anthropological work, 101,
108–14, 124
hearing tests on, 79–80
smelling tests on, 86, 87
Royal Commission into Aboriginal
Deaths in Custody, 151
Runne's clock, 78–9
Ryan, W, 156–67

Saibai Island, 112
saltiness (taste), 90
Samoa, Jimmy, 3–4, 5
Sarawak, 28
Sassoon, Siegfried, 127
Saussure, Ferdinand de, 33, 37–9, 41
schooling, *see* education
scientific research, *see* research
sea, association of word for 'blue'
with, 60, 61, 62
sea cucumber fishing, *see* marine
industry
sea rights, 150, 181
Second World War, 139, 143,
144–5, 162
secondary education, 6, 7, 145
seeing and vision, 43–75, 91
segregation and separate
development, 131, 136–41

Index

in schooling, 6, 167, 168
self-employment, 135–6
self-management, 140–1, 147–51, 178
Seligmann, Charles S, 28–9, 42, 100
  anthropological work, 101, 124;
  magic and religion, 114, 116–18;
  taboos, 107, 108
  hearing tests on, 80
  taste experiments, 89–90
semantics, 38–9, 173–4
sensitivity to pain, 95–6, 100
separate development, *see* segregation and separate development
sexual relations, 108, 113, 122–3, 137
  see also marriage
Sharp, Noni, 130, 138–9, 141–4
shipwrecks, 18–19, 123
Shnukal, Anna, 173
short-sightedness (myopia), 49–50, 51
sight and vision, 43–75, 91
size–weight illusions, 96–8, 100
skin sensations, 92–6
skulls, preservation of, 117–18
sliding rule estimates, 72–4
smell, 84–9
Snellen's letter test-types, 47–8
Snellen's No. LIV method, 48
social etiquette, 110–11, 143–4
social organisation, 101–28
  MacFarlane's observations, 21–4
  see also standpoints
sociology, 158
  symbolic interactionist, 165–7
sorcery/magic, 113, 114–17, 125, 206
souls, 117
South Sea (Pacific) Islanders, 20, 127, 146
  in marine industry, 133
spatial perception, 67–85
speech, *see* languages and linguistics
sphygmometers, 99
spirits *(mari)*, 117

spiritualism, *see* religion
squints, 45
standpoint theory, 213–17
standpoints, Islander/Indigenous, 1–2, 142–7, 196–7, 203–4, 208–17
  consideration by educational historians, 160–3, 170–1
  culture as disciplinary concept and, 180–1
state dependency, 136–8
stealing, 122
strabismus, 45
susceptibility to pain, 95–6, 100
suserisuseri, 64
sweetness (taste), 90
symbolic interactionist sociology, 165–7
synchronic dimensions of languages, 39–40

taboos, 107–8, 113, 119
tactile discrimination, 92–5
taste, 89–90
teacher-supervisors, 131, 137, 138
teacher training, 160, 167
  Murray Island institute, 174
teachers, 1, 6, 160, 167–8
  English as a Second Language, 165
  Naghir Island, 4, 5
  see also curricula
temperament, 92, 123, 126–7, 156
  clan members, 113–14
  see also warfare and fighting
temperature spots on skin, 95
terra nullius, 143
testing of Torres Strait Islanders, 42–100
theft, 122
theoretical constructions, 195–217
thresholds of pain, 95–6, 100
Thursday Island, 1, 5, 137, 148
  Cambridge Anthropological Expedition on, 29, 77
  Government Resident, 131, 134
  schools, 4, 6–7

tintometer tests, 65–6
tone-difference, 82–3
Torres Strait, 18
Torres Strait Creole (Kriol), 6, 176
Torres Strait Regional Authority (TSRA), 148
totems and totemism, 112–14, 118–19
touch and feeling, 92–8, 100
trade and commerce, 121–2, 134–5
traditional ceremonies, *see* ceremonies
traditional knowledge, *see* Indigenous Knowledge
transmigration of souls, 117
travel restrictions, 6, 131, 137, 149
trepang fishing, *see* marine industry
tuning forks, 82–3

United Nations, 183–6
United Nations Development Programme (UNDP), 184
United Nations Educational, Scientific and Cultural Organisations (UNESCO), 156
university education, *see* higher education
upper limit of hearing, 81–2

Verran, Helen, 188
vertical line drawing tests, 70–2
viewpoint, *see* standpoints
violet (colour), 57, 60, 61, 66
vision and seeing, 43–75, 91
visual acuity, 46–54
visual illusions, 44, 67–85
visual powers, 53–6
visual purple, 51
vocabulary, *see* nomenclature
Volosinov, Valentin Nikolaevi□, 39
'voodoo dolls', 116

wages and earnings, 134, 136–7, 161–2

Walker, Rev Fred, 134–5, 146
warfare and fighting, 114, 123–4, 127
    beliefs and ceremonies accompanying, 108, 116
    cannibalism, 16, 18–20, 21, 23, 25, 123
water, association of word for 'blue' with, 60, 61, 62, 64
Watson, Helen, 172–5
weight, discrimination of small differences in, 96–8, 100
welfare state dependency, 136–8
Wemyss, Thomas, 18–19, 123
western Islands and Islanders, 104–5
    Augud, 112–13, 118–19
    colour blindness, 57–8
    kinship system, 109–12
    language, 32–7, 40; adultery, words for, 122–3; colour nomenclature, 61
    trade, 121
    see also Mabuiag Island/Islanders
white men, *see* Europeans
Whitlam government, 140–1, 158
Wilkin, Anthony, 28–9, 101, 114, 122, 123–4
Williamson, A, 160–72
women
    colour nomenclature, 58
    colour preferences, 66–7
    eyes' physiological condition, 46
    married, 110, 122
    size–weight illusions, 97, 98
    see also childbirth and pregnancy; marriage
words, *see* nomenclature
World War II, 139, 143, 144–5, 162

yellow (colour), 59, 60, 61, 65
    preference for, 66, 67
yellow–blue blindness, 58

Zogo, 118–19

www.ingramcontent.com/pod-product-compliance
Lightning Source LLC
LaVergne TN
LVHW041959060526
838200LV00038B/1291